362.29 MAC ~~MAC~~

DATE DUE			
4/8/15			
20/11/15			
14/4/17			

Responding to Drug Misuse

Responding to Drug Misuse provides a unique insight into the current shape of the drugs treatment system in England.

Reporting findings from research linked to the government's ten-year drugs strategy Tackling Drugs to Build a Better Britain, the book places these in the context of policy, practice, and service development. It goes on to discuss the implications of these findings for the government's new strategy Drugs: Protecting Families and Communities. Throughout the book contributors reflect on current debates on drug strategies and social policy and consider the relevance of the findings for policy and practice. Topics discussed include:

- recent trends in drug policy and how these link to crime
- responses of dedicated drug treatment services
- service users' perceptions and suggestions for improvement
- the impact of drug misuse on children, families and communities.

This timely addition to the literature on drug misuse will be essential for substance use practitioners, including social workers, psychiatrists, psychologists and nurses. It will also supply helpful guidance for health and social care commissioners and policy providers.

Susanne MacGregor holds a Leverhulme Emeritus Fellowship at the Centre for History in Public Health at the London School of Hygiene and Tropical Medicine and is the Programme Coordinator for the Department of Health's Drug Misuse Research Initiative.

Responding to Drug Misuse

Research and policy priorities in
health and social care

Edited by Susanne MacGregor

Routledge
Taylor & Francis Group

LONDON AND NEW YORK

First published 2010
by Routledge
27 Church Road, Hove, East Sussex BN3 2FA

Simultaneously published in the USA and Canada
by Routledge
270 Madison Avenue, New York, NY 10016

*Routledge is an imprint of the Taylor & Francis Group,
an Informa business*

Typeset in Times by RefineCatch Limited, Bungay, Suffolk
Printed and bound in Great Britain by
TJ International Ltd, Padstow, Cornwall
Cover design by Andy Ward

British Library Cataloguing in Publication Data
A catalogue record for this book is available from the British Library

Library of Congress Cataloging-in-Publication Data
Responding to drugs misuse: research and policy priorities in health
and social care / edited by Susanne MacGregor.
      p. cm.
   Includes bibliographical references and index.
   ISBN: 978–0–415–47470–2 (hardback)
   1. Drug abuse—Great Britain.   2. Drugs—Social aspects—
   Great Britain.   3. Drug addicts—Rehabilitation—Great Britain.
   I. MacGregor, Susanne.
   HV5840.G7R47 2009
   362.29′15—dc22
                                                    2009007386

ISBN: 978–0–415–47470–2 (hbk)

Contents

17 Evidence and new policy questions   203
SUSANNE MACGREGOR

Tables

Figures

Boxes

Contributors

Kostas Agath is a Consultant Psychiatrist at Westminster Substance Misuse Services, Central and North West London NHS Foundation Trust.

Ron Alcorn is a Consultant Psychiatrist at Specialist Addiction Services, East London Foundation (NHS) Trust.

Thomas Barnes is Professor of Clinical Psychiatry at Imperial College London.

James Bashford is a General Practitioner in Staffordshire and a Lecturer in the School of Pharmacy and Medicines Management, Keele University.

Tom Carnwath is an Independent Consultant Psychiatrist.

Vikki Charles is a Research Associate at the Institute of Psychiatry.

Daniel Clay is Director of Action Research Limited. He worked previously for the Tavistock Institute and the Policy Research Bureau.

Alex Copello is Professor of Addiction Research at the University of Birmingham and Consultant Clinical Psychologist in Substance Misuse Services, Birmingham and Solihull NHS Mental Health Care Trust.

Judy Corlyon is a Principal Researcher at the Tavistock Institute.

Michael J. Crawford is Reader in Mental Health Services Research at Imperial College London and Honorary Consultant Psychiatrist at Central and North West London NHS Foundation Trust.

Peter Croft is Professor of Primary Care Epidemiology and Director of the Primary Care Musculoskeletal Research Centre at Keele University Medical School.

Ilana Crome is Professor of Addiction Psychiatry, School of Medicine, Keele University.

Michael Donmall is Reader in Addictions Research and Director of the National Drugs Evidence Centre within the School of Community-Based Medicine at the University of Manchester.

Colin Drummond is Professor of Addiction Psychiatry at the National Addiction Centre, Institute of Psychiatry, King's College London and Honorary Consultant Psychiatrist, South London and Maudsley NHS Foundation Trust.

Karen Duke is a Principal Lecturer in Criminology at Middlesex University.

Qulsom Fazil is a Lecturer in the Department of Psychiatry, University of Birmingham.

Jeffrey Fehler is a Consultant Psychiatrist at Hillingdon Drug and Alcohol Services based at the Central and North West London NHS Foundation Trust.

Martin Frisher is Senior Lecturer in the School of Pharmacy and Medicines Management, Keele University.

Christine Godfrey is Professor of Health Economics and Head of Department in the Department of Health Sciences at the University of York.

Jude Goyder is a Trainee Clinical Psychologist at University College London.

Hermine Graham is a Lecturer in the School of Psychology at the University of Birmingham.

Jo Hart is a doctoral student at the Institute of Psychiatry.

Christos Kouimtsidis is Honorary Senior Lecturer in Addiction, St George's University of London and the Institute of Psychiatry, King's College London and Consultant Psychiatrist at NW Herts Community Drug and Alcohol Team, Hertfordshire Partnership Foundation Trust.

Brynna Kroll is an independent researcher with ARTEC Enterprises Ltd, a specialist substance misuse training and consultancy service in Exeter.

Susanne MacGregor is Leverhulme Emeritus Fellow at the Centre for History in Public Health at the London School of Hygiene and Tropical Medicine, and Programme Coordinator for the Department of Health's Drug Misuse Research Initiative.

John Macleod is currently a General Practitioner in Hartcliffe, Bristol. He is also Reader in Clinical Epidemiology and Primary Care in the Department of Social Medicine, University of Bristol.

Majid Mahmood was a Research Associate in the Department of Psychology, University of Birmingham, working on the Good Practices Project.

Orsolina Martino is a Research Fellow in the School of Pharmacy and Medicines Management, Keele University.

Sheryllin McNeil was a Research Associate in the Department of Psychology, University of Birmingham, working on the Good Practices Project.

Mani Mehdikhani is a Specialist Clinical Psychologist (Addictions) University Hospital Aintree, Merseyside.

Nicola Metrebian is Senior Research Fellow at the National Addiction Centre, Institute of Psychiatry, King's College London.

Tim Millar is Research Fellow at the National Drug Evidence Research Centre and researches on drugs and drugs misuse in the Health Methodology Research Group, University of Manchester.

Joanne Neale is Professor of Public Health in the School of Health and Social Care at Oxford Brookes University.

Jim Orford is Emeritus Professor of Clinical and Community Psychology at the University of Birmingham.

Steve Parrott is a Research Fellow in the Department of Health Sciences at the University of York.

Sue Patterson is a Research Fellow at Imperial College London.

Polly Radcliffe is Research Associate at the European Institute of Social Services, University of Kent.

Duncan Raistrick is a Consultant Addiction Psychiatrist at Leeds Addiction Unit.

Gary Roberts is a Consultant Clinical Psychologist, Birmingham and Solihull NHS Mental Health Care Trust.

Sue Ruben is a Consultant Psychiatrist at North Wales NHS Trust.

Louise Sell is a Consultant Addictions Psychiatrist and Service Director at Greater Manchester West NHS Foundation Trust.

William Shanahan is Consultant Psychiatrist and Lead Clinician, the Addictions Directorate, CNWL NHS Foundation Trust.

Laura Sheard is a Research Fellow at Leeds Primary Care Trust.

Amanda Simon was a Research Associate in the Department of Psychology, University of Birmingham, working on the Good Practices Project.

Alex Stevens is Senior Researcher at the European Institute of Social Services, University of Kent.

Gerry V. Stimson is Executive Director of the International Harm Reduction Association, London, UK.

Andy Taylor is an independent researcher with ARTEC Enterprises Ltd, a specialist substance misuse training and consultancy service in Exeter.

Gillian Tober is a Consultant in Addiction Psychology at Leeds Addiction Centre. She is a clinician and head of the Addiction Unit Training Department.

Charlotte Tompkins is a Research Fellow at Leeds Primary Care Trust.

Peter Tyrer is Professor of Community Psychiatry at Imperial College London.

Hameera Waheed was a Research Associate in the Department of Psychology, University of Birmingham, working on the Good Practices Project.

Tim Weaver is Senior Lecturer in Mental Health Services Research at Imperial College London.

Preface

This edited volume brings together seventeen specially written chapters providing up-to-date, research-based evidence on key issues relating to the health needs, treatment and care of drug misusers in England. The focus of the book is on illicit or harmful drug use and it presents some of the findings from the Department of Health's (Policy Research Programme) Drug Misuse Research Initiative (DMRI). The implications of these data are discussed within the context of the UK Ten Year Drugs Strategy, which operated from 1998, and with reference to the new strategy announced in 2008. The chapters report original findings but are also discussion papers where authors offer their own opinions on policy directions. The intention is to extend the forum of debate to a wider public and all those concerned to improve responses to harmful or illicit drug use. The chapters focus primarily on health and social care needs and policy responses. Currently the criminal justice aspects of the problem tend to dominate debate – this book deliberately aims to redress this imbalance.

The overriding message is that problematic drug use, or drug misuse, is a complex condition and there are no easy solutions. A number of common themes are addressed. Is the current arrangement of services appropriate? What kinds of and how many services are needed for drug misusers and how should these services inter-relate? What has been the influence of increased attention to the drugs–crime link on treatment services? What actually happens in drugs treatment services, do they work and are they cost-effective? Are there any remaining unmet needs? What do service users think about services and does involving them in services make a difference? As drug use has become more widespread, is it sufficient or appropriate to leave responses to specialized, separate services or should attempts be made to mainstream provision, involving mental health services, GPs, or children and young people's services, for example? Given the current emphasis on inter-agency working and joined-up policy and practice, how can this be improved and what are the barriers to effective cooperation?

The findings reported here are based primarily on work carried out through the DMRI. The DMRI was funded through the Department of Health's Policy Research Programme (PRP) whose role at the time was said to be to:

commission high-quality research that seeks to provide a knowledge-base for health services policy, social care policy and central policies directed at the health of the population as a whole. Particular attention is paid to the social dimension, including consideration of the communities that we live in and our lifestyle choices. PRP priorities are regularly reviewed to reflect Departmental priorities.

Research commissioned by the PRP is principally to inform 'policy customers' (as first defined by the 1972 Rothschild report) and assist them in reaching decisions in the immediate and medium term in negotiation with ministers and other departments within the limits of existing budgetary constraints and government priorities and values.

Initially around £2.4 million was prioritized over five years to fund research into drug misuse. The purpose was to help answer some of the questions highlighted in the 1998 strategy *Tackling Drugs to Build a Better Britain* in relation to treatment needs and delivery, and prevention of harm. In the first phase, fourteen projects were commissioned, covering issues relating to the cost-effectiveness of drug treatment, co-morbidity (dual diagnosis), waiting lists, treatment and prevention for young people, the impact on young people and patterns of long-term cannabis use.

The topic of young people was considered in both phases of the programme to be a priority. Co-morbidity was also identified as a key problem: the background policy concern here was that a group of people might be slipping through the net of care. The importance of providing timely and appropriate treatment was also prioritized with attention to waiting lists. National policy emphasized increasing the number of drug misusers participating in effective treatment and early identification and treatment of young people with drug problems. In both phases of the DMRI, there was policy interest in access to services and in how to improve the retention of service users in services after referral and assessment.

The 1996 Task Force to Review Services for Drug Misusers had pointed to the paucity of research on the effectiveness of treatment (DH 1996). Added to this was increasing interest driven by the Treasury in the cost-effectiveness of treatment: this dimension figures in a number of projects funded through the DMRI which together have helped to accumulate data on this issue. In addition, services were known to sometimes fail to attract certain users into treatment, some opiate-dependent injecting drug users failed to benefit and there was little consensus of opinion on how best to manage these patients. Research on prescribing injectables to these patients and on barriers to access to services for particular sub-groups was of interest to policy makers.

In the second phase of DMRI, the overriding issue was to assess the impact of the additional investment in drug treatment services. Ten projects were funded at a cost of £1.2 million, focusing on routes into and through services and the experiences of service users: this reflected increased attention to delivery in later years of the Ten Year Strategy. Key topics were experience of treatment and service configuration; and children, young people, families and communities. Phase two covered the years following the *Updated Drug Strategy 2002*.

Research funded via the PRP was not of course the only government-funded research being carried out to support the Drugs Strategy. Other sections of the Department of Health funded particular projects and the Home Office, along with the National Treatment Agency (NTA), commissioned a large body of research. Topics investigated with funds provided from these sources since 1998 have included attention to reducing drug-related deaths, the treatment of problems relating to crack use, and heroin prescribing.

The chapters that follow report findings from the DMRI and discuss the implications for policy and practice. Chapter 1 sets the context of perceptions of the drug problem and the development of policy responses. In Chapter 2, Duke asks: how did the connection between drugs and crime become more prominent in UK drugs policy from the mid-1990s? What is the 'drugs–crime link' and how did this emerge as a key issue? How did the criminal justice system become a major gateway into drug treatment and rehabilitation? And how did the belief that coerced treatment was just as effective as voluntary treatment shape policy and practice?

Given the ambition of evidence-based policy and practice, in Chapter 3, Macleod indicates some of the principles which should guide our interpretation of research evidence. He asks: what do we know and what do we not know about the psychosocial consequences of drug use? How adequate is the reasoning and understanding of science that underlie much discussion of this question? In particular, what is the evidence on the relation between psychosis and cannabis use?

The next eight chapters (4–11) focus on the response of dedicated drugs treatment services; those which deal with the core clientele referred to services, including injecting drug users. These chapters pay attention also to the question of the cost-effectiveness of services and discuss the ways in which research findings play into good practice guidelines, including those from the NTA and the National Institute of Health-care and Clinical Effectiveness (NICE).

In Chapter 4, Raistrick and colleagues ask what treatment is usually provided in a range of the most common drug treatment services. What is actually happening in substance misuse treatment agencies? Given that methadone prescribing has now become an integral and standardized part of drug treatment, what are the costs of providing treatment and is treatment cost-effective?

Weaver and colleagues ask, in Chapter 5, what is current practice nationally, especially what is case management? What are the objectives of this approach? Why is it appropriate to treatment of drug misuse? From a survey of 455 services across all Drug Action Team areas in England, what can be seen about the way care coordination has been implemented in drug treatment services?

In Chapter 6, Donmall and Millar report on the OWL (outcomes of waiting lists) study and answer the question, what is the effect of being put on a waiting list? Are drug users less likely to take up the treatment offer? Are they more or less likely to be engaged in treatment if they have had to wait?

Chapter 7 by Radcliffe and Stevens reports on the actual rate of retention in treatment services. This is important given the aim to retain people in drugs treatment for twelve weeks. How can we explain drop-out from treatment both between assessment and treatment entry and between entry and thirty days in treatment?

Chapter 8 by Neale and colleagues focuses on injecting drug users (IDUs) and asks what happens when IDUs try to access support and treatment. What are their perceptions of services? Considering recent renewed interest in the potential of treatment using injectable opiates (methadone or heroin), Metrebian and colleagues in Chapter 9 review the history of injectable opiate treatment in the UK and show how policy and practice have changed. They ask how feasible it would be to provide injectable opiates and how feasible is it to conduct research trials on this topic.

In Chapter 10, Kouimtsidis and Drummond ask: what is the effectiveness of use of cognitive behaviour therapy in methadone maintenance treatment? What lessons can be learned from the attempt to conduct a pragmatic randomized controlled trial for the practical implementation of NICE guidelines in real clinical settings? This study collected economic data as well as data on clinical outcomes. Together with information from other studies in the DMRI, including those reported by Raistrick and colleagues (Chapter 4) and Neale and colleagues (Chapter 8), these data contribute to a growing body of information on the costs and effectiveness of treatment.

But there are other ways to evaluate services than in terms of cost-effectiveness, including attention to the views of the public and patients. A number of chapters include information on service users' perceptions but the next chapter focuses specifically on accessing the expressed wishes and opinions of the clientele of services. So in Chapter 11, Crawford and colleagues ask what factors promote or hinder the process of user involvement in drug misuse services.

Then five chapters (12–16) look at the wider impact of drug misuse on other health and social services and on children, families and communities, shedding some light on relatively neglected issues. Chapter 12 by Weaver and colleagues asks: what is the prevalence of mental illness and substance misuse co-morbidity among patients who attend substance misuse or mental health treatment services? In Chapter 13, Frisher and colleagues use the General Practice Research Database to answer the question, how many co-morbid patients are there? What health care is being provided to co-morbid patients through General Practice?

As well as the individual patients and clients of drug treatment services, mental health and GP services, other people are affected by drug misuse, especially parents, siblings and children. What is it like to be a family member of a drug-misusing person? Chapter 14 by Orford and colleagues describes what happened when a model of intervention focusing on family members (and developed and utilized with other groups affected by substance misuse) was disseminated to two minority ethnic communities – one composed of Pakistani/Kashmiri families and the other of African Caribbean people. What benefits can be derived from receiving support from an intervention designed for family members?

In Chapter 15, Clay and Corlyon ask: what services are available in England to support the children of substance misusers. How do they operate and what issues do they deal with? Do they appear to be meeting clients' needs? And Kroll and Taylor in Chapter 16 ask: what dilemmas are encountered in attempts to intervene effectively in families where there is parental drug misuse. What are the views and experiences of children and parents and of professionals and practitioners involved in their care?

Finally in Chapter 17, MacGregor summarizes some common findings identified in these chapters and relates them to current debates on drugs strategies and social policies. Recognizing that policies have developed in an iterative way and that the process of decision making is complex, it is nevertheless hoped that the evidence provided in this volume will contribute to more enlightened public debate on this important social issue.

Susanne MacGregor
January 2009

Acknowledgements

Contributors to the DMRI research programme wish to thank the Department of Health (Policy Research Programme) for funding their research. All views expressed in this volume are however those of the authors and not necessarily shared by the Department of Health.

Susanne MacGregor wishes to thank The Leverhulme Trust for the award of an Emeritus Fellowship and Ingrid James of LSHTM for help with the production of the manuscript. Greatest thanks go to the collaborators in drug treatment and related services professionals and service users who made these research projects possible.

1   Policy responses to the drugs problem

Susanne MacGregor

Policy developments

An account of New Labour's drugs policy can usefully start with the claim made repeatedly by Paul Hayes, Chief Executive of the National Treatment Agency (NTA), that it was only by stressing the link between crime and drugs that increased resources for drugs treatment were levered from the Treasury. It is worth noting also the role played by Tony Blair in these changes. As Prime Minister, he made a personal commitment to the crime and drugs strategy, keeping the issue in the public eye and giving it high priority.

Spending rose substantially. In 1993/4, £526 million was being spent in total on tackling drug misuse across the UK: within this, £61 million was devoted to treatment and rehabilitation. In 1994, about 67,000 people were counted as in treatment; by 2004/5, this number was 160,450; and by 2006/7, 195,000 (MacGregor 2006a, 2006b; NTA 2007a). In 2007/8, £398 million was allocated for the pooled treatment budget provided by the Department of Health and Home Office (NTA 2007a). [The total spend on treatment in 2005/6 was estimated to be £508 million (Reuter and Stevens 2007: 56).]

Underlying this was the confident claim that 'treatment works' and that it is cost-effective. It was said that for every £1 spent on treatment at least £9.50 would be saved in crime and health costs (Godfrey *et al.* 2004; HM Government 2008: 51–52). Treatment was the way to break the link between drug misuse and crime. The vehicles for rolling out this strategy at local level are drug partnerships [which now take a variety of forms such as Drug Action Teams (DATs) or Crime and Drug Reduction Partnerships (CDRPs)]. The Home Office is responsible for coordinating the drug strategy across government at a national level.

Continuities with Conservative policies

The origins of New Labour's approach to illicit drugs lie in the policies of the previous Conservative government. *Tackling Drugs Together: A Strategy for England 1995–1998* (HM Government 1995) set the template for drugs policy. This introduced DATs and Drug Reference Groups. The key aim was to take effective action by vigorous law enforcement, accessible treatment and a new emphasis on education and prevention, in order to:

- increase the safety of communities from drug-related crime;
- reduce the acceptability and availability of drugs to young people;
- reduce the health risks and other damage related to drug misuse.

This White Paper entrenched the division between alcohol and drugs as separate strategies. *Tackling Drugs Together* (TDT) marked a shift from the harm-reduction approach which had dominated from the 1980s onwards – an approach which had been influenced by recognition of the then new problem of HIV and AIDS. TDT stated clearly that the principal objective of treatment services should be to assist drug misusers to achieve and maintain a drug-free state. But it added, 'whilst abstinence remains the ultimate aim, steps will continue to be taken to reduce the spread of HIV and other communicable diseases by drug misusers' (HM Government 1995: 1.6).

TDT emphasised the link between illicit drugs and crime. The Conservative strategy also established ideas of partnership, aiming at an integrated response. There would be a joined-up policy, coordinated from the centre of government. Statutory and voluntary sectors would work together and health and social care would be linked to the criminal justice system. The details of policy would be worked out at the local level through the newly established DATs, taking advice from their Drug Reference Groups.

At the same time, a link to community concerns was made in TDT. John Major, the then Prime Minister, in his introduction to the Strategy, referred to the idea that drug misuse 'blights individual lives, undermines families and damages whole communities' – themes which were periodically reiterated by both Conservative and Labour ministers in forewords to policy initiatives.

One year on from TDT, on 1 May 1996, the *Effectiveness Review* was published (DH 1996). This reported on a fundamental review of treatment services and their effectiveness, informed by input from commissioned research and expert papers and judged by a specially selected panel. The main conclusion was that 'treatment works'. (This choice of phrase should be understood within the context of the dominance in political debate at the time of the notion that 'prison works'. 'Treatment works' was deliberately counter-posed to this phrase.)

The Chairman of the Review, Dr Polkinghorne, concluded:

> Drugs misuse is a complex and diverse issue. It causes immense harm to individuals and to society. Our review clearly shows that treatment works in reducing harm. It also makes clear that there are no 'magic bullets' and that treatment must be matched to the needs of individuals. A key finding is that to be effective, treatment must embrace care in the widest sense.

This might include addressing housing needs, child care issues, retraining for employment and general support.

(Press release, 1 May 1996)

Polkinghorne also said that:

> drug misuse is a chronic relapsing condition and ... a number of attempts may be needed before an individual can become drug free. ... Syringe exchanges and the prescribing of substitute drugs help minimise harm and need to be firmly at the centre of the overall approach to treatment. ... We hope that the critical examination of the effectiveness of treatment approaches which we have begun will be built on through a continued programme of rigorous research and evaluation.

(Press release, 1 May 1996)

There are clear continuities therefore in the New Labour strategy with what went before. The Conservatives' initiatives laid the groundwork for the new policies, although some changes were introduced. One important feature of New Labour's strategy was precisely that it was a ten-year strategy rather than the three years of TDT. The ideas would be given time to bed in and to develop, and sufficient monies would be devoted to implementation.

The New Labour approach

The Ten Year Strategy rested on the existing classification system for illegal drugs. It was based on the key assumption that 'treatment works'. But, more emphatically than in earlier Conservative initiatives, it stressed the use of diversion into treatment from the criminal justice system. Over time, and markedly by the time of the *Updated Drug Strategy* in 2002 (Home Office 2002), the main focus of attention was to be on the 'hard-core' of problematic drug users – the 'PDUs', including injecting drug users and users of crack and opiates.

This Drug Strategy set out a range of interventions that concentrated on the 'most dangerous drugs', the 'most damaged communities' and individuals whose addiction and chaotic lifestyles were most harmful. Later developments increased the use of testing to trigger diversion into treatment. The expanded services, supported by increased expenditure, would be rigorously monitored through the use of systems of performance management: only thus could such additional expenditure be justified to the Treasury and to the wider public. Underlying concepts, typical of the Third Way approach to social policy, were those of partnership and community involvement. In these arrangements, commissioning would have a key role with clearly separated funds and distinct institutions.

Influenced by the advice of Senior Medical Officers, and building on consensus views from experts in the field, 'Orange Guidelines' on treatment were issued in 1999 (DH 1999a). These made recommendations and referred to the responsibilities of all doctors to provide care to drug users for both general medical needs and for drug-related problems, improved safety through good assessment procedures, urine analysis, dose assessment where possible, regular reviews and shared care working, reducing diversion through daily dispensing and supervised ingestion, provision of evidence based interventions and the need to work within a shared care framework.

(Gerada 2005: 75)

These guidelines were revised and updated in 2007 (DH 2007) and operated along with a series of further guidelines from the NTA and from NICE to provide the frameworks within which medical practitioners and others were expected to make clinical decisions in order to develop good practice and maintain cost-effectiveness.

One organisational difference between the Conservative and Labour strategies was to shift prime responsibility at local level from health authorities to local authorities. Another significant contextual aspect flowed from devolution – one of the most important features of the changes wrought by New Labour to British politics and society. In implementing the Drug Strategy, there have developed some differences in arrangements in England, Scotland, Wales and Northern Ireland. But the broad goals of the UK strategy until 2008 were supported by all administrations.

Tackling Drugs to Build a Better Britain, published in 1998, aimed to:

- help young people resist drugs;
- protect communities from drug-related anti-social and criminal behaviour;
- enable people with drug problems to overcome them and live healthy and crime free lives; and
- stifle the availability of illegal drugs on the streets.

(HM Government 1998)

The most distinctive new element however was drawn from evidence from the USA, where it was observed that treatment delivered through the criminal justice system could be effective: this approach was transplanted into British policy. The key principle was that coerced treatment is as effective as voluntary treatment and offending could be reduced in this way.

New Labour also aimed to improve the procedures of government and the delivery of public services through the adoption of more modern systems of management, with a stress on performance and innovation (Cabinet Office 1999). Key aims here were that policy making would be more joined up and strategic; that public service users, not providers, would be the focus; and that public services would be delivered efficiently and be of high quality. Core competencies were developed for civil servants so that they would become forward-looking, outward-looking, innovative and creative, use evidence, be inclusive, work jointly across departments, establish the ethical and legal basis for policy, evaluate, review and learn lessons. A great deal of stress was placed on using the evidence base to decide what works. Public Service Agreements were introduced in 2001. Equally in the drugs field as in other social policy areas, initially a great deal of emphasis was placed on the value of a 'pragmatic' and evidence-based approach to policy and practice. This included funding new research and testing ideas in pilots before rolling them out. There would also importantly be more service user involvement, as users were seen as a counterweight to a heavy producer interest in public services.

The anti-drugs strategy is a cross-government initiative. It was initially coordinated by the Anti-Drugs Coordination Unit (son of the Conservatives' Central Drugs Coordination Unit), located in the Cabinet Office and led in its early years by a Drug Czar (Keith Hellawell) and Deputy Drug Czar (Mike Trace). With the arrival of David Blunkett as Home Secretary, the *Updated Drug Strategy* in 2002 gave overall responsibility to the Home Office for delivery. But other departments such as the Department of Health and the (then) Department for Education and Skills would also have key roles.

In April 2001, the NTA was set up with the remit of expanding the availability and quality of drug treatment. Some saw this as an astute compromise between the care and control lobbies, giving attention to treatment but masking the shift of power from the Department of Health to the Home Office. The new Chief Executive, Paul Hayes, came from a background in the probation service. The NTA is responsible for monitoring expenditure of the pooled treatment budget. This pooled budget was introduced in 2001/2 with £129 million available in that year. As we have seen, this budget rose substantially over subsequent years. In addition, there was approximately £200 million of mainstream local expenditure available for drug treatment.

The updating of the Drug Strategy in 2002 was influenced by a policy review by the Home Affairs Select Committee (2002). This review contained some criticisms of the former 'Drug Czar' approach. The committee accepted the benefits of focusing on the relatively small group of PDUs and stressed that policy should concentrate here, where harms were greater, rather than on the larger numbers whose drug use poses no serious threat to their own wellbeing or that of others (Home Affairs Select Committee 2002: para. 38). They also recommended a review of the classification system with regard to the less harmful drugs. They were critical of the overly ambitious targets contained in the original strategy and they wished to see more attention to treatment for cocaine and crack users, substantial increases in funding for treatment for heroin addicts, and for methadone therapies to be widely available. They also favoured a proper evaluation of heroin prescribing and a pilot programme of safe injecting houses. The Select Committee also recommended that a target be added to the National Strategy explicitly aimed at harm reduction and public health.

A key aim of the 2002 *Updated Drug Strategy* was to reduce the harm that drugs cause to society – communities, individuals and their families – and so it concentrated on the 'most dangerous drugs and most dangerous patterns of use' – most dangerous being defined as class A drugs (which include ecstasy as well as heroin and cocaine). Strategy focused on the 'most damaged communities' and on 'those individuals whose addiction and chaotic lifestyles are the most harmful both to themselves and others', i.e. the then estimated 250,000 PDUs in England and Wales. And it focused particularly on the young, especially the 'most vulnerable' young. It was to involve a selective and targeted approach. In particular, the revision involved dropping many of the over-ambitious performance targets set out in the 1998 strategy.

A key element of these later developments was the aim to increase the participation of problem drug users in drug treatment programmes by 55 per cent by 2004 and 100 per cent by 2008 and to increase year on year the proportion of users successfully sustaining or completing treatment programmes.

Policies aiming to deal with drugs and crime in local communities have included: arrest referral schemes; Drug Treatment and Testing Orders (DTTOs); Drug Rehabilitation Requirements (DRRs); intensive community-based programmes; Progress2work, a JobCentre Plus initiative which helps recovering drug users find jobs; Communities Against Drugs; and the Drugs Interventions Programme (DIP). The aim in addition is to provide comprehensive programmes of throughcare and aftercare for treated drug misusers returning to the community from prison, including post-release hostels. (These initiatives are discussed more fully by Duke in Chapter 2.)

November 2004 saw the launch of *Tackling Drugs: Changing Lives* (Home Office 2004). This involved a plan of action through to 2008. The Prime Minister, Tony Blair, said that tough measures were needed to deal with drug dealers and offer more support to users. The policies aimed to:

> get as many drug addicted offenders into treatment as possible. The measures already in place to test offenders at the point of charge are working well but need to be strengthened to increase the number who take up this offer of help . . . so we will introduce testing at arrest as well as charge and require a person who has tested positive for a specified class A drug to attend an assessment by a drugs worker. Those who are assessed as needing further assistance or treatment will be required to attend a follow up appointment to draw up a care plan . . . we will introduce a new presumption that those caught in possession of more than a certain amount of drugs are guilty of intent to supply rather than possession for personal use . . . tough on dealers but support for those who need a way out of the vicious circle of drug-related crime.
>
> (Prime Minister's speech, 25 November 2004)

The head of the NTA, Paul Hayes, commented on this 'most significant increase in Government investment . . . [which] has enabled more drug misusers to access treatment more quickly than ever before' (press statement, 28 September 2004).

So in the years after 1998, the numbers in drug treatment doubled and the government invested £1.5 billion in its Drug Strategy. The aim was also to shift provision of drug treatment more towards the voluntary and community sector. In 2001, 80 per cent of drug treatment places were provided through the National Health Service (NHS); by 2005, this had reduced to 65 per cent, with 35 per cent of the cost of drug treatment going to third-sector providers.

There is no doubt that this period witnessed unparalleled attention to the issue of drug misuse with substantial investment of funds, energy and attention in improving responses and, it was hoped, making a noticeable impact. Over time, for researchers, concern shifted from demonstrating need to ways of expanding and improving services and thus the outcomes of treatment. An important additional moment was the publication of *Hidden Harm* in 2003 (ACMD 2003), which marked a change in perspective from attending solely to the needs of the service user to recognising also those of service users' families and especially the children of drug-using parents.

In 2005, the NTA launched its treatment effectiveness agenda, emphasising however that the focus would remain on the service user (NTA 2005). The aim was also to reinvigorate harm reduction. Critical success factors would be to improve the client's journey through treatment, improving engagement with treatment, retention and completion. 'The NTA does not advocate enforced reduction regimes or enforced detoxification', but they wanted staff to be more ambitious for their clients and to aim at reintegration, and by this they meant getting them into employment, education and housing. The retention target would become part of the performance management of the NHS, thus giving it more influence over commissioners and managers. The aim was also that each client would have an identifiable and written care plan and better aftercare (Dale-Perera 2005).

After time, of course, the strategy was no longer about ambitions but could be judged by results. Initially, the biggest criticisms of the strategy were about implementation. Later, challenges to the central goals began to be voiced. A range of evaluations of the strategy have appeared, including those responding to consultation on the new 2008 strategy and reports published by RSA and UKDPC (Reuter and Stevens 2007; RSA 2007). One criticism has been that policy focused too much on numbers in treatment with less attention being paid to outcomes of treatment, although one should note (as mentioned above) that the NTA had already in 2005 begun to switch attention to the quality of services and treatment outcomes (NTA 2005).

The 2008–2018 drug strategy has four strands:

- protecting communities through tackling drug supply, drug-related crime and anti-social behaviour;
- preventing harm to children, young people and families affected by drug misuse;

Table 1.1 Key events 1995–2008

1995	*Tackling Drugs Together*
1996	*Task Force to Review Services for Drug Misusers*
1997	New Labour government elected
1997	*Modernising Government*
1998	*Our Healthier Nation*
1998	*Tackling Drugs to Build a Better Britain*
1999	*The Orange Guidelines – Drug Misuse and Dependence – Guidelines on Clinical Management*
1999	*Patient and Public Involvement in the New NHS*
2000	Drug Misuse Research Initiative phase one
2000	ACMD *Reducing Drug Related Deaths*
2000	*Criminal Justice and Court Services Act*
2000	DH *Framework for the Assessment of Children in Need and Their Families*
2001	NTA established
2002	Home Affairs Select Committee Report
2002	*Updated Drugs Strategy*
2002	NTA Waiting Times guidance
2002	NTA *Models of Care*
2002	Audit Commission report *Changing Habits*
2003	*Hidden Harm* ACMD report
2003	Drug Interventions Programme launched
2004	*Tackling Drugs: Changing Lives*
2004	Cannabis reclassified from class B to C
2005	DfES *Every Child Matters*
2005	Drug Misuse Research Initiative phase two
2005	RCPsych/RCGP Report: *Roles and Responsibilities of Doctors in the Provision of Treatment for Drug and Alcohol Misusers*
2006	*Models of Care* update
2006	DfES *Common Assessment Framework for Children and Young People*
2006	NTA guidance on user and carer involvement
2007	ACMD *Hidden Harm Three Years On*
2007	RSA Commission on Illegal Drugs, Communities and Public Policy
2007	NTA guidelines on clinical management updated
2007	NICE guidelines on psychosocial interventions; opioid detoxification; and management of opioid dependence
2008	Cannabis reclassification from class C to B announced
2008	UKDPC report: *Reducing Drug Use, Reducing Offending*
2008	DCFS *Care Matters*
2008	New Drugs Strategy – *Drugs: Protecting Families and Communities*

- delivering new approaches to drug treatment and social re-integration;
- public information campaigns, communication and community engagement.

(HM Government 2008)

It thus maintains the focus on the PDU and the differentiation between alcohol and drugs. It continues to prioritise the links between drugs misuse and crime but gives greater emphasis to the impacts of PDU on others, especially children and families. There are continuities with the past but some shifts in direction: these are in part responses to changing perceptions of the problem and partly influenced by new evidence deriving directly from research.

Perceptions of the problem

Prime Minister Tony Blair described how the issues were perceived by his government when it came to power:

> Britain by 1997 had undergone rapid cultural and social change. . . . Much of this was necessary and good. Rigid class divisions and old-fashioned prejudices were holding Britain back. But some social change had damaging and unforeseen consequences . . . family ties were weakened. Communities were more fractured, sometimes as a result of desirable objectives like social mobility or diversity, sometimes as the consequence of mass unemployment and failed economic policies. Civil institutions such as the church declined in importance. At the start of the 20th century, communities shared a strong moral code. By the end of the century, this was no longer true. As society changed so too did the nature of crime. There was an explosion in crime and in particular violence fuelled by drug abuse. There were more guns in circulation and far less reluctance to use them . . . the criminal justice system was stuck . . . it was failing every reasonable test that could be applied.
>
> (*Observer*, 11 December 2005)

For some time, regular British Crime Surveys had shown real worries about public safety, drug-taking and associated theft and debris, especially in council estates and poorer residential areas (see also Leitner *et al.* 1993; Duke *et al.* 1996: 74–84; Shiner *et al.* 2004). One leading criminologist, Elizabeth Burney, has laid the blame partly on increased drug-taking:

> if one is looking for one feature of modern life not found in the past which is associated with nuisance behaviour and fear of crime, it must surely be drug dealing and use. Most other types of incivility have long been present in one form or another but the rise of hard drug cultures over the past thirty years has introduced a new element of disorder on the streets and residential areas . . . heroin use is still associated with poverty and it is yet again poor neighbourhoods where people are most likely to suffer the effects of drug dealing in their midst, including associated violence.
>
> (Burney 2005: 76)

Evidence from a range of surveys of young adults shows that use of all illicit drugs has increased sevenfold since the 1960s and Britain is at the top of the league in Europe on this measure, with rates comparable to those found in the USA and Australia (Newcombe 2007: 16–18). Steep rises occurred in the 1980s and again in the 1990s. An increase in supply was part of the explanation – from wider availability of heroin to the appearance of crack cocaine and domestic cannabis farms. Also important were factors influencing the demand for illicit drugs. For many young people growing up in Britain today, drugs form part of the landscape in which they live. For deprived young people, the landscape is particularly bleak (M. Rutter and Smith 1995; Rowlingson 2001).

The context in which policies on drugs are discussed today is one in which there has been – and most likely will continue to be – a ready supply and availability of drugs, in spite of the best efforts of law enforcement and border agencies. In the UK in recent years, 'drugs' have been increasingly framed through the link with crime. But drug-taking is a complex social phenomenon. All those familiar with the field – professionals, policy makers, practitioners, affected families and communities, and drug users themselves – are aware of this, informed as they are by evidence and experience. The topic is however often discussed publicly in rather simplistic and moralistic terms. Heroin in particular is seen as the demon drug and has been blamed for a host of problems. But other drugs like crack cocaine and 'skunk' (a stronger form of cannabis) have periodically been awarded the title 'most evil and feared' of substances. When experts point out that alcohol and tobacco also cause huge harm without always being similarly vilified, the public become perplexed and such arguments seem to have little impact on the dominant taken-for-granted assumptions (Nutt *et al.* 2007).

More sophisticated debate within the policy networks which take particular interest in drugs issues has focused on a number of themes and choices. These include: whether drug-taking has become 'normalised' (if not shared in by most young people, at least being something they are all familiar with among their contemporaries and referred to in consumer and youth culture); or whether it is a symptom of 'marginalisation' – while larger numbers may experiment with drugs at some point, only a minority continue and even fewer go on to exhibit secondary harms (physical, mental, social and legal) associated with frequent or excessive use. 'Marginalised' sub-groups, it is thus argued, are likely to share a number of characteristics and factors in their backgrounds, such as genetic predisposition, disrupted families, disturbed education, and other mental or physical conditions.

Similarly, other aspects of the debate discuss whether attention and policy should focus on the larger number of 'recreational' users – who might (especially if using along with alcohol) exhibit anti-social behaviours, or who, through accident or ignorance, might sometimes suffer very adverse consequences such as sudden death – or should focus instead, given scarce resources, on those who cause the most problems to themselves and others – the so-called PDUs. This term originates in an earlier ACMD (Advisory Council on the Misuse of Drugs) definition of the 'problem drug taker' as 'a person who experiences social, psychological, physical or legal problems related to intoxication and/or regular excessive consumption and/or dependence as a consequence of his own use of drugs or other chemical substances (excluding alcohol and tobacco)' (ACMD 1982: 34). The definition grew out of a recognition of the increasingly poly-drug problem, the rise in numbers using drugs, the geographical spread of use, the increased availability of illicit drugs, the growing proportion who claimed to be addicted to heroin and the increased proportion of addicts being seen by doctors in private and general practice. The new perspective thus questioned the former disease-based notion of addiction or dependence, noting that, while many drug misusers do incur medical problems through their use of drugs, some do not. In future, services should be geared to solve common problems rather than be merely substance- or diagnosis-centred (Mold 2008: 75).

This concept hardened during the course of the Ten Year Strategy with the focus on the most problematic drugs, most problematic users and most problematic communities. The PDU, on whom services are now encouraged to focus attention, is someone who suffers negative effects from his or her own drug use, in particular those who use opiates or crack. Measures relate to substances used, frequency and patterns of use.

Other questions are whether policy and practice should focus on 'harm reduction' or 'abstinence'. Harm reduction has usefully been explained by Russell Newcombe. He notes that there is no overarching theory of harm reduction and various models can be *observed* (Newcombe 2008). The main point is to distinguish between drug *use* itself, its causes and effects – which is the main question for the abstentionists – and discussion of the risks of drug use. Harm reductionists assume that drug use cannot be abolished and that in all societies some forms of substance use can be observed. When they talk about substances, they include not just illicit drugs but prescribed drugs like tranquillisers and, importantly, alcohol and tobacco. They think it more useful to pay attention to the different types of risk and benefit involved in drug-taking. Newcombe has identified seven key aspects, all of which involve different ranges of risk. These are: *context*; *amounts*; *methods*; *patterns*; *mixtures*; *access*; and *product*. All these factors should be taken into account in designing public policies and thinking through how to respond intelligently to the phenomenon of substance use in society (Newcombe 2008).

Abstentionists take a simpler approach: they argue for zero tolerance, giving up drugs altogether – there is no 'safe' pattern of use. Whether this would include ceasing to take any alcohol, tobacco or prescribed or over-the-counter drugs is a key issue here, total abstinence being an ideal rarely attained and some would say not even desirable. Discussion sometimes focuses on whether these are quite distinct approaches or part of a continuum. Some argue that a more realistic ambition would be for controlled or reducing use, among the general public and treated drug users alike.

In criminal justice responses, much has been made of the distinction between 'users' and 'dealers', although research often finds that, especially at lower levels in the supply chain, this distinction can be difficult to apply. And increasingly, debate has paid attention to the relative merits of voluntary or 'coercive' treatment. To enter into this debate involves deciding what exactly these terms mean, as coercion can be subtle and informal as well as enforced through the implements of courts and policing (Stevens *et al.* 2005).

Are there any agreed 'facts' in this complicated debate? What is the evidence on the current situation?

In 2008 there were estimated to be approximately 332,000 PDUs (crack and/or opiate users) in England (HM Government 2008: 8). In addition, there are about 55,800 PDUs in Scotland, 800 in Northern Ireland and 8,000 in Wales (Eaton *et al.* 2005). Eighty-six per cent of the estimated number of PDUs are users of heroin (Hay *et al.* 2007). The median age of those in treatment is about 30 years (Reuter and Stevens 2007: 28). Crack use has increased and the estimated number of crack users in London is now almost as large as that of heroin users (Reuter and Stevens 2007: 29). Seventeen per cent of school children aged 11–15 years had used an illegal drug in the past year (HM Government 2008: 8), most usually cannabis.

Deaths related to drugs in Great Britain in 2004 numbered over 1,700 (Reuter and Stevens 2007: 35) and in 2005 there were over 9,000 known cases of hepatitis C infection from injecting drug use (ibid.: 38). In 2004/5, 85,000 people were arrested for drug offences in England and Wales (ibid.: 51), and Reuter and Stevens estimate the total spend on enforcement of the *Misuse of Drugs Act* in 2004/5 to be £23.67 billion (ibid.: table 4.1).

It is notable that in public discourse so much attention is devoted to illicit drug-taking and that hard drugs, especially heroin and crack, are seen as the root cause of so many social problems. This is quite remarkable given that less than 1 per cent of adults have ever used opiates (Reuter and Stevens 2007: table 2.1, drawing on the 2005/6 BCS). The highest proportion is in the 25–29-year-old age group and even here it reaches only 1.9 per cent (ibid.). But heroin has increasingly penetrated British society and is found in cities, towns and rural communities. Users have become younger and are not necessarily deprived. In the 1990s and early twenty-first century, researchers emphasised that what they observed was use of many other substances as well and they described a 'polydrug' culture, which included use of alcohol.

Conclusion

Policies are shaped by the way a 'problem' is perceived. For 'drugs' the field is defined primarily by the *Misuse of Drugs Act 1971* which identifies certain substances as 'illicit' and ranks them in order of harms in a classification system from A to C. This identification of the issue has remained fundamental over time. However, within this the policy response has shifted periodically, from focusing on notions of 'addiction', to concerns about public health and diseases linked to injecting drug use, to the current focus on a selected group of opiate and crack users (PDUs) involved in criminal behaviour. Most recently, the impact of drug users' behaviour on their children and families has begun to receive more attention. Over this period, the amount of research on drug misuse has increased exponentially, influenced partly by advances in survey methodologies and in computing. Hopes to achieve at least evidence-*informed* policy and practice have paralleled these developments. It is in this spirit that the following chapters were written.

2 The focus on crime and coercion in UK drugs policy

Karen Duke

Introduction

From the mid-1990s, the interconnections between drugs, crime, punishment and treatment became increasingly refined and reinforced within drugs policy. The so-called 'drugs–crime link' became the catalyst for the expansion and investment in drug treatment and testing at every point in the criminal justice process. Various surveys showed that problem drug users are more likely to have had contact with the criminal justice system than have the general population. For example, national estimates in 2005/6 indicated that 1 per cent of the general population aged 15–64 years in England could be classified as problem opiate and/or crack cocaine users (Hay *et al.* 2007). This compared to 13 per cent of the arrestee population who were dependent on heroin and 8 per cent who were dependent on crack in 2005/6 (Boreham *et al.* 2007). Similarly, high rates of problem drug use were also reported within the sentenced population with over one-third (39 per cent) of male prisoners and over a quarter (27 per cent) of men serving community sentences experiencing problematic drug use (Budd *et al.* 2005). For many of these problem drug users, the criminal justice system has now become the main gateway into drugs treatment and rehabilitation.

A key principle of Labour drugs policy development was that 'coerced treatment is just as effective as voluntary treatment'. Drawing upon published research, evaluations and commentaries, this chapter will examine the increasing merger between drugs and criminal justice, and the issue of coercion in the Drug Interventions Programme (DIP) which has established treatment and testing initiatives at every point of contact in the criminal justice process. It will explore the conflicts, tensions and ethical dilemmas surrounding the introduction of coerced treatment and testing and their wider impact on developments in drugs treatment.

Policy developments and context

Historically, the criminal justice system has not had a prominent role in British drugs treatment systems. However, these areas have become increasingly interconnected in recent years. Prior to the mid-1990s, various scholars argued that the criminological approach to drug issues was not particularly well developed in Britain (see Downes 1988; Pearson 1990; South 1994). This was a consequence of the domination of the medical-disease model of addiction and the clinical and medical origins of British drugs policy (Berridge 1990). It also reflected the large proportion of addict cases which were either 'therapeutic' or 'professional' in origin prior to the 1960s. British research has tended to focus on epidemiological issues, treatment and services. Until recently, this historical context led to a lack of research on and understanding of the relationship between drugs and crime and of the position of drug users within the criminal justice system.

Prior to the 1995 drugs strategy, the focus in drugs policy was on the development of services and the introduction of harm reduction initiatives. For example, the Central Funding Initiative (CFI) created a new layer of drug agencies and specialists within the community during the 1980s (MacGregor *et al.* 1991). Very few of these drug services engaged directly with the criminal justice system but they would treat drug-using offenders and ex-offenders if they self-referred themselves. For the most part, the criminal justice system and drug treatment providers existed independently of each other. This earlier phase of policy was also profoundly affected by the HIV/AIDS crisis and the discourse of harm reduction, which changed the ways in which drugs services in the community operated. Accessible services which operated outreach, open-door and user-friendly policies were developed, and ambitious targets, such as abstinence, were replaced with more limited targets and a hierarchy of goals (Stimson 1990). By the late 1980s, there were also indications that drug issues in the criminal justice system were moving into mainstream drugs policy debates as a result of the pressure to deal with HIV and secure a public health response. In a series of reports on AIDS and drugs use, the Advisory Council on the Misuse of Drugs (ACMD) highlighted the special problems around the link between HIV and injecting drug use and the opportunities for intervention in the criminal justice system, particularly in prisons (ACMD 1988, 1989, 1993). By 1990, the Criminal Justice Working Group of the ACMD was appointed to examine various aspects of the criminal justice system in relation to drug users and measures to improve effectiveness, resulting in three major reports dealing with probation, police and prisons (see ACMD 1991, 1994, 1996).

The 1991 *Criminal Justice Act* represented one of the first attempts at using the criminal justice system as a site for drugs treatment. The Act pursued a bifurcated approach which allowed for harsh punishments for drugs traffickers and treatment and diversion from custody for less serious offenders with drug problems. Sentencers were enabled to attach an additional requirement to probation orders – that an offender should undergo treatment for drug or alcohol dependency. In theory, this meant that more drug users would be brought into contact with treatment services and drug problems would be prioritized over crime problems (Collison 1993). Under the Act, funding of voluntary organizations, some of which dealt with drug issues, would be passed from the Home Office to local probation services. As a result, probation services would have more of a role in commissioning. However, research conducted by Lee (1994) suggests that within the first six months after the commencement of the 1991 Act, very few conditions of treatment were made and it was debatable whether those which were imposed were actually being used as alternatives to custody. Various factors could have contributed to these low take-up rates, including: (a) the lack of credibility of the conditions of treatment amongst sentencers as a sentencing package for more serious offenders; (b) competition between the various types of community punishments; (c) financial constraints on both probation services and drug agencies; (d) problems around assessment and disclosure of drug problems amongst offenders; and (e) questions regarding the motivation of offenders towards treatment (Collison 1993; Lee 1994). One of the key objections to using the requirements was that this amounted to coercive treatment, which many probation officers and drug workers were fundamentally opposed to on ethical and ideological grounds.

The publication of the 1995 drugs strategy, *Tackling Drugs Together*, signalled an important transformation within British drugs policy. The criminal justice system began to feature more prominently in drugs issues. The focus on HIV and harm reduction for the individual user was overshadowed by a new emphasis on the so-called 'drugs–crime link' and protecting communities from drug-related harm. In their prescient conclusion regarding the future direction of drugs policy in 1994, Roger Howard and his colleagues argued that the criminal justice system would be at the forefront of changes in terms of tackling drug misuse (Howard *et al.* 1994). Other policy subsystems and the 'community' were drawn into the management of the contemporary drug problem as the concepts of 'partnership' and 'multi-agency working' became important themes. A distinctive feature of these new partnership structures was the closer alliance between the criminal justice system and other agencies.

Although tackling drug-related crime was a key strand of the strategy, there was little in relation to expanding treatment *within* the criminal justice system under the 1995 strategy. The four key objectives were: to ensure that the law is effectively enforced; to reduce the incidence of drug-related crime; to reduce the public's fear of drug-related crime; and to reduce the level of drug use in prisons (HM Government 1995: 1). The police, customs, probation and prison services were to develop strategies for tackling drugs use and drug-related offending. For the first time, mandatory drugs testing was introduced within the Prison Service, despite criticism from various commentators. One of the key objections was that the testing procedures were not underpinned by adequate treatment provision (K. Duke 2003). The introduction of drug testing in prison was an important shift in policy and marked the beginning of testing throughout the criminal justice system and the possibility of testing in other institutions.

It was not until the Labour victory in 1997 that the criminal justice system developed an important role in terms of treating drug users. For Labour, the problems of drugs and crime were viewed as inextricably linked and their policy on drugs would attempt to 'break this vicious circle' (Labour Party 1996). The goal of their policy was crime reduction through the development of treatment initiatives within the criminal justice system. Drawing upon selected pieces of research, new drugs policy would be underpinned by treatment-oriented principles: drug treatment works; drug treatment is cost-effective; coerced treatment is just as effective as voluntary treatment; drug testing helps to identify those with drugs problems and to ensure they conform to treatment regimes; and offenders should be kept in treatment for a minimum of three months. The 1998 drugs strategy, *Tackling Drugs to Build a Better Britain*, marked the beginning of the proliferation of new treatment programmes within the criminal justice system. For example, Drug Treatment and Testing Orders (DTTOs) were introduced in 1998 to 'break the links between drug misuse and other types of offending' (HM Government 1998: 3). These community sentences involved testing and treatment components supervised by the probation service. Further attempts at drug testing were introduced by the *Criminal Justice and Court Services Act 2000* with the Drug Abstinence Order (DAO) and Drug Abstinence Requirement (DAR) which required offenders to be tested for drug use as part of community sentences. Another example of the expansion of treatment within the criminal justice system under the new strategy was the development of an integrated counselling, assessment, referral, advice and throughcare service (CARATS) in the Prison Service. The budget for drug treatment in prisons has increased dramatically since then, from £7 million in 1997/8 to £80 million in 2007/8 (UKDPC 2008).

In 2002, the *Updated Drug Strategy* focused further on the links between drug use and crime and tackling the harm drugs caused communities. The entire strategy rests on the assumption that there is a direct link between drug use and crime. As various authors have shown, the drugs–crime link is much more complicated and the evidence base does not show this direct relationship (see Seddon 2000, 2006; Stevens 2007). The updated strategy enhanced the development of drug testing and treatment within the criminal justice system through the DIP which aimed to get offenders 'out of crime and into treatment'. It provides treatment opportunities at every point of the criminal justice process including arrest, bail, sentencing, imprisonment and aftercare in the community. The related targets of the strategy were to reduce drug-related crime by measuring the number of offenders testing positive on arrest and increasing the number of problem drug users in treatment by 55 per cent by 2004 and 100 per cent by 2008, as well as improving rates of retention in treatment programmes and completion. By January 2008, over 3,750 offenders a month were entering treatment via DIP (UKDPC 2008). The cost-effectiveness of this approach was based on the National Treatment Outcome Research Study (NTORS) finding that for every £1 spent on treatment at least £9.50 is saved in crime and health costs (Godfrey *et al.* 2004). These figures have been repeated like a mantra throughout the official documentation as a justification for the current approach of using the criminal justice system as a site for drug treatment. However, it is important to acknowledge that only approximately half of the NTORS sample were offenders and all entered existing treatment services within the community on a voluntary basis.

The DIP was initially set up as a three-year programme from 2003 to 2006 with a budget of £165 million per year, and was further extended. In 2006/7, the budget for drug interventions within the criminal justice system was over £330 million in England and Wales (UKDPC 2008). Since 2003, DIP has introduced a myriad of different initiatives. In 2005, DTTOs, DAOs, and DARs were replaced by the Drug Rehabilitation Requirement (DRR) and US-style drug courts were piloted in Leeds and west London to deal with offenders who had been sentenced to DRRs. Under its 'Tough Choices' initiative, drug testing on arrest and charge for those detained on 'trigger offences' (i.e. acquisitive crime) has also been introduced. Those who test positive for the use of heroin, crack or cocaine are required to be assessed for drug treatment. Failure to comply with the testing or assessment component is an offence. Restrictions on bail have also been introduced, which reverse the presumption of court bail for those who have tested positive for class A drugs unless they undergo an assessment of their drug use and any follow-up treatment. In addition, conditional cautioning has been introduced, which involves attaching a condition to a police caution to encourage the user to seek treatment and rehabilitation. For the individual users who are subject to these new interventions, there is very little choice involved. If they fail to comply with the order or initiative, they can be subjected to various sanctions. Nolan (1998) refers to this as 'therapeutic coercion' where failure to comply with the programme and to fully accept and engage with its perspective results in a penal sentence.

Coercion in drugs treatment

There is a long history of debate regarding the locus of responsibility for the control of drugs and whether it should be dealt with as a medical, moral or criminal justice problem. Analyses of drugs policy illustrate the constant balancing between the aims of treatment on the one hand, and punishment on the other (Stimson and Oppenheimer 1982; Smart 1984; Dorn and South 1994; Berridge 1999). The balance has shifted over time and has been influenced by the definition of the drugs problem and by the social, political and institutional contexts. At the heart of the New Labour strategy is the focus on tackling drug-related crime by utilizing the criminal justice system as a site for drugs treatment. Many commentators have argued that these recent developments in drugs policy represent a 'new drugs interventions industry' (see Parker 2004) involving a treatment/punishment hybrid (Stevens 2004) and indicate an increasing 'criminalization' of drug treatment and rehabilitation (K. Duke 2006).

Under the new initiatives, the criminal justice system has been given powers to coerce drug-dependent offenders into treatment. It is important to distinguish this type of coercion from compulsion which involves the removal of choice and decision making. With the new forms of legal coercion, drug-using offenders still retain some choice, but it is constrained (Seddon 2007). However, those who reject the treatment option or fail to comply with the treatment regime may be subjected to sanctions or end up in prison. Similarly, we also need to distinguish this type of coercion from other forms of coercion which may be operating in relation to 'voluntary' treatment, such as pressure from family, friends and employers (Bean 2004). A useful definition comes from the work by Stevens *et al.* (2003: 2) in their international review of the literature on drugs, crime and treatment which defines quasi-compulsory treatment (QCT) as 'treatment of drug-dependent offenders that is motivated, ordered or supervised by the criminal justice system and takes place outside regular prisons'.

Research on the effectiveness of coerced treatment has not been consistent and has failed to produce a clear consensus (see Stevens *et al.* 2003 for an international review). The evidence base has been dominated by US research with the exception of a few studies, such as the evaluation of QCT of drug-dependent offenders in six countries in Europe (see McSweeney *et al.* 2006). Research from the United States generally concludes that legally coerced treatment has at least the same level of effectiveness as 'voluntary'-based treatment (see Gostin 1991; Hall 1997; Farabee *et al.* 1998; Wild *et al.* 2002). A pan-European study by McSweeney *et al.* (2007) comparing 'coerced' and 'voluntary' drug treatment options showed similar reductions between the two groups in terms of drug use, injecting risk and offending behaviours and improvements in mental health. Drug treatment which is motivated, supervised or ordered by the criminal justice system did not have better retention or different outcomes compared to 'voluntary' treatment. In relation to the UK, in their review of programmes, UKDPC (2008) concluded that the general principle of using criminal justice-based interventions to encourage engagement with treatment is supported by the evidence. However, despite the huge investment which has been made in these initiatives, very little is actually known about what works, for whom, and in which contexts. Several key themes emerge from the reviews of literature and evaluations on coerced treatment, including (a) the importance of motivation in terms of retention and engagement with treatment, (b) the content, quality and context of treatment, and (c) effective interagency working between criminal justice and health agencies.

It is simplistic to reduce the debate to a stark dichotomy between coercion and voluntarism (Seddon 2007; Webster 2007). Coercion is a multi-dimensional concept and needs to be conceptualized along a continuum. Elements of coercion have always been present in community-based, harm reduction-oriented treatment through drug testing mechanisms and compliance agreements between the 'client' and the drug agency. A recurring theme within the literature is the overriding importance of motivation and its relationship to coercion (Stevens *et al.* 2003). As Seddon (2007) argues, the concept of coerced treatment is very complex and there is a need to draw a distinction between motivation to *enter* treatment and motivation to *engage* in treatment. There is clear evidence from the various evaluations which have been completed that criminal justice interventions can be effective in terms of motivating drug-dependent offenders to enter treatment. For example, the evaluation of the 'Tough Choices' initiative has demonstrated that testing on arrest and mandatory drug assessment have increased the numbers being tested and entering treatment, with 79 per cent of those tested on charge and 74 per cent of those tested on arrest being retained in treatment for twelve weeks (Skodbo *et al.* 2007). However, the evaluations of DTTOs have shown low completion rates with only around one-third of offenders completing their orders (see Turnbull *et al.* 2000; Hough *et al.* 2003); but those who do successfully complete their orders reduce both their drug use and their offending. There were clear differences in the reconviction rates between those who did not complete the orders (91 per cent) and those who completed their orders (53 per cent) (Hough *et al.* 2003). In 2004, about half (49 per cent) of DTTOs in England and Wales were breached and significant numbers (44 per cent) ended up in prison as a result (Home Office 2005). Based on their review of the research, McSweeney *et al.* (2008) argue that lower breach rates and better retention, engagement, completion and reconviction rates were found in the Scottish DTTO pilots due to greater flexibility and discretion by practitioners regarding supervision and sanctions in relation to non-compliance. There is little evidence supporting responses which further punish and criminalize drug users.

In the early phases of the strategy, effectiveness was measured primarily by focusing on the numbers of people entering treatment rather than treatment outcomes. Research and evaluations also need to emphasize the more subtle aspects of success, such as reducing drug use, using drugs more safely, switching to less harmful drugs, and reductions rather than cessations in offending. A key reminder within all the research conducted is that problem drug use is a chronic, relapsing condition which requires a range of different types of support, including help with housing, education, training, unemployment and mental health issues. This is particularly the case with drug users in contact with the criminal justice system who present with specific needs. For example, the Drug Treatment Outcomes Research Study (DTORS) was undertaken in the context of the growth of criminal justice referrals and examines the effectiveness of treatment in terms of whether or not the client was referred by the criminal justice system. Of the overall sample, 35 per cent were criminal justice system referrals and this group was characterized by more complex patterns of offending, higher levels of crack use, unstable housing, and separation from children, and individuals were more likely to come from black minority ethnic groups. They were more likely to be male, to have left school early, and to be unemployed. Although this was not their first episode of drugs treatment [the majority (73 per cent) had previous experience of treatment], the baseline report concluded that these types of referrals through the criminal justice system do re-instigate treatment for a 'difficult' group (Jones *et al.* 2007: 12).

The independent United Kingdom Drug Policy Commission (UKDPC), which was established in 2007 to provide objective analysis of drug policy, concluded that after a period of focusing on quantity and expansion, attention should now focus on quality of provision and outcomes (UKDPC 2008). There is a need to concentrate on the multiple problems experienced by drug-using offenders, in terms of deprivation, homelessness, unemployment and mental health issues, and to develop holistic interventions which address these complex needs. At present, the criminal justice system and the treatment providers are limited in their ability to deal with these wider social structural issues (McSweeney *et al.* 2008). The quality of assessments and treatment is important, particularly in relation to follow-up provision and aftercare. Webster (2007) suggests that criminal justice-based treatment programmes are problematic because the criminal justice system is not concerned with rehabilitating offenders beyond the duration of their sentences. This creates problems because drug treatment is a lengthy process which requires longer term intervention with follow-up and aftercare. This is illustrated clearly by the problems regarding continuity of care and resettlement experienced by drug users on release from prison (see Burrows *et al.* 2000; Ramsay 2003).

The new forms of legal coercion have led to much debate as to whether drug treatment should always be entered into on a voluntary basis and whether coercive treatment can be effective. Although there has been a dramatic change in attitudes and growing acceptance of coerced treatment, many professionals and practitioners in the drugs field remain fundamentally opposed to the use of legal coercion in treatment. For them (many of whom come from a non-coercive harm reduction background), the criminal justice system is not seen as an appropriate site for treatment and therapy. It is not a question of whether coerced treatment is effective but of the conflicts and tensions it raises in terms of the underpinning values and ideologies.

Under the new initiatives, treatment providers have been forced to work within a criminal justice framework and its requirements. They have been expected to form partnerships with criminal justice staff. Working in partnership is difficult when agencies and organizations do not share the same aims and ideologies. For example, the introduction of DTTOs resulted in difficulties in terms of interagency working between the two groups (see Turnbull *et al.* 2000; Hough *et al.* 2003; National Audit Office 2004). Conflicts erupted between the working procedures, practices and ideologies of those professionals working within a health and welfare framework who were tasked with the counselling, treatment and rehabilitation elements of the orders and those working within a criminal justice and punishment-oriented framework who were responsible for enforcing the sentence (Barton 1999; Quinn and Barton 2000; Barton and Quinn 2002). These tensions related to the legal coercion involved in the treatment initiatives and the conflicting ideologies of care versus control and abstinence versus harm reduction. Difficulties have also arisen regarding issues of confidentiality and information sharing. Health care professionals work within a framework of informed consent and confidentiality. Under the criminal justice initiatives, drug-using offenders are limited in their ability to give proper informed consent. The initiatives also rely on information sharing between agencies, which breaks guidelines around client confidentiality which operate outside the criminal justice system.

A key question which arises from the focus on providing treatment within the criminal justice system is how far this welfarist, harm reduction outlook has been eroded within health and social services and drug agencies with the increasing links and partnership with the criminal justice system. Before the prioritization of crime within drugs policy, these two systems worked mainly independently of each other with very little overlap. Compared to ten years ago, there has been a sea change in terms of the willingness of drug treatment providers to accept contracts and to work in partnership with criminal justice agencies. As part of these new alliances, there has also been an acceptance of the new forms of legal coercion. Based on the British evaluations and research of the various treatment initiatives, Hough (2002) argues that the risk of implementation failure is high due to the problems of interagency working. He argues that more knowledge and understanding are required regarding how to strike the correct balance between sanction and toleration of non-compliance. He also argues that more understanding is needed around how to encourage health services and criminal justice agencies to work better together.

Future directions for policy, practice and research

Since 1997, a plethora of treatment and testing initiatives have been developed within the criminal justice system involving various forms of legal coercion. The shift towards the crime focus has also brought unprecedented increases in terms of resources into the drugs field. The new 2008 drugs strategy, *Drugs: Protecting Families and Communities*, reinforces further the merger between drugs treatment and the criminal justice system and the continued obsession with drug-related crime. Some of the key aims of the strategy are: to increase the number and range of offenders brought into contact with the DIP by extending the programme locally; to maximize the use of DRRs; to increase conditional cautioning; to further expand the Integrated Drug Treatment System; and to extend the use of drugs courts. The strategy emphasizes more informal social control by extending the responsibility and involvement in drugs control to families and communities. Other forms of coercion are creeping in as drug users are seen as having 'a responsibility to engage in treatment in return for the help and support available' (HM Government 2008: 5). Drug users will be threatened with benefit cuts if they do not engage with drug treatment programmes. As DrugScope (2008) commented, 'The stick of coercion and threats to remove benefit will be counter-productive without positive support, well-trained advisers and tackling the reluctance of employers to recruit former drug users.'

A key claim of providing quasi-compulsory drugs treatment within the criminal justice system is that it diverts drug-using offenders out of the prison system and therefore reduces levels of imprisonment. As Stevens (2004) argues, one of the risks of QCT is that it can become an expensive precursor to imprisonment rather than an alternative. As discussed above, this was clearly the case with the high breach rates on DTTOs and subsequent custodial sentences imposed. Net-widening and further criminalization are significant dangers with the expansion of treatment initiatives in the criminal justice system. The UKDPC (2008) warns against further net-widening through extending the use of drug testing in police custody suites to include testing additional groups of drug-using offenders (i.e. non-problematic, recreational users), and expanding the range of trigger offences. The UKDPC report concluded that drug initiatives within the criminal justice system should be reserved only for those with severe drug problems and drug-related offending behaviour.

By focusing on coercion and crime reduction goals, another danger is that harm reduction measures to contain blood-borne viruses such as HIV and Hepatitis C will become sidelined. The emphasis in drug treatment has shifted from a focus on the individual and reducing health-related harm towards focusing on the wider community and protection from crime-related harm. There is a long history of difficulties in delivering harm reduction in the criminal justice system relating to the overriding importance placed on abstinence and the problems of implementing some initiatives such as needle exchanges and methadone maintenance, particularly in prisons (K. Duke 2003). Successful outcomes in treatment in the criminal justice system need to be re-defined, and containing drug use rather than eliminating it may be a more realistic goal. As Reuter and Stevens (2007) argue, the focus on crime has overshadowed harm reduction and there is still a need for a wider range of services for drug users, including needle exchange, methadone mainten-ance, heroin-assisted treatment and drug consumption rooms.

With the conflation of drug treatment and criminal justice and increasing coercion, the real risk is that drug treatment will become viewed solely through a criminal justice lens, distorting the principles and practice of the treatment process (Seddon 2007: 277). Various commentators have argued that there is a danger that the criminal justice system will become the front-end of drug treatment at the expense of expanding and improving the quality of community-based services (see K. Duke 2003; Parker 2004; Stevens 2004; Reuter and Stevens 2007). As Parker (2004: 385) argues, the drugs–crime–treatment project has the potential to undermine mainstream community drug services: 'The mainstream treatment sector will continue to be more important in crime reduction than this new criminal justice project.' The preoccupation with crime also raises the issue of the inequity of provision – drug-using offenders may receive faster access to better care and support than non-offending drug users in the community – resulting in the absurd situation where people may be committing offences in order to avoid the waiting lists for treatment through community routes (RSA 2007). Turning Point, a large social care organization providing services to drug users, has argued that the two systems of referral need to be improved – by introducing a more public health/harm reduction-oriented approach in criminal justice treatment, and by ensuring rapid access and integrated approaches in community drugs treatment (Turning Point 2004).

Given the substantial investment in the provision of criminal justice-based drug treatment, the weaknesses and absences identified in the evidence base are surprising and impede the development of effective policy and practice (see McSweeney *et al.* 2008). Much of the research and evaluation of initiatives thus far has been hampered by the sheer speed at which they were implemented and has therefore focused on pilot studies and short-term assessments (UKDPC 2008). There is a need to look at longer-term outcomes in relation to coercive measures and the processes and conditions involved in treatment over time. There are important caveats and complexities in the research and evidence base which require a broader view of the factors affecting treatment. As Parker (2004: 381) warns, 'the unconditional Treatment Works slogan is thus somewhat dangerous. Treatment can work reasonably effectively under certain conditions but the factoring is complex and requires sophisticated, holistic interventions.' The UKDPC suggests a substantial increase in funding to develop a coordinated research programme and identifies a number of key areas for future study, including: (a) research into the assessment and matching of interventions to individuals; (b) the development of a typology of drug-using offenders; (c) evaluation of the DIP and of interventions not yet evaluated; (d) production and publication of data, including outcome measures for drug interventions within the criminal justice system; (e) comparative evaluation of DTTOs/DRRs and drug courts and any added value of court supervision; (f) consideration of the impact of interventions on women and black and minority ethnic groups; (g) assessment of the process and outcomes with regard to drug-dependent offenders discharged from prison and the identification of good practice; and (h) comparative study of the costs and benefits of community and prison sentences for drug-dependent offenders (see UKDPC 2008: Annex A). Politicians and policy makers must now prioritize and properly resource research in these areas which would help to enable more effective evidence-based policy and practice.

3 Drug-taking and its psychosocial consequences

John Macleod

This chapter outlines some features of the general context of drug-taking in contemporary Britain and indicates what we know and what we do not know about the psychosocial consequences of drug use. A key conclusion is to urge caution about taking observational evidence at face value.

The main arguments of the chapter can be simply set out. They are that:

- the use of nearly all psychoactive drugs is associated with increased risk of adverse psychological and social outcomes;
- this association is stronger the more extreme the pattern of drug use;
- socioeconomic disadvantage is associated both with increased risk of adverse psychological and social outcomes and with more extreme patterns of drug use;
- the challenge to researchers, policy makers and practitioners is to distinguish between (a) situations where drug use mediates the association between disadvantage and psychosocial harm, (b) situations where drug use causes harm irrespective of any association with disadvantage, and (c) situations where drug use is mainly a marker of a toxic environment that causes harm through other pathways;
- failure to recognise this key question of causality may be part of the reason why policy to reduce the psychological and social harms associated with drug use has been less successful than hoped.

Introduction

The association between people's use of drugs (psychoactive substances taken with recreational intent) and adverse health and social outcomes has been recognised for hundreds of years. Until the early twentieth century, concerns around this phenomenon were related mainly to alcohol and tobacco and were often expressed in terms of moral disapproval with certain patterns of drug use seen as markers of character weakness, indolence, fecklessness and criminality (Meylan 1910; Sandwick 1912). Over the twentieth and twenty-first centuries, much has changed. These changes include an expansion of the repertoire of popular psychoactive drugs used and their routes of administration, changes in the regulatory framework around drug use, and 'epidemics' of drug use amongst younger people. Drug use and 'addiction' are now more widely considered within a medical than a moral explanatory model, though the appropriateness of this paradigm shift continues to be discussed (Szasz 1976; Dalrymple 2006). Since the 1980s, UK policy around injection drug use has reflected the framework of 'harm reduction' – a pragmatic approach that arose largely because of concerns that injection drug users might provide a conduit for the spread of the Human Immunodeficiency Virus (HIV) into the general population (ACMD 1988). Harm reduction has involved a substantial expansion of services providing treatment interventions intended to reduce drug-related harm experienced by drug users, people close to them and the wider community. The harm reduction philosophy has subsequently been applied to types of drug use unlikely to be associated with substantially increased risk of HIV transmission and now includes consideration of interventions intended to reduce harms of licit as well as illicit drug use. The common characteristic of all harm reduction interventions is their aim to modify drug use, whether by preventing initiation of use, increasing cessation or reduction of use, or encouraging use of controlled substitute drugs via alternative routes of administration. All these policies are predicated on the assumption that the association between harm and the type of drug use intervention is aimed at is *causal*. This assumption may not always be stated explicitly but its implicit acceptance is essential since modification of drug use that is not causally related to the harm it is intended to reduce will not lead to any effective harm reduction.

Causes

The study of causes is the quantitative science underpinning evidence-based health policy: identifying and then manipulating causes is how intervention policy influences health. Any discussion of health policy should start from this point. Traditionally causes are identified through experiment because this is the only reliable way to eliminate the influence of *confounding*, hence the ascendancy of randomised controlled trials in the hierarchy of medical evidence. There are many situations, however, where experiment is impractical or unethical and in these situations the main source of evidence is systematic observation of free-living humans. Causal attribution in relation to associations between environmental risk factors and health outcomes in observational data is one of the most complex areas in epidemiology. Other than chance there are, broadly, three non-causal mechanisms by which a drug exposure (A) can come to be associated with a psychosocial outcome (B). The first is *confounding*, where the association reflects the fact that both A and B are related to a third factor C but this relationship does not involve any common causal pathway. Reverse causation refers to the situation where B causes A rather than vice versa – for example somebody who was previously 'teetotal' may start to drink heavily after becoming depressed. The third non-causal mechanism involves measurement bias where measures of both A and B tend to be simultaneously inflated or deflated such that they appear to vary with each other – for example some young people may claim extensive involvement in both drug use and criminal behaviour, when in fact their involvement in both is minimal.

Confounding is the most difficult of these to circumvent. George Bernard Shaw neatly summarised the issue in his introduction to *The Doctor's Dilemma:*

> It is easy to prove that the wearing of tall hats and the carrying of umbrellas enlarges the chest, prolongs life, and confers comparative immunity from disease, for the statistics show that the classes which use these articles are bigger, healthier, and live longer than the class which never dreams of possessing such things.
>
> (G. B. Shaw 1911)

Shaw was of course referring to confounding and his implicit subtext was that no sensible person would base a public health strategy around the distribution of tall hats and umbrellas. His 'common sense' observations carry an important message for policy makers and practitioners hoping to reduce drug-related harm.

It was through the study of effects of tobacco use in observational data that many of the key methodological and interpretational problems of causal attribution in observational data were worked out and it was Austin Bradford Hill who first proposed a set of criteria to guide causal inference, following his work on the British Doctors Study (Hill 1965). However, whilst studies on effects of tobacco use on risk of physical disease have grown in epidemiological sophistication, not least because of a need to counter the misinformation of the tobacco industry, evidence on the effects of illicit drugs has often been interpreted less critically. This is particularly true in relation to the effects of illicit drug use on psychological and social outcomes, where it often seems that epidemiological evidence serves a mainly rhetorical purpose as support for a particular ideological position for or against drug use.

Reliably identifying adverse psychological and social effects of drug use, both licit and illicit, is difficult, for several reasons. Causation is probably most straightforward to establish in relation to associations observed between drug use and physical disease outcomes. It is not now generally contested that tobacco use *causes* respiratory cancers, probably through a direct physiochemical effect, nor that opiate use causes increased risk of death from opiate overdose, nor that injection use of any drug, which involves the sharing of injection equipment, causes increased risk of contracting blood-borne infections. The situation with psychological and social outcomes is different, mainly because the causal processes leading to these adverse health destinations are, in general, poorly understood. One of the few consistent observations that can be made in this regard is that adverse psychosocial outcomes such as poor educational attainment, mental health problems, criminal and antisocial behaviour, reduced economic success and lower workforce participation, are all intrinsically linked with general socioeconomic disadvantage, particularly when this is experienced in childhood. The fact that poorer people experience poorer health in relation to most classes of morbidity and mortality seems to be a fundamental epidemiological truth, and the general association between drug problems and social position is no different. With perhaps the exception of problem alcohol use amongst adults, all the patterns of licit and illicit psychoactive substance use conventionally seen as problematic (i.e. either out of control or very dangerous) appear to be associated with early social disadvantage, where data are available to examine this question. Since this adversity was experienced in childhood and preceded the drug misuse in question, reverse causality is not an issue. Thus the strongest predictor of whether a child will have initiated smoking by the age of 10 is whether their father had a manual as opposed to a non-manual job around the time of their birth (Macleod *et al.* 2008). A strong predictor of heavier cannabis use in adolescence is social disadvantage experienced in early childhood (Poulton *et al.* 2002). Over half of heroin injectors presenting to one practice in Edinburgh were excluded from primary school because of behavioural problems (Robertson *et al.* 2007). Since all these types of childhood adversity are known to be strong predictors of later poor psychosocial outcomes, it is inevitable that the drug use they are also predictive of will itself be associated with psychological and social problems. The challenge is to distinguish between instances where drug use is part of the causal chain between childhood disadvantage and later adverse health and social situations and those where the drug use, irrespective of the fact that it may be harmful in other ways, is essentially a 'noise factor' that makes little if any causal contribution to the health or social problems we wish to prevent. Another question to consider here is that only 'visible' drug use is available for study. For various reasons drug use amongst the socially disadvantaged may be more likely to be visible: the disadvantaged tend to be more likely to be subject to official surveillance and to have less reason or opportunity to hide their drug use. This notwithstanding, it seems unlikely that the association between problem drug use and disadvantage is purely a product of 'ascertainment bias'.

Cannabis use and mental health

These issues are perhaps best illustrated by consideration of an association between drug use and psychosocial harm that recently exercised policy makers – the question of whether cannabis use causes psychosis and the most appropriate policy response.

Psychosis is a symptom of severe mental illness characterised by impairment of thought and perception leading to disconnection with objective reality. In particular, psychosis is a feature of schizophrenia, estimated to be the fourth most important cause of life years lost through disability in the world and described as the 'leading unsolved disease afflicting humans' (Carpenter 2003). Both genetic and environmental factors seem to influence risk of schizophrenia; however, which genes, what aspects of the environment and whether these interact in important ways remain unclear (Maki *et al.* 2005). An association between cannabis use and psychosis was first observed several decades ago (Negrete 1988). More recently, results from several large, general population-based, prospective observational studies have reported associations between a range of cannabis use phenotypes and a variety of measures of psychotic experience. We reviewed this evidence as part of the Department of Health's Drug Misuse Research Initiative (Macleod *et al.* 2004a, 2004b). In the largest, and oldest, of the studies we identified, cannabis use in late adolescence was associated with an increased risk of a subsequent diagnosis of schizophrenia (Andreasson *et al.* 1987).

If this association is causal, it is important. Since the late 1960s, cannabis use seems to have increased substantially in most developed countries (Hickman *et al.* 2007). Cannabis is now well established as the third most widely used psychoactive drug (after alcohol and tobacco) in Europe, the USA and Australasia (ACMD 2006). In the UK, around half of adolescents will use cannabis at least once and approximately one-fifth of them will use it regularly (monthly or more frequently) in young adulthood. Assumptions that most of these will subsequently 'grow out' of this use pattern have no firm evidential basis (Macleod 2008). The competing, though not necessarily mutually exclusive, reasons why an association between cannabis use and psychosis might be apparent and the policy implications should be considered against this background.

The first, and perhaps most obvious, possibility is that cannabis may cause psychosis. Plausible mechanisms for such an effect, involving neurochemistry or social factors related to cannabis use, are not hard to find (Hall and Solowij 1998; Maki *et al.* 2005), though apparent mechanistic plausibility can be seductive and misleading for epidemiologists in search of causes and, as Bradford Hill himself originally suggested, plausibility is generally the weakest test of any causal hypothesis (Hill 1965; Petitti 2004).

It is also possible that psychosis may cause cannabis use – for example, people who are psychotic may use cannabis to ameliorate in some way the unpleasant aspects of their experience (Macleod 2007). It seems unlikely that this self-medication would be directed at positive psychotic symptoms *per se*, since acute cannabis intoxication increases rather than decreases unusual thoughts and perceptions. Cannabis use, however, may have other effects valued by users, either drug effects or those arising out of social situations surrounding use (Gregg *et al.* 2007).

Part of the association between cannabis use and psychosis could also conceivably be an artefact of measurement bias. This would arise if people who were more (or less) inclined to talk about their cannabis use were similarly more (or less) inclined to report unusual thoughts and perceptions. In certain youth subcultures 'weirdness' appears to have a certain cachet attached to it. Reporting bias is subtler than the conscious telling of untruths and its effects can be misleading to the unwary (Macleod *et al.* 2002).

However, the most serious alternative explanation for the association between cannabis use and psychosis is that it arises through confounding (Davey Smith and Ebrahim 2002). In other words, it is real (as opposed to an artefact of bias) but has no causal basis. For example, coffee drinking is genuinely strongly associated with risk of lung cancer, not because coffee drinking causes lung cancer, but because both coffee drinking and lung cancer are independently associated with smoking (Ames and Gold 1997). This issue of causality is crucial in the context of effective prevention. Preventing coffee drinking would not be an effective public health strategy to reduce rates of lung cancer. Aspects of adversity in early life may underlie both risk of certain patterns of cannabis use (heavier use and earlier use) and risk of psychosis without the three being linked by a common causal pathway (Maughan and McCarthy 1997). In this situation, the target for *effective* prevention of psychosis would be the early life adversity, not the cannabis use.

As discussed above, causal inference is a sub-specialty itself within observational epidemiology (Hill 1965; Rothman 1976; Susser 1991; Parascandola and Weed 2001). Many attributes of an association make its causal basis more or less likely but it is extremely unusual for observational evidence to be able to prove causality 'beyond reasonable doubt', basically because of the problem of residual confounding. The fact that it is not feasible to identify independent effects of strongly correlated known risk factors, given plausible levels of measurement error, can be demonstrated mathematically (Davey Smith and Phillips 1990, 1992; Phillips and Davey Smith 1991), and further confounding by unanticipated factors is always possible. In some senses, it seems surprising that some people appear to believe it is possible to overcome these problems in observational data through sophisticated analysis. If this were true, there would be no need for randomised controlled trials to determine whether treatment interventions were effective. Randomisation is used to eliminate the problem of confounding by known and unknown factors. Its importance has been learned through the hard lesson of getting things wrong through reliance on observational evidence. The best-known recent example is that of hormone replacement therapy (HRT) and its supposed protective effect on heart disease risk, where huge numbers of women now seem to have been subjected to *increased* risk of heart disease and other harms by an over-enthusiastic health industry (Lawlor *et al.* 2004).

Measuring cannabis use, psychotic illness and the various factors that might confound this association is no less challenging than measuring use of HRT, heart disease and socioeconomic position amongst middle-aged women. If the basic issue is that people who use illicit drugs such as cannabis may be different from people who do not in ways other than the fact of their cannabis use, and that measuring and adjusting for all the relevant dimensions of this difference may be difficult, then observational studies on effects of cannabis use will be very problematic to interpret. Moreover, the evidence that cannabis use causes clinically important psychotic illness is not as extensive as some have suggested. Only one large, prospective, general population-based study has examined the association between adolescent cannabis use and later schizophrenia (Andreasson *et al.* 1987; Zammit *et al.* 2002). Three further studies of adolescent cannabis users and three of adult cannabis users have subsequently reported effects on a variety of self-reported psychotic symptom phenotypes (Tien and Anthony 1990; Arseneault *et al.* 2002; van Os *et al.* 2002; Fergusson *et al.* 2003; Henquet *et al.* 2005; Wiles *et al.* 2006). These studies are summarised in Table 3.1.

Overall, they show varying, but invariably increased, relative risks for whatever psychosis outcome phenotype was measured in relation to whatever their most extreme cannabis exposure category was. But it is important to note that these relative risks are generally substantially attenuated on adjustment for whatever potential confounding factors were measured. Typically these adjustment factors are broad indices of (a) social position, (b) use of other drugs, and (c) history of mental health problems. This attenuation, along with the magnitude of the remaining association, is strongly suggestive of probable residual confounding.

Our systematic review did not only consider evidence on cannabis use and psychosis. We searched for the best available evidence for effects of any illicit drug use on any adverse psychological or social outcome (Macleod *et al.* 2004a). In general, this evidence showed that, with a few exceptions, drug use was associated with subsequent bad outcomes – poorer mental health, lower educational achievement and adverse scores on various indices of social functioning. This association was largely non-specific, that is, these adverse outcomes were seen to be associated with the use of a range of different drugs and use of each of these drugs predicted a variety of adverse outcomes. In most instances, adjustment for obvious potential confounding factors, insofar as this was possible, led to considerable attenuation of the strength and size of these 'effects'. Inevitably most of the evidence we found related to cannabis use since, amongst illicit drug users, cannabis users are easiest to study in large population samples.

Systematic reviews are essentially just another form of observational research where the units of observation are studies rather than individuals. As such, they are subject to most of the potential biases that afflict any observational study and their interpretation is substantially subjective. However, it is worth noting that the numerous recent reviews of the evidence on cannabis and psychosis have come to very similar conclusions (Arseneault *et al.* 2004; Macleod *et al.* 2004a; Smit *et al.* 2004; Semple *et al.* 2005; Degenhardt and Hall 2006; Moore *et al.* 2007). These are that, while evidence is compatible with a causal link between cannabis use and psychosis, it is currently inconclusive, mainly because of the possibility of residual confounding. Different reviewers have only varied in how emphatically they have

Table 3.1 Prospective observational studies examining the association between cannabis use and subsequent psychotic symptom experience

Study and site	Participants	Follow-up period	Most extreme cannabis exposure considered	Psychotic experience outcome*	Adjustment factors**	Unadjusted effect estimate***	Adjusted effect estimate
Studies considering adolescent exposure							
Swedish conscripts study (Sweden) Zammit *et al.* 2002	Males aged 18–20 conscripted to the military in 1969	Subsequent 27 years	Lifetime use more than 50 times	Hospitalisation for schizophrenia	Prior mental health, IQ, social integration, prior disturbed behaviour, smoking, other drug use, place of upbringing	6.7 (4.5 to 10.0)	3.1 (1.7 to 5.5)
Dunedin birth cohort (New Zealand) Arseneault *et al.* 2002	Young people born in 1972/3	Until age 26	Any use by age 15	Diagnosis of schizophreniform disorder based on self-reported symptoms	Other drug use, psychotic symptoms at age 11	4.50 (1.11 to 18.21)	3.12 (0.73 to 13.29)
Christchurch birth cohort (New Zealand) Fergusson *et al.* 2003	Young people born in 1977	Until age 25	Cannabis dependence at either age 18 or age 21	Self-reported symptoms	Symptoms and cannabis use at previous assessments, prior mental disorders, family functioning, deviant peers, prior sexual abuse, antisocial behaviour, neuroticism, sensation seeking, self-esteem, IQ at 8, other drug use	Dependence at 18, 3.7 (2.8 to 5.0) Dependence at 21, 2.3 (1.7 to 3.2)	Dependence overall, 1.8 (1.2 to 2.6)

Study	Population	Follow-up period	Cannabis use	Outcome*	Adjustment factors**	Effect***	Effect***
Munich study (Germany) Henquet et al. 2005	Young people aged 16–24 in 1995	Subsequent 4 years	Almost daily use	Self-reported symptoms	Urbanicity, history of childhood trauma, psychotic symptoms at baseline, use of other drugs, tobacco, and alcohol	2.57 (1.52 to 4.34)	2.23 (1.30 to 3.84)
Studies considering adult exposure							
Epidemiologic Catchment Area (ECA) study (USA) Tien and Anthony 1990	Individuals aged 18–49 years in 1981–1985	Subsequent year	Daily use	Self-reported symptoms	Baseline mental health	Not reported	2.4 (1.54 to 3.70)
Netherlands Mental Health Survey and Incidence Study (NEMESIS) (Netherlands) van Os et al. 2002	Individuals aged 18–64 years in 1996	Subsequent 3 years	Top third of the distribution amongst people reporting some cannabis use	Self-reported symptoms	Ethnic group, marital status, education, urbanicity and level of discrimination	11.32 (3.29 to 38.99)	6.81 (1.79 to 25.92)
National Psychiatric Morbidity Study (UK) Wiles et al. 2006	Individuals aged 16–74 years in 2000	Subsequent 18 months	Cannabis dependence	Self-reported symptoms	Area, tobacco and alcohol use, mental health at baseline, IQ, marital status, life events	3.40 (1.50 to 7.73)	1.47 (0.42 to 5.19)

* Self-reported psychotic symptoms were measured using different instruments in the different studies.

** For full range of adjustment factors see papers; in addition to factors listed most studies also adjusted for age, sex and some measure of social position.

*** Effects are reported in terms of different measures of relative risk, most commonly odds ratios; 95% confidence intervals are presented in brackets – these indicate precision of the estimate; this is mainly a reflection of study size. Confidence intervals that include values less than 1.0 indicate that an effect in the opposite direction, i.e. a protective effect of cannabis use on psychosis, cannot be discounted on the basis of this evidence.

acknowledged this possibility. These 'inconclusive conclusions' seem to have irritated some politicians and lobbyists who were perhaps looking to science to confirm their existing prejudices and convictions.

Other perspectives

These questions of causes can be considered in other ways. Ecological studies focus on populations rather than individuals. Thus population changes in cannabis use over time may be compared with subsequent rates of psychosis. If, as some have suggested, cannabis use genuinely doubles or even trebles risk of psychosis over a relatively short period from exposure to effect, then populations where cannabis use has increased should see increases in psychosis, all other influences on psychosis being equal. The ability to test this hypothesis depends on the availability and quality of data on rates of cannabis use and psychosis in a population. Both are often suboptimal. However, using Australian data, Degenhardt and colleagues found little evidence to suggest that apparently substantial changes in cannabis use had been followed by the increases in psychosis one might expect if cannabis use caused psychosis (Degenhardt *et al.* 2003). More recently, Hickman and colleagues looked at the same question using UK data (Hickman *et al.* 2007). Their results were more equivocal. Large increases in cannabis use between the early 1970s and the late 1990s were apparent. However, the biggest increases amongst young people were relatively recent. Reliable data on incidence of psychosis in the UK were also relatively recent. Therefore a possible prior influence of cannabis on this incidence could only be modelled. Model projections suggested that increases in psychosis might have been less substantial, and consequently less noticeable, than some had assumed. They also suggested, however, that a truly causal relationship would lead to larger increases, unlikely to go unnoticed by reliable surveillance, by around 2010.

Can we obtain better evidence?

The evidence summarised above indicates that cannabis use might be an important cause of mental health problems and may therefore provide a rational target for effective primary prevention. This question is important, given the extent of cannabis use and the human cost of psychosis. It should therefore also be important that scientists seriously attempt to find a reliable answer.

Compared to evidence on causes of other chronic disease, evidence on cannabis use and psychosis is limited both in quantity and quality. This in turn limits our capacity to develop interventions worth evaluating in randomised trials. Better evidence should ideally come from longitudinal research that commences early in the life course, before either cannabis use or psychosis is present, in order to address the question of direction of causality. Studies should also include repeated measures of all the important socio-environmental and temperamental factors that might confound an association between cannabis use and psychosis, if they are to consider the influence of such confounding. If they are to detect subtle effects that might be obscured by exposure misclassification, they need to include repeat assessments of both frequency and quantity of cannabis use. In order to address the question of possible reporting bias, these qualitative and quantitative self-reports should be corroborated with toxicological assessments (Wolff *et al.* 1999). Psychosis outcomes should be assessed with standard psychometric instruments and these assessments should be augmented with data on actual clinical events, probably obtained through linkage to clinical databases. This may seem like a lot to ask, though it is the approach that many scientists have recognised the importance of taking.

Other approaches may also help, most notably genetics. Patterns of drug use in the population are probably mainly a reflection of environmental factors, given the timescale over which drug 'epidemics' wax and wane in the population. However, this does not imply that genes are unimportant. Indeed several strands of evidence suggest they are important, probably because genes influence aspects of drug metabolism that have a bearing on how an individual experiences a particular drug, in turn shaping his or her pattern of drug use (Nestler and Landsman 2001). The immediate relevance of these genes to interventions is likely to be limited as any one genetic influence will typically be small compared to the influence of environmental factors. Nevertheless, genes that genuinely influence level of drug use may provide invaluable instruments to study effects of drugs in a way that largely overcomes the problem of confounding since genes are, in effect, randomly allocated (Davey Smith and Ebrahim 2003). Genome wide association studies (GWAS) have recently transformed the ability of genetic epidemiologists to identify genuine genetic influences on common health phenotypes and risk markers (Morton 2008). If there are genes that influence level of cannabis (or other drugs) use, it seems likely that they will be discovered soon through GWAS-based approaches. This may lead to clarification of questions around whether cannabis use causes a range of outcomes, including psychosis.

Evidence-based policy

If policy makers were to wait for unequivocal epidemiological evidence in relation to every policy action they were considering then not much would be done. Whilst this might be a good thing in relation to harmful policies, it would also almost certainly mean that much good would be forgone. However valuable better evidence might be, it is not necessary to wait for it before taking public health action. Prevention of cannabis use by young people has a strong public health justification, because of its reinforcing relation with tobacco use (Amos *et al.* 2004; Patton *et al.* 2005) and because it exposes users to risks of criminalisation. The issue is not whether we should try to prevent cannabis use but how we should achieve this aim – ideally through humane, effective interventions that are acceptable to the people receiving them and which do not generate disproportionate collateral harm (Gray 2001; Macleod 2008). Unfortunately the evidence base for interventions likely to meet these criteria is currently limited, making their development and evaluation that much greater a priority. Two approaches have recently shown some promise. In terms of primary prevention, peer-led interventions appear to be effective in reducing uptake of smoking amongst adolescents (Campbell *et al.* 2008). Their application to cannabis prevention could be evaluated. Motivational interviewing has also shown evidence of effectiveness in secondary prevention of cannabis use amongst young adults (McCambridge and Strang 2004). Larger-scale evaluation of both these approaches in experimental studies would not only guide rational investment in policy to reduce known harms of cannabis use. If the interventions proved to be effective, such studies would provide more robust evidence on true causes. Individuals whose level of cannabis exposure has been successfully manipulated in an experimental study should show concomitant changes in their experience of harms that are genuinely caused by (rather than just associated with) level of cannabis exposure.

Current policy

Policy around drug use is fractured along historical and ideological lines, partly reflecting the old dichotomy as to whether drug consumption is viewed as a health issue or a question of personal choice and morality. Policy around personal injection drug use (as distinct from entrepreneurial activity around injectable drugs) has substantially embraced the medical model to the extent that injectors within the criminal justice system are now often offered treatment. Community-based Drug Treatment and Testing Orders may be used as an alternative to custodial sentences and some injectors serving custodial sentences may access substitution therapy (Hunt and Stevens 2004). The rationale for this policy is mainly that treatment of injection drug use will reduce drug-related crime, a strategy also predicated on the assumption that the strong association between drug injection and criminality is predominantly causal.

Policy around non-injection illicit drug use is, in contrast, still firmly rooted within a non-medical model. This model seems to assume that, if the social consequences of choosing to use drugs are made sufficiently unpleasant, people will choose not to use drugs. Thus, in the UK, the main policy response to personal cannabis use, by far the most common form of illicit drug consumption, is currently based in the criminal justice system. Public information campaigns, such as the 'Talk to Frank' initiative, and school-based educational interventions such as 'Blueprint' have also been components of official policy around cannabis (see http://drugs.home office.gov.uk), though investment in these non-criminal justice interventions has been proportionately much smaller. Further there is no strong, or even moderate, evidence that any of these interventions have any influence on levels of cannabis use.

Arguments around the pros and cons of different policy approaches to drug use have been extensively rehearsed (Single 1989; Strang *et al.* 2000a; Wodak *et al.* 2002). However, it seems impossible to remove the consideration of the short-term political concerns of policy makers from the equation. These obstacles to evidence-based policy were recently exemplified in the UK in relation to the policy response to cannabis use.

Following the events of September 2001, the 'war on terror' appears to have supplanted the 'war on drugs' as the dominant rationale politicians invoke when wishing to justify potentially contentious spending decisions and policy related to limitations on personal freedom. Ironically, the entrepreneurial opportunities afforded by the illegality of many drugs continue to provide one of the most reliable sources of finance for criminal and terrorist organisations. Against this background, one UK Home Secretary appeared to consider the disproportionate amount of criminal justice, particularly police, resources that were then being consumed by activity directed at personal cannabis use, and decided that priorities had changed (May *et al.* 2007). A reclassification of cannabis within the UK *Misuse of Drugs Act* (from 'class B', where the maximum tariff for a possession offence was five years' imprisonment, to 'class C', where it was two years) was announced in 2003 and implemented in 2004. David Blunkett's main intention with this essentially symbolic gesture (very few convicted cannabis users ever received custodial sentences) seemed to be to signal to the police that they now had more important priorities than the pursuit of cannabis users. Unfortunately his relatively minor reform was widely represented as a significant policy shift by both supporters and opponents of the liberalisation of cannabis use in the UK (May *et al.* 2007).

Most of the evidence showing an association between cannabis use and psychosis emerged prior to the announcement on cannabis reclassification. Indeed reports from the only study to have found an association with increased risk of schizophrenia were first published in 1987. These facts notwithstanding, lobbyists representing various factions embarked on a media campaign to suggest that new and stronger evidence of adverse effects of cannabis use on mental health had recently appeared and that this evidence meant that the decision on cannabis classification should be reconsidered. In 2005, the ACMD (the government's expert advisory group on drug policy) was asked to review the evidence and make recommendations based on it. They concluded that evidence supported the possibility of a causal link between cannabis and psychosis but that cannabis use appeared to be falling and there was no rationale for a reversal of the decision on classification. They also recommended support for better research into the possible harms of cannabis use and for health education (ACMD 2005). Following a change of Prime Minister in 2007, the expert group was again asked to provide evidence-based policy advice in 2008. The rationale for this further re-examination of the evidence was partly a suggestion that UK-produced herbal cannabis of relatively high potency had achieved market dominance following reclassification. Whether cannabis potency is an important consideration in relation to possible harmful effects of cannabis is not clear. Again the advisory group acknowledged the possibility that cannabis use might cause psychosis, though also noted that data from primary care appeared to show that rates of psychosis were falling. Evidence that changes in the cannabis market since reclassification had led to a general increase in cannabis potency was felt to be patchy. Again their conclusion was that there was no evidence to support a policy of reclassification and that both better research and more health education were needed (ACMD 2008). Following this advice, an unpopular administration beset with various domestic political problems and apparently anxious to seem decisive about something that now appeared to be a potential political liability, announced that cannabis would be restored to its 'class B' status.

Summary and conclusions

Illicit drug use is associated with a wide range of psychological and social harms the reduction of which would lead to a healthier and happier society. The extent to which drug use causes these harms and consequently the scope for their effective reduction through prevention of drug use, assuming the means to do this effectively were available, is unclear. Taking the particular example of psychotic illness, schizophrenia has a huge impact on individuals, families, services and the wider community. Because of limited understanding of the causes of psychosis, attempts to ameliorate this impact have met with limited success. Against this background, evidence of an association between cannabis use and psychosis has emerged. By normal epidemiological conventions, evidence that this association has a causal basis is currently not strong. However, cannabis may cause psychosis and this possibility presents a tantalising glimpse of a means to effectively reduce the population burden of psychiatric disease (McGrath and Saha 2007). Irrespective of this possibility, there are good reasons to develop effective interventions for the primary and secondary prevention of cannabis use now. Rigorous evaluation of these interventions along with better basic epidemiological research should clarify whether cannabis use causes psychosis and if preventing cannabis use can prevent psychosis. Unfortunately, however, policy around illicit drug use continues to be driven by political and ideological considerations. Whilst scientists and public health practitioners may have to accept this reality, they should also insist that any public investment in policy at least be accompanied by the rigorous evaluation needed to demonstrate cost-effectiveness. Basic science, at both the population and individual level, to clarify causes and consequences of drug use, licit and illicit, should be a priority within biomedical research because drug use is a widespread environmental exposure and because its association with key unexplained diseases such as schizophrenia may mean that such research leads to important general insights about causes of ill health. Scientists and practitioners should however be realistic about the probable influence of their findings on policy, as on current evidence this is likely to be minimal.

4   'Treatment as Usual'

Duncan Raistrick, Gillian Tober,
Christine Godfrey and Steve Parrott

Expectations created by *Models of Care*

Such is the interest in drug misuse that almost everybody has an opinion on the right way to deal with it. Unsurprisingly, these opinions differ widely and range through 'war on drugs' rhetoric to outlandish claims for the success of specific interventions. What might be the implications of this wide range of views for attempts to reach a consensus on best practice or even standard practice?

To explore this question, we studied a range of drug misuse treatments offered in seven very different treatment agencies across the north of England as we found them in 2006. We will discuss the thinking behind the design of the study and the issues raised later in this chapter but first we will give some background on how policy has moved us towards thinking in terms of *Treatment as Usual*.

The first state-funded centres for the treatment of drug misuse were established in the 1960s and 1970s and operated under the so-called British System (Strang and Gossop 1994). The activity of clinics was monitored by the Home Office Drugs Branch but clinicians had freedoms beyond those found elsewhere in the developed world. Inevitably this led to some idiosyncratic practices. Equally, many of these clinics were doing pioneering work and laying down the evidence base that is well known today. As the problems of drug misuse grew in the 1980s and 1990s so did treatment services and there was a shift in emphasis from in-patient and residential rehabilitation units to community-based services. The British System stood in contrast to the heavily regulated clinics of North America and Australasia and, in the eyes of politicians, was seen to be failing in its ability to contain or reduce problems of drug misuse. The government of the day was opposed to the expansion of methadone programmes and set up a Task Force, which reported in 1996, to review services. Many in the treatment field believed a victory had been won when the Task Force went on to support methadone as the mainstay of treating opiate dependence (DH 1996: 58–66). A Pyrrhic victory because, in truth, the report began the first steps in a process through which government would increasingly try to micro-manage the way in which methadone was made available to opiate drug users – for how many, for how long and in what quantities – a process which has arguably been damaging to the service user journey.

The tension between individual treatment and the public good was exposed. By the 1990s, drug misuse, complicated by the arrival of HIV and added to by drug-related crime, had reached such a level of public and political concern that a national strategy was required. This was not the only driver towards standardised treatments. The need for evidence-based practice was generally accepted as a rational way to proceed, as was the need to contain health care costs by ensuring scarce funds were channelled into cost-effective interventions. The Task Force review was followed up by Department of Health guidance on commissioning effective treatment (DH 1997). Findings from the National Treatment Outcome Research Study (NTORS) were used to inform commissioning decisions. In 1998, the government published its Drug Strategy and later the National Treatment Agency (NTA) was established to guide treatment practices. One of the first actions of the NTA was the production of *Models of Care for the Treatment of Adult Drug Misusers* (NTA 2002b). This set out a comprehensive framework for commissioning services. Four tiers of service were described:

- Generic services
- Open access to drug treatment services
- Structured community drug treatment services
- Residential treatment services (in-patient and rehabilitation)

The tiers, which seem to have face validity, describe different levels of specialisation across an integrated treatment system. *Models of Care* also adopted treatment modalities which were pragmatically generated by NTORS to describe the main treatment packages available in the UK at the time. The four original modalities have been expanded to twelve and form the basis for producing aggregate national statistics. However, there are difficulties in applying them at local agency level. There are two main problems: (a) modalities are conceptually confused in that they cut across specific interventions, the setting, and whether or not the intervention is structured; (b) modalities separate psychosocial therapies and pharmacotherapies whereas evidence-based good practice guidance stipulates the use of pharmacotherapy as an enhancement to a psychosocial intervention (Carroll 1997). A key problem is that modalities as currently defined appear to have been used as a tool by commissioners to create competition rather than cohesion in the local treatment system – probably not the original intention. Alternatively, however, modalities that have conceptual integrity and applicability in routine practice could form the basis of routine (treatment) practice – what we could call *treatment as usual*.

Investigating *Treatment as Usual*

The aim of our study was to examine the extent to which the policy initiatives described above had created standardised treatment modalities and to what extent these were visible in 2006. Very little is known about what actually happens in substance misuse treatment agencies. There are some insights from major trials, such as the UK Alcohol Treatment Trial (UKATT Research Team 2005), where a 'gold standard' treatment, motivational enhancement therapy in the case of UKATT, was compared with a new treatment expected to be as good as or better than the 'gold standard'. *Treatment as Usual* is sometimes used as the 'gold standard', and so, from an ethical standpoint, it is of interest to know what validity can be attached to *Treatment as Usual* as an effective intervention which might then be a control group treatment.

Participants were recruited from seven agencies in Yorkshire and Lancashire, catering for different populations and providing different services and treatments. To ensure generalisability, the selection of agencies was designed to yield a cohort of participants who would be recognised as the kinds of people seeking help from agencies across the UK. The agencies were located in areas with different socio-demographic characteristics, including ethnic mix and deprivation indices, and were health service and voluntary sector, and from both primary and secondary care. Some services stood alone and would be recognised as providing a single treatment modality as defined by the NTA; other services provided a mixture of modalities but saw it as convenient to report themselves as providing a single modality. For the *Treatment as Usual* study, agencies were invited to define and describe their own interventions, thereby generating a list for each agency. All baseline data were collected at the first appointment at the agency and one treatment session per participant, based on agency-defined most usual treatment, was recorded.

The methods used for estimating the costs and economic consequences of treatment were developed from previous work (Coyle *et al.* 1997). Each contact with service users, called an *event*, is recorded and timed. The cost per minute for each member of staff is calculated and overheads apportioned to estimate the cost of each event. Finally, health and social gains or losses during treatment are measured. Data collection requirements are:

- *service functions*: a breakdown of the agency's activities by functions (e.g. clinical work, management, training), required to apportion overheads;
- *service overhead costs*: costs of buildings and equipment – for health agencies met through a capital charge and for voluntary agencies by rental payment;
- *staff costs*: gross staffing costs, including all employer payments in terms of National Insurance contributions and pensions;

- *activity data*: the intervention, staff involved, duration and location of each service user contact (events data);
- *outcome measures*: baseline to follow up change in key domains (see rating scales below) and service utilisation (from structured interviews);
- *process rating*: a measure of the adherence to the specified intervention and the quality of delivery (from video recording sessions).

Outcome measures

There is a consensus in addiction research that the key outcome domains for substance misuse are:

1 Substance use
2 Substance dependence
3 Substance-related problems
4 Psychological health
5 Physical health

There are standardised instruments to measure all of these domains (Raistrick *et al.* 2006). It is, however, difficult to find a consensus on which particular outcome measures to use within domains or how to present a profile of outcomes. The likely reason for this is that investigators have different perspectives and follow different agendas. For example, there are public health issues relating to injecting behaviour, mental health issues that have particular impact at an individual level, problems related to intoxication which may have particular relevance to driving and child protection, and broader social concerns, notably reducing crime. An effective outcomes package will:

- measure key and distinct domains;
- measure change;
- be universal across social groups and substances;
- be brief and written in plain language;
- use instruments with proven psychometric properties.

Data collection for the *Treatment as Usual* study was based on a standardised package called RESULT which can equally well be used for routine evaluation.

Semi-structured interview

The semi-structured interview was the format used to collect drug use, demographic and service utilisation data. Information on up to six drugs used was collected. The interviewer prompts for use of alcohol, cigarettes and cannabis. Items for each drug are: (a) frequency – number of days used in last thirty; (b) amount – pounds sterling for illicit drugs; (c) route or method of use. Service utilisation data estimate use of the criminal justice system, health and social care facilities – and are not collected in routine use of the package. The time frame was the previous six months.

Dependence – Leeds Dependence Questionnaire (LDQ)

The Leeds Dependence Questionnaire (Raistrick *et al.* 1994; P. Ford 2003) is a measure of dependence which is positively but not perfectly correlated with current substance use and able to measure dependence in periods of abstinence (Tober 2000). Dependence, understood as a measure of the strength of a substance use habit or addiction, is an important variable for treatment planning, measuring change and predicting outcome.

Social problems – Social Satisfaction Questionnaire (SSQ)

Eliciting social problems has some utility in terms of individual treatment plans. However, social problems tend to be idiosyncratic and the significance of each problem depends substantially on an individual's socioeconomic status. For these reasons, the package includes a scale of Social Satisfaction (Raistrick *et al.* 2007), which can be universally applied.

Psychological health – Clinical Outcome in Routine Evaluation (CORE)

The Clinical Outcome in Routine Evaluation scale (Evans *et al.* 2002) gives a measure of psychological morbidity across four subscales: (a) wellbeing, (b) symptoms, (c) functioning, (d) risk. This scale is specifically designed to measure outcomes of psychological treatments.

Physical health – Symptom Checklist (SCL)

For agencies lacking the capability of undertaking physical health checks, a brief Symptom Checklist is a useful alternative (Marsden *et al.* 1998).

Global rating – EuroQol (EQ-5D)

RESULT includes EuroQol (EuroQol Group 1990) which allows for comparison of health states between people with substance misuse and other health problems. EuroQol, with population values for different health states, is used for calculating quality-adjusted life years (QALYs). QALYs are the outcome measure used by the National Institute for Health and Clinical Excellence (NICE) to determine whether or not specific treatments should be recommended on the strength of cost-effectiveness evidence.

Treatment Perceptions Questionnaire (TPQ)

The TPQ was given at follow-up. The TPQ was developed at the National Addiction Centre to assess treatment satisfaction (Marsden *et al.* 2000). It is a ten-item questionnaire producing a total score in the range 0–40 with an invitation to add comments at the end.

Process rating

The only way to know whether a particular intervention has been delivered in line with treatment protocols is to video or audio-record treatment sessions. If claims are to be made that the outcomes for the service user were a consequence of treatment, there must be evidence that the treatment was delivered. To rate the amount and quality of the delivery of *Treatment as Usual*, a process rating scale is required. The Treatment as Usual Process Rating Scale (TAUPRS) was adapted from two validated instruments (S. Ball *et al.* 2002; Tober *et al.* 2008) and contained thirty-three items in total. Thirty-one content and style items measured: (a) *relevant session content*, covering components of agency treatment protocols and rated for frequency and quality; (b) *non-relevant session content*, rated for frequency and given as a ratio of total session content; and (c) *therapist style*, rated for therapist behaviours known to have therapeutic value, namely reflective listening, an empathic style as described in motivational interviewing, and those style items associated with enlisting social support. Item 32, *frustration*, referring to negative behaviours on the part of the practitioner, such as expressing impatience or being judgemental, carried only a frequency rating. Item 33 was a *session content/activity checklist* which did not carry a frequency or quality rating.

Findings of the study

Baseline characteristics of participants

The baseline characteristics showed that different kinds of agencies see people with different needs and, broadly speaking, those needs matched the declared role of the agency. A total of 401 participants were recruited for the study. The average age of the participants was 31 years and very similar across all agencies. The gender ratio was generally 3:1 male:female with one exception – in one agency, 46 per cent were females, a reflection of the proportion of participants attending that agency's specialist pregnancy and parenting service. The proportion of service users who had received further education ranged from 15 per cent to 46 per cent. For most agencies 45–50 per cent of service users had children – the highest number was 75 per cent. The number of service users in employment varied considerably, from 5.3 per cent, for an agency working exclusively with people in the criminal justice system, up to 31 per cent. There were generally high numbers receiving state benefits: all agencies had more than 20 per cent of service users in this category, the highest level being 43 per cent. [Unemployment in the UK was 5.4 per cent at the time of the study (National Statistics 2006).]

The referral drug varies markedly between agencies. Two agencies, which had criminal justice system roles, were almost exclusively seeing heroin users (97 per cent of all their service users). One agency in a large town had the fewest heroin users, 26 per cent, but the most cannabis users, 34 per cent. A secondary care service picked up 11 per cent methadone referrals, mainly from primary care – the next highest was 2.7 per cent. Very high numbers were tobacco smokers: in three agencies, 100 per cent of service users were reported to be smokers and the lowest report was of 87 per cent smokers in two agencies. [This compared to 28 per cent in the general population (Goddard and Green 2005).]

Six-month outcomes

At the six-month follow-up, 98.8 per cent (396) of the 401 study participants were accounted for: 66.8 per cent (268) were interviewed and a full data set collected. Follow-up rates varied between sites, ranging from 45.8 per cent to 76.9 per cent. Those followed up had similar baseline characteristics to those not followed up: the only significant difference was a fall in the number of amphetamine users seen at follow-up. The follow-up methodology has been described by Tober *et al.* (2000). The outcomes were measured using the four key domain scales described above.

Overall, statistically significant improvements were made in all four measures from baseline to six months (see Table 4.1). All sites produced significant reductions in substance dependence and psychological and physical health symptoms and all but one improved social satisfaction. The significance of the amount of reduction in dependence scores was that on average they fell to

Table 4.1 Outcome measures at baseline and six-month follow-up

	Baseline		Month 6		Change		p
	Mean	(SE)	Mean	(SE)	Mean change	(95% CI)	
LDQ total n = 268	16.21	(0.49)	8.64	(0.49)	−7.57	(−8.64 to −6.49)	<0.001
SSQ total n = 268	13.84	(0.35)	15.50	(0.32)	1.66	(0.99 to 2.34)	<0.001
SCL total n = 266	15.70	(0.49)	11.94	(0.50)	−3.76	(−4.72 to −2.80)	<0.001
CORE total n = 268	56.34	(1.44)	45.23	(1.49)	−11.11	(−13.99 to −8.23)	<0.001

within two standard deviations from the population norm and this has been described as one of the methods of establishing that clinically significant change has occurred (Jacobson *et al.* 1999). More gradual changes would be expected in the other domains, with psychological and physical symptom scores decreasing over weeks and improvement in social satisfaction scores lagging further behind. The point of measuring a range of outcomes, including the social and the psychological, is that these are domains commonly and significantly affected by substance misuse, and they are, or should be, targeted in treatment (Tober 2000). Social satisfaction may be further impaired during and immediately following a period of treatment and it may be the case that psychological functioning never fully returns to pre-morbid levels. Improvement did not necessarily mean abstinence from illicit drugs or even abstinence from opiates where a substitute prescription has been given. Of the 278 individuals followed up, 271 gave saliva samples for a toxicology profile and a high proportion of these were positive.

The mean item scores on the TPs ranged from 2.32 to 3.22 (the maximum item score was 4), suggesting overall satisfaction with treatment. Of the 268 who completed this questionnaire, 90 (33.6 per cent) took the opportunity to add comments. The majority of free response comments were positive but a number of negative themes also emerged:

- Waiting too long for treatment to begin
- Staff not offering support or listening to individual needs
- Need for more clinics and more flexible appointments
- Difficulty contacting keyworkers or staff
- Wanting smoking rooms
- Wanting to change keyworker
- Errors with prescriptions

The EQ-5D was used primarily to calculate change in QALYs. The EQ-5D mean value for the general population aged between 25 and 34 is 0.93 (sd 0.15). Participants' mean score at baseline was 0.74, compared with 0.81 at follow-up. Thus participants had much poorer health status compared to the population norm but improved during the treatment period, albeit to a level that remained below the population norm.

Costing treatment and other service use

Costs for 268 service users were computed at baseline and six-month follow-up. Table 4.2 shows the costs for health services, social services, addiction treatment and crime for the six months before baseline, the six months before follow-up and the change in costs between baseline and follow-up. All costs are in 2005/6 prices.

The results illustrate an increase in health care, social care and addiction service costs during the six months after entering treatment compared to the

Table 4.2 Overall service utilisation, derived from participants' questionnaires and unit cost estimates, 2005/6

	Baseline		Follow-up		Change in costs	
	Mean £	Std deviation	Mean £	Std deviation	Mean £	Std deviation
Health care	1,040	4,461	1,197	5,210	+157	6,629
Addiction services	401	1,951	757	2,000	+355	2,779
Crime	3,897	11,030	2,084	4,788	−1,812	10,233
Social care	74	268	93	302	+18	360
Total societal cost	5,412	12,312	4,131	7,242	−1,282	12,450

six months prior to entering the service. However, this increase in costs is more than offset by a reduction in the costs to the criminal justice services. The mean cost change was a reduction of £1,282, with a standard deviation of £12,450, illustrating the huge variation in costs across individuals. It is to be expected that getting service users into health care and housing would be among the initial benefits of treatment and that these costs would fall over time. Keeping people out of the criminal justice system would be a more sustained saving if treatment of the addiction problem was successful. The seven agencies had different levels of involvement with criminal justice services and, therefore, different potential for making societal cost savings for this domain.

Calculating an average ratio of net cost per outcome change for the treatments delivered involves combining changes in treatment costs and service utilisation with changes in health outcome data aggregated across the seven sites. This is thought to be the most appropriate approach since the study was designed to look at the *range* of services likely to be found in an integrated treatment system. It is not legitimate to compare one agency against another as the study did not have a controlled design. Rather, the calculations illustrate changes in the treatment system as a whole, which could be compared to the results achieved in research studies. For example, the mean QALY gain was 0.031 (95 per cent CI 0.013, 0.049) across the seven agencies. These QALY gains are of a similar magnitude to those found in the UKCBTMM study: 0.0347 for Methadone Maintenance alone and 0.0315 for Methadone Maintenance and CBT (UKCBTMM Project Group 2005). Expressing the combined costs and outcomes as a ratio yields a net cost per QALY gained of £27,372 considering treatment costs alone. If other public sector service costs are included then there was a net saving of £31,176 for each QALY gained. Similar calculations from the UKCBTMM study would yield figures of a net cost per QALY of £22,506 for treatment alone and a net saving of £138,139, taking account of resource savings for the enhanced treatment and net costs per QALY of £15,378 and £849 for the control updated to 2005/6 prices. Given the small sample size in the UKCBTMM study, these comparisons should not be over-emphasised. The economic evidence base recently reviewed by Belenko *et al.* (2005) reveals that drug treatments yield more economic benefits than costs compared to no-treatment alternatives.

The treatment process

The essential flaw with *Models of Care* is that it assumes that individuals have a definable need for a particular level of care, or indeed specific intervention, at particular times in the service user journey. Insufficient account is taken of the importance of building a therapeutic alliance, something which is known to facilitate service users' progress through stages of change and to enhance motivation for abstinence. When it is the case that services are commissioned to deliver solely harm reduction, solely cessation or solely prescribing, the therapeutic relationship is institutionally fragmented.

Process rating provides an essential insight into the nature, content and quality of the delivery of interventions and the basis for making comparisons between what agencies and staff claim to do and what actually occurs. Treatment fidelity has been shown to improve the quality of interventions and is enhanced by staff training in the delivery of specific interventions when followed by supervised practice (Carroll *et al.* 1994, 2000; W. R. Miller *et al.* 2004; Tober *et al.* 2005; Baer *et al.* 2007). Baer and colleagues have reviewed the available methods for rating treatment fidelity and emphasised the importance of this practice, using validated instruments that can adequately rate the variety of treatments (Baer *et al.* 2007). Training followed by supervised practice has been shown to be inexpensive (Tober *et al.* 2005) and effective.

In this study some agencies describe their activities in practical terms, such as prescribing and triage assessment, and some describe a therapeutic intervention. The conclusions of process rating were that agency staff did some of what they said they did and did not transgress stated boundaries of care. One of the surprises was the division between those agencies offering practical rather than therapeutic help and those agencies offering therapeutic but not practical help. Given the very different content of sessions, it is likely to be misleading to use a generic term like treatment and to compare agency activity under this heading. Rather the range of interventions provides components of a treatment *system*, including short-term, practical activities designed to engage service users in a process of change that may ultimately result in moving to agencies where abstinence and long-term stability are supported. Current service models undervalue the importance of continuity in this process and may actively disrupt it.

Treatment costs and cost-effectiveness

As well as exploring variations in treatment costs, the *Treatment as Usual* study examined the link between treatment costs, service utilisation and outcomes. The following formula is used to calculate cost to outcome ratios: cost of treatment/QALY. For example, if a treatment costs £2,000 and delivers one QALY then cost per QALY is £2,000. However this does not take account of the fact that a person's health may improve or deteriorate without treatment. If, without treatment, health would have deteriorated by, say, 0.2 QALY then treatment has actually delivered 1.2 QALYs and the cost per QALY would be £1,667. If, without treatment, health would have improved by 0.2 QALY then treatment has delivered only 0.8 QALY and the cost per QALY is then £2,500. The cost to outcome ratios presented here should be interpreted with caution. Without a control group it is not possible to say whether either of these conditions would prevail. A true cost-effectiveness study would include a no treatment control group. As this would be unethical in practice, *Treatment as Usual* could be taken as a reference treatment in future UK studies.

The costs and savings reported from *Treatment as Usual* compare the six months before and the six months after entry into treatment. It is possible that both these periods are unrepresentative. The six months before treatment may have seen an accumulation of drug-related problems leading the service user into treatment. By definition, for those referred through the criminal justice system, there will have been criminal activity which may have been at a higher level than usual. Use of emergency health and housing services may also have been higher than usual. Once in treatment, the use of regular health and housing services would be expected to increase. However, the increase should be short-lived as benefits accrue. It is, in short, valid to compare these two six-month periods but it is not valid to extrapolate beyond the six-month limits. Longer-term cost-effectiveness depends upon successfully moving people through the treatment system.

Research in practice settings

The *Treatment as Usual* study showed that it is feasible to conduct good quality research in drug services across different care sectors. There were some significant differences between the response of front-line staff and that of the parent organisation. Some organisations saw the research as an opportunity to improve data collection and treatment delivery while others saw a commercial threat to any disclosure. On the front line, secretarial, administrative and clinical staff were universally helpful and interested while expressions of interest and support from finance and service managers were more mixed.

Equally there were spin-off benefits to service users. Participants who had dropped out of treatment at the follow-up stage and were still misusing illicit drugs were often keen to re-engage in treatment. Rapport was built at the initial meeting and many participants were able to confide in the researcher, who had time to listen and give advice or put them back in touch with the service. Researchers were able to answer questions about other services which had not been accessed. This was a rewarding aspect of the researchers' role.

Agencies themselves were able to learn from participating in the *Treatment as Usual* study. For example, some agencies were surprised at the extent to which they had underestimated their non-attendance rate. Researchers made 1,204 appointments which resulted in 561 people attending at least one appointment and 417 people not attending (within the study period). One of the larger agencies experienced substantial changes in its commissioned drug misuse services and recruitment fell short of what had been likely at the time of writing the research proposal. Unexpected changes of commissioning arrangements are a new threat to research projects and some contingency should be put in place when planning projects. In summary, 978 individuals were referred to agencies and were, therefore, potential participants for the study; of the 561 attenders 108 (19.3 per cent) did not want to participate and researchers were unavailable to see 52 (9.3 per cent), leaving a recruitment rate of 71.4 per cent (401). This raises the important questions of how representative are help-seekers of drug users more generally and why do so many never reach services (although some non-attenders reported here may have entered treatment after the recruitment period).

Concluding comments

1   The study demonstrated a marked variability between agencies in terms of (a) the kinds of help-seekers attending; (b) the range of interventions offered; (c) the capabilities of staff available; (d) the governance procedures in place.
2   All agencies made a positive response to help-seekers and delivered statistically significant health and social gains. Service users had generally positive experiences of the participating treatment agencies.
3   The service user population is significantly impaired compared to the general population on measures of physical and psychological health, and drug and alcohol use and dependence, is significantly at risk from smoking and shows low educational achievement and high unemployment. Thus the positive impact of the interventions delivered is noteworthy.
4   Societal costs excluding crime increased in the six-month follow-up period. This is to be expected as a consequence of increased access by service users to health care and housing. When crime reduction is taken into account, there are overall savings.
5   The size of the 'treatment effect' is similar to that found in other areas of health care and within the NICE benchmark cost limit.
6   Agencies claimed to offer a variety of interventions. In reality, most of the time, only a few were actually delivered and some of these were without protocols or guidance notes available. If interventions were to be specified in protocols or manuals and supported by training and routine supervision of video-recorded practice then it is reasonable to expect there might be a shift to more uniformity of treatment delivery and possibly better outcomes.

7   It has been shown to be possible to conduct good quality research in practice settings. The measures used in the *Treatment as Usual* study delivered meaningful results, have value as motivational change tools and are important measures of treatment progress.

8   There were tensions between attempts by commissioners to micro-manage service delivery and clinicians' desire to exercise their knowledge and skills as they felt best for service users. Service managers were often caught in the middle, fearing that contracts would be lost if targets were not met. Arguably, more would be achieved at less cost if a more collaborative approach between central direction and treatment delivery was itself a target.

What are the policy implications?

There are three policy implications: (i) a need to reverse the fragmentation of services; (ii) a need to adopt clinically meaningful outcome measures such as the RESULT outcomes package; and (iii) a need to train and supervise practitioners to deliver evidence- and protocol-based interventions.

5 Care co-ordination in drug treatment services

Tim Weaver, Jude Goyder, Jo Hart, Jeffrey Fehler, Nicola Metrebian and Michael J. Crawford

Background

The notion that complex social problems required joined-up policy solutions was one of the key principles driving social policy in the late 1990s. The first ten-year Drug Strategy (HM Government 1998) was a powerful expression of this principle. While relatively brief about the specifics of how UK drug treatment services should develop, the strategy was clear that treatment was part of a response to drug use in society. The strategy addressed issues of both supply and demand for drugs and argued that treatment needed to be co-ordinated with the activities of the criminal justice system. The key 'treatment element' of the Drug Strategy was the establishment of the National Treatment Agency for Substance Misuse (NTA) in 2001. The role of the NTA was to oversee an increase in the availability, capacity and effectiveness of drug treatment services. In 2002, the NTA published *Models of Care for the Treatment of Adult Drug Misusers* (hereafter referred to as *Models of Care*) which proposed a national framework for the commissioning of drug treatment services (NTA 2002b).

Development of local service systems with the capacity to meet the multiple needs of people who misuse drugs was central to *Models of Care* and it recognised that:

- a range of drug treatment interventions and modalities needed to be available through local services in order to match the differing needs of clients;
- treatment would be most effective if provided alongside general health, social care and criminal justice interventions that address factors contributing to drug misuse as well as its consequences;
- services needed to be integrated so that this range of interventions could be provided in a co-ordinated way.

(NTA 2002b)

To achieve these objectives *Models of Care* placed responsibility with local Drug Action Teams (DATs) to commission local services that provide a range of interventions at each of four tiers (tier 1: non-drug services; tier 2: open access drug services; tier 3: specialist community services offering structured treatments; tier 4: residential or in-patient services). In turn *Models of Care* required services offering structured treatment programmes (i.e. tier 3 or tier 4 services) to practise a form of case management known as 'care co-ordination'. Care co-ordination was introduced to achieve a 'joined-up' response to the multiple and complex needs of drug users at the individual patient level (NTA 2002b).

Although the introduction of care co-ordination was novel in UK drug treatment services, which had a limited tradition of case management, it was not a radical innovation in health care policy. Care co-ordination is a variant of case management. It is beyond the scope of this chapter to review the history and development of case management but, since being introduced to mental health care in the 1960s, it has been extensively applied, refined and re-invented in a range of treatment settings. Indeed, *Models of Care* emphasises the consistency and complementarity of care co-ordination to the Care Programme Approach (CPA) practised in mental health services in the UK, which itself is a form of case management (DH 1998a).

What is case management?

Case management describes a generic approach to the longitudinal, clinical management of clients with complex, chronic, enduring or relapsing health problems. Case management may be required (a) if the needs of clients are multiple not singular, (b) if the effectiveness of core treatment interventions is influenced by the presence of other co-morbidity (clinical or social), and/or (c) there is some form of joint clinical or medico-legal management responsibility. In any of these circumstances, there may be a requirement to ensure co-ordination of interventions. Drug misuse fits this description in that it is a chronic relapsing condition (Gossop *et al.* 1998) for which treatment, prognosis and recovery are commonly complicated by concurrent social problems, criminal justice issues, poly-substance use (Home Office 2002), and physical and psychiatric co-morbidities (Weaver *et al.* 2003). As drug treatment has expanded, services have increasingly been required to manage clients with these multiple, complex and variable health and social care needs. This requires not only a range of interventions to be provided but also input (ideally co-ordinated) from a number of care agencies. Hence, treatment agencies also need to pursue 'joined-up' solutions.

The generic aims of case management are (a) to maintain contact (engagement) with clients, and (b) to improve defined measures of health status and social functioning. The precise clinical and service-level aims of case management may vary according to treatment setting and client group. However, an implicit objective of all case management schemes is to enhance patient outcomes by improving the co-ordination of service delivery and increasing access to needed services (Onyett 1992). This is achieved through two mechanisms:

- First, overall responsibility and accountability for the 'management of a case' is clarified by assigning that case to a caseload of a designated 'case manager' or (under certain circumstances) a case management team.
- Second, the aims and objectives of case management are pursued through implementation of a process of care. The case manager has responsibility for assessing the patient's needs, developing a care plan to meet those needs and ensuring that those needs are met, monitored and reviewed (Figure 5.1).

Models of Care and subsequent developments in care coordination

The implementation of 'care co-ordination' within tier 3 drug treatment services ensures that care and treatment employ case management principles.

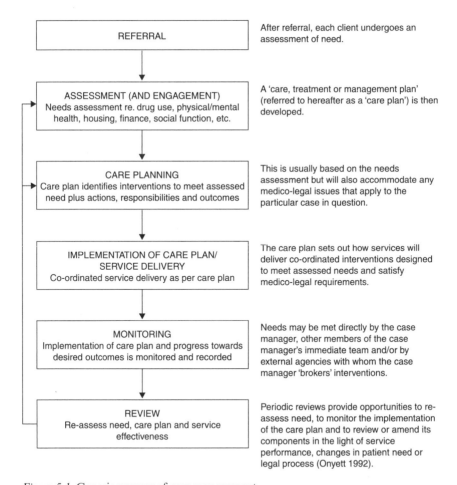

Figure 5.1 Generic process of case management.

Although *Models of Care* gives specific and separate emphasis to the processes of assessment and care planning, they nevertheless represent key elements of a longitudinal care co-ordination process that involves:

- identification of a named care co-ordinator to organise care across health and social care agencies and maintain contact with the client;
- systematic and ongoing assessment of health and social care needs;
- care planning which responds to these needs;
- regular reviews of the care plan.

As care co-ordination is intended to be 'needs-led', the intensity of care co-ordination will depend on the range and complexity of individual need. *Models of Care* originally differentiated 'standard' and 'enhanced' models of care co-ordination. The latter was distinguished by the need for co-ordination with a partner agency with specific competencies and medico-legal responsibilities – either mental health services (for those with severe mental illness) or a criminal justice agency. However, the 2006 update to *Models of Care* removed 'enhanced' and 'standard' from the care co-ordination lexicon, recognising instead that 'clients have a range of needs, from simple to highly complex, and this must be reflected in the care plan and the intensity of care co-ordination' (NTA 2006a).

Key research questions for the drug misuse research initiative

The development of care co-ordination is viewed by policy makers as a critical element in the development of a modern, integrated and effective drug treatment service, which responds appropriately to shifting patterns of drug use and the shift of drug policy to centre-stage in the government policy agenda (NTA 2002b). However, there is no significant tradition of case management in UK substance misuse services and limited information about how differently configured services were interpreting, practising and developing care co-ordination.

The research described in this chapter represents an attempt to benchmark current practice nationally.

The National Study of Care Co-ordination in drug treatment services (NatSOCC)

The study method

The NatSOCC study aimed to examine the implementation of care co-ordination (case management) within drug treatment services (both statutory and non-statutory) and to describe models of case management and variations in practice. To achieve these aims, we completed a national postal survey of adult drug treatment services providing tier 3 interventions (alone or in conjunction with tier 2 or tier 4 interventions). Private treatment clinics, young persons' services and any Drug Interventions Programme (DIP) services not integrated within a treatment service offering tier 3 interventions were excluded. At completion in December 2006, the survey population included 455 services across all DAT areas in England.

The survey questionnaire included items related to service characteristics including number and professional background of staff, interventions provided, and the size and characteristics of the client population. Data regarding the extent to which key elements of case management (assessment, care planning, monitoring and review) had been implemented were also sought. A further series of questions explored the way in which case management was operationalised at a team level and definitions of case management responsibilities.

Completed questionnaires were received from 337 (74.1 per cent) services. Brief data obtained for all services (i.e. caseload size, intervention provision, managing organisation) enabled comparison of the characteristics of respondents and non-respondents. There were no significant differences between non-respondents and respondents in relation to statutory or non-statutory management, aggregate caseload size or prescribing status. Nine services were excluded from further analysis because they did not meet inclusion criteria: for example tier 4 services providing aftercare ($n=5$), non-specialist services providing limited drug treatments ($n=2$) or small satellite clinics of primary care-based services ($n=2$). Hence the analysis described below was completed with a population of 328 services.

Study findings

National profile of tier 3 drug treatment services

Services were diverse but could be characterised on the basis of team composition and interventions provided. We developed a typology comprising four distinct service types (see Table 5.1) which was used in our analysis. Services were characterised as:

- structured *prescribing services* with no structured day programme;
- structured *prescribing services with a day programme*;
- non-prescribing, structured *counselling services*;
- non-prescribing *structured day programmes*.

The vast majority of prescribing services were managed by a statutory provider (NHS Mental Health or Primary Care Trust). However non-statutory agencies provided over a third (16/44, 36.4 per cent) of prescribing services that also offer structured day programmes. Structured counselling was also provided by two-thirds of services ($n=220$, 67.1 per cent). Whilst prescribing services with or without a day programme and non-prescribing day programmes commonly reported provision of structured 1-2-1 counselling, we characterised services as 'counselling' where that was the sole intervention provided. Of the 110 (33.5 per cent) non-prescribing services, 64 (19.5 per cent) provided a structured day programme, while 46 (14 per cent) provided counselling only. Non-statutory agencies are the main providers of non-prescribing services (100/110, 90.9 per cent). Prescribing services provided the widest range of tier 3 interventions while the majority of (non-prescribing) counselling services and structured day programmes concentrated on their single main mode of intervention. Local authorities managed eight services (2.4 per cent) of varying types.

Table 5.1 shows that a majority of services provide interventions for users of both opiate and non-opiate drugs, while nearly half also provide services to primary alcohol users (44.8 per cent, $n=147$).

Virtually all prescribing services offered care-planned prescribing (97.2 per cent) and most (86.7 per cent) also offered community detoxification. Just over half provided low threshold prescribing (51.4 per cent). A small minority of non-prescribing services (9/110, 8.2 per cent) were involved in shared care prescribing arrangements, providing non-medical interventions to clients medically managed by a partner agency.

The majority of services ($n=219$, 66.8 per cent) also provided tier 2 interventions to clients. This was particularly common amongst counselling services (43/46, 93.5 per cent) and prescribing services with structured day programmes (37/44, 84.1 per cent). A minority ($n=46$, 14 per cent) also provided tier 4 services.

Staffing and team composition

Our findings revealed a diverse workforce and varying team composition and structure across services. Virtually all medical posts we identified [210.3 of 216 whole-time-equivalent (WTE) posts, 97.4 per cent] were based in prescribing services.

The aggregate workforce with case management responsibility totalled 3,654 posts. Nursing was the most commonly represented discipline, comprising more than a third of the aggregate workforce ($n=1,402$, 38.4 per cent), and the highest proportion of keyworkers in prescribing services. Staff with qualifications in social work ($n=518$, 14.2 per cent), community work ($n=319$, 8.7 per cent), counselling ($n=281$, 7.7 per cent), criminal justice work ($n=246$, 6.7 per cent), psychology ($n=198$, 5.4 per cent), and without health care qualifications comprise the remainder.

Non-prescribing services had the highest proportion of staff with counselling backgrounds. Workers without health care qualifications represented a prominent minority of staff in both prescribing and non-prescribing services (14 per cent and 20 per cent, respectively).

Three types of teams were identified in prescribing services. All were medically led and included nursing staff. Differentiation was made on the basis of inclusion of team members from non-medical disciplines. Three variants were identified:

- *Comprehensive teams* included social care *and* psychotherapy (psychologists and counsellors) clinicians and in some instances other allied health staff as keyworkers.
- *Medical and psychotherapy teams:* as above but without staff who have social care qualifications.
- *Medical and social care teams* included social care professions but no psychotherapy clinicians specifically delivering psychosocial interventions. Other allied health professions may also be represented but no psychologists or counsellors.

Table 5.1 shows the distribution of the above team types between differently configured prescribing services.

Non-prescribing services could be categorised according to a primary focus on social care or psychosocial interventions:

- *Social care teams:* these teams comprise staff from a social care background. They may include staff delivering psychosocial interventions (including nurses working in this capacity) plus keyworkers from other allied health professions. However, they provide no medical interventions.
- *Psychosocial teams:* these teams consist primarily of staff trained in counselling, psychology and psychotherapy. The team may include some nurses, keyworkers from other allied health professions and keyworkers without professional health care qualifications who are given appropriate training to deliver psychosocial interventions.

The organisation of case management at service level

Services reported team sizes ranging from one to fifty-one WTE keyworker posts with a median of seven and diverse caseload sizes. Generally, prescribing services reported larger teams and higher aggregate caseloads but ranges were wide both between and within service types. For each service, we calculated the mean caseload by dividing the total caseload by the figure obtained for WTE keyworkers employed. Table 5.1 shows that the mean caseload per WTE keyworker also varied widely. The mean caseload was highest in prescribing services (28 drug clients, 31.5 drug and alcohol clients) where the range was between 5 and 230.

The distribution of the mean keyworker caseloads we calculated for each service was very skewed. Hence, we considered the median values and the range of (mean) keyworker caseload sizes in our further analysis by service type. In this analysis, we found that the median keyworker caseload in prescribing services with a structured day programme was 16 drug clients, rising to 18.6 when alcohol clients were also included. The range in keyworker

Table 5.1 Typology of tier 3 adult drug treatment services based on interventions provided for clients, also showing team composition, target client group, caseload management policies and ratio of clients to keyworkers

	All services (N=328)		Structured prescribing (N=174)		Structured prescribing + day programme (N=44)		Non-prescribing counselling (N=46)		Non-prescribing day programme (N=64)	
	n	(%)	n	(%)	n	(%)	n	(%)	n	(%)
Team composition										
Comprehensive team	80	(24.4)	59	(18.0)	21	(6.4)	0	–	0	–
Medically led team, no social care	77	(23.5)	62	(18.9)	15	(4.6)	0	–	0	–
Medically led team, with social care	61	(18.6)	53	(16.2)	8	(2.4)	0	–	0	–
Social care team, non-medical	62	(18.9)	0	–	0	–	22	(6.7)	40	(12.2)
Psychosocial therapies team, non-medical	48	(14.6)	0	–	0	–	24	(7.3)	24	(7.3)
Target population										
Primary opiate users only	58	(17.7)	54	(31.0)	2	(4.5)	1	(2.2)	1	(1.5)
Primary non-opiate users only	10	(3.0)	0	–	0	–	5	(10.7)	5	(7.8)
Primary opiate and non-opiate users	260	(79.3)	120	(69.0)	42	(95.5)	40	(87.0)	58	(90.6)
Also manages primary alcohol clients	147	(44.8)	72	(41.4)	26	(57.7)	23	(51.1)	26	(40.6)

Caseload management

	Median	(Range)	Median	(Range)	Median	(Range)	Median	(Range)	Median	(Range)
Personal caseloads	79	(24.1)	43	(24.7)	9	(20.5)	14	(30.4)	13	(20.3)
Personal caseloads + some shared cases	239	(72.9)	126	(72.4)	35	(79.5)	31	(67.4)	47	(73.4)
Team shares entire caseload	10	(3.0)	5	(2.9)	0	–	1	(2.2)	4	(6.3)
Internal brokerage reported*	111	(33.8)	63	(36.2)	9	(20.5)	19	(41.3)	20	(31.3)
Sharing of casework reported**	37	(11.3)	18	(10.3)	4	(9.1)	10	(21.7)	5	(7.8)
	Median	(Range)	Median	(Range)	Median	(Range)	Median	(Range)	Median	(Range)
N drug clients per WTE keyworker	20	(2–230)	28	(3–230)	16	(4–158)	9.7	(2–55)	6.6	(2–33)
N drugs and alcohol clients per WTE keyworker	23.3	(2–230)	31.5	(5–230)	18.6	(8–158)	14.2	(4–55)	8.8	(2–33)

* Internal brokerage: workers provide specialist input to clients not on their caseload.
** Sharing of casework: either by sharing caseloads or internal brokerage.

caseload sizes was again marked amongst this group of services with a low of 8 and a high of 158.

Aggregate caseloads of non-prescribing services were typically smaller, although there were examples of such services with large caseloads. (Counselling services: median 50; range 4–400. Structured day programmes: median 40; range 5–700.) Over one-fifth of non-prescribing services had a caseload that exceeded 100 current clients with drug problems (24/110, 22 per cent). The median keyworker caseload in counselling services was 9.7 drug clients (range 2–33), rising to 14.2 (2–33) when alcohol clients were also taken into account. Two-thirds of such services had keyworker caseloads of less than 20 clients (31/46, 67.4 per cent).

The median keyworker caseload in non-prescribing services with a structured day programme was 6.6 drug clients (range 2–55), rising to 8.8 (range 4–55) when alcohol clients were also included. A majority of services had keyworker caseloads of less than 15 clients (45/64, 70.3 per cent).

There were fifteen services with keyworker caseloads of less than five. All of these were non-prescribing services. One was a counselling service providing brief intensive specialist counselling. The other fourteen services had a structured day programme.

Mean keyworker caseloads exceeded fifty in twenty-nine services and seventy in nine of these. These were all structured prescribing services with large aggregate caseloads (more than 250 clients). In each team doctors 'keyworked' clients and provided medical management to a medical and psychotherapy team but not medical and social care teams or comprehensive teams. PCTs managed seven of the nine services with caseloads exceeding seventy. In these services, medical management was provided by non-specialised GPs. While there was no significant difference in the median caseloads of structured prescribing services with comprehensive as opposed to non-comprehensive teams, it was apparent that *all* services that could be defined as 'extreme outliers' at either end of the range of median keyworker caseloads (i.e. less than 15 or more than 70) had non-comprehensive staff teams as defined above.

Allocation of case management responsibility

Table 5.1 shows that in the vast majority of services (n=318, 97 per cent) keyworkers were allocated a personal caseload, commonly coupled with shared team responsibility for a proportion of cases (n=239, 72.9 per cent). In seventy-nine services (24.1 per cent), the allocated keyworker had sole responsibility for the case management of allocated clients. A small number of services (n=10, 3 per cent) reported that keyworkers were not allocated a caseload and responsibility for care was instead shared across the team. There was no significant relationship between service type, team composition and the method for allocation of case management responsibility.

Amongst the 318 services where keyworkers were allocated a personal caseload of clients, two-thirds (217/318, 68.2 per cent) reported that some form of internal brokerage operated within the team whereby keyworkers provided specialist input to clients not on their caseload. This was most common in services where there was also formal sharing of case management responsibility for a proportion of cases, but was also reported in half of the seventy-nine services (*n*=42, 53.2 per cent) which identified the allocated keyworker as the person solely responsible for case management of allocated clients. However, prescribing services with a comprehensive team were more likely to report internal brokerage (66/80, 82.5 per cent) than were those with non-comprehensive teams that were either nurse-led (44/77, 57.1 per cent) or which included social care staff (36/61, 59 per cent) ($\chi^2$2df=13.8, p=0.001).

In only thirty-six services (11 per cent) was there no within-team sharing of casework for individual clients. Examples of all service types with this arrangement could be identified but counselling services had the highest proportion where this arrangement was reported (9/46, 19.6 per cent).

Policies for the management of keyworker caseload size

Respondents were asked whether the service had any policy guiding caseload size. Data were provided by 308 of the 318 services where keyworkers carried personal caseloads. One-quarter (*n*=81, 26.3 per cent) reported that they had no policy in relation to caseload size, just under a third reported operating some form of caseload weighting system (*n*=98, 31.8 per cent), while 41.9 per cent (*n*=129) reported operating a simple minimum and/or maximum number of cases that a keyworker could be allocated pro rata. There was no significant relationship between service type and policy. However, different service types reported markedly different caseload limits. For example, the median figure for the maximum caseload size reported by structured prescribing services was thirty-five cases (range: 13–90). For counselling services and structured day programmes the comparable median figure for the maximum caseload size was twenty cases (range: 9–37) and ten cases (range: 4–32), respectively.

We were able to compare reported caseload with policy concerning minimum and/or maximum caseload in 121 cases. This comparison demonstrated that the stated policy was often a poor guide to actual caseloads. Mean caseloads fell within the designated range reported in seventy-two services (59.5 per cent), below the minimum figure in eighteen services (14.9 per cent) and above the maximum in thirty-one services (25.6 per cent). There was no significant difference between service types in the proportions of services where keyworker caseloads fell outside the range defined by policy.

The case management process

Our findings showed that the vast majority of services (306/316, 96.1 per cent) completed some form of *assessment* with more than 90 per cent of their caseload and that overall an estimated 96.1 per cent of the aggregate tier

3 treatment population had been assessed at the time of the survey. However, assessment arrangements differed. For example, counselling services reported less emphasis on comprehensive assessment as opposed to triage than other service types. Moreover, while most services reported that assessment was 'open-ended' or 'variable', a quarter of services reported that the process was time-limited. Services of all types reported these differing practices and there was no statistically significant difference in the proportion of the four service types reporting these different assessment arrangements. Similarly high proportions of patients (more than 90 per cent) across all service types were reported to have been subject to *risk assessment*.

Assessments were used to generate care plans for the majority of clients except in three (0.9 per cent) non-prescribing services which reported not completing any care plans. Care plans, described as brief or comprehensive, were completed for nearly nine out of ten clients (89.4 per cent) in the aggregate treatment population. There was some evidence that counselling services placed more emphasis on brief care plans, and comprehensive plans were more likely in non-prescribing day programmes. The proportion with a care plan was lowest in counselling services (83.5 per cent) but did not differ markedly between other service types. With the exception of forty-nine services (15.4 per cent), the care planning process was not time-limited. Services of all types reported varied practices. There were no apparent differences between the services operating these different arrangements in terms of the size of their total aggregate caseload or the median size of individual keyworker caseloads.

Approximately 90 per cent of tier 3 clients had care plans monitored by keyworkers. The proportions of 'monitored clients' were highest in structured prescribing services (94.3 per cent) and lowest in counselling services (83.5 per cent). Care plan reviews were reported for 85.5 per cent of the total aggregate tier 3 treatment population. The proportion receiving a review was lowest amongst counselling services (76.6 per cent) and highest in structured prescribing services (87.1 per cent) and non-prescribing day programmes (87.5 per cent).

Outreach was employed as a strategy for both monitoring clients and promoting their retention in treatment in a substantial minority of drug treatment services. Outreach client visits were reported by nearly a third (n=105, 32 per cent) of services where clients failed to attend for assessment, and by slightly more (n=120, 36.6 per cent) when treatment appointments were missed. Prescribing services with a structured day programme were more likely to visit clients to encourage attendance at assessment (35.5 per cent) whilst prescribing services without a structured day programme were most likely to visit clients to encourage attendance at treatment (39.1 per cent). When team composition is accounted for, prescribing teams with medical and social staff were the most likely to carry out visits for clients who fail to attend assessments (39.3 per cent of services will carry out some home visits) and treatment appointments (50.8 per cent will carry out some home visits).

For most services reporting the use of outreach, this was a mechanism to maintain contact with clients irrespective of referral route. However, a small number of services reported that they would only practise outreach with clients referred into treatment through criminal justice system agencies. Fourteen services (4.3 per cent) reported this policy in relation to clients defaulting on assessment appointments, and nine (2.7 per cent) reported the same policy in relation to clients defaulting on treatment appointments. Although the use of outreach is not limited to criminal justice system clients, services are slightly more likely to carry out home visits for clients if the service has a relationship with a local DIP team.

Discussion

The development of care co-ordination is viewed by policy makers as a critical element in the development of a modern, integrated and effective drug treatment service, which responds appropriately to shifting patterns of drug use (NTA 2002b). The findings of the NatSOCC study provide important new evidence about the early development of care co-ordination but certain study limitations should be acknowledged before the implications for policy and service development are described.

The most important limitation of the survey is its descriptive rather than evaluative nature, which thus provides a cross-sectional examination of a potentially dynamic practice. In short, we do not know whether the developing approaches we observed were effective. Nor do we know to what extent guidance issued since data collection (NTA 2006b, 2007b) may have impacted on the observed practices.

Notwithstanding these limitations, the study does achieve its important objective of benchmarking the progress of services towards implementation of the case management process. A positive finding is that an overwhelming majority of services have embraced case management principles and are undertaking assessments and developing care plans which they both monitor and review. Moreover at most of these services a large majority of the patients are subject to these procedures. However, behind these encouraging reports some extreme variation in practice is evident. Given that tier 3 drug treatment services are themselves a heterogeneous group, this was not unexpected, but many of the differences we observed were independent of service type or even the professional composition of the team. Services providing the same range of interventions to the same client groups appear to be approaching this in quite different ways. The most striking differences are related to caseload size. Some services treat a small number of clients relative to the number of keyworkers and some services treat a very large number of clients with relatively few keyworkers. While the mean caseload of prescribing services is around thirty clients, clinicians in around one in seven prescribing services operate with a personal caseload of more than fifty clients. There has to be some assessment of the appropriateness of service intensity relative to the clients' needs at either end of the range of caseload sizes, whether the worker is responsible for over fifty clients or fewer than five clients. It is important to stress that our study does not provide answers to these questions but, given the variations we have observed, there is a need for outcome-based research to address questions about optimal caseload sizes and the critical components of case management.

Unfortunately, there is no UK evidence about the effectiveness of care co-ordination in drug treatment, and limited data from other settings. While the USA has seen a number of schemes implemented and evaluated, there has been limited fidelity to any one model and generalisability to the UK situation is uncertain. In the USA, case management tends to be seen as an intervention, which is an adjunct to treatment, rather than an overall framework for service delivery.

We have noted above that care co-ordination in drug treatment services shares certain key characteristics with the CPA used in mental health services. CPA is seen as a brokerage model of case management, in which managers who may be directly involved in the delivery of interventions are also required to 'broker' the delivery of needed interventions through other specialist agencies, as opposed to within a comprehensive team. It has been argued that brokerage models of case management have a weak evidence base compared to alternative intensive, team-based approaches which stress outreach rather than monitoring and supervision (*Lancet* 1995; Marshall 1996; Marshall *et al.* 1998, 2003). In this context, the finding that significant numbers of services are beginning to embrace outreach principles is significant. This is a clear area for development and further investigation.

Trials of the UK CPA in mental health services have shown consistent reductions in 'loss to follow-up', but clinical gains and reductions in the use of in-patient care have proved difficult to achieve (Marshall *et al.* 1995, 2003; Tyrer *et al.* 1995; Burns *et al.* 1999). Care co-ordination is built on similar principles to the CPA. But while the allocation of a 'personal caseload' of clients to a keyworker is an almost universal characteristic, our findings also suggest that in three-quarters of services there is a degree of shared responsibility for clients. Given the evidence from the mental health field, this may provisionally be viewed as a positive finding. It is perhaps to be expected that services with comprehensive teams (i.e. a broad multi-disciplinary mix) should engage in more internal sharing of casework but, beyond this, there is little evidence that caseload management policies are strongly related to the characteristics of the service.

Taken as a whole, these findings suggest that there is a lack of consensus and consistency around some key aspects of case management practice but nevertheless some interesting and potentially positive developments are in process. These need to be fostered and rigorously evaluated so that policy and practice guidance, and local DAT commissioning decisions, can be guided by good outcome-based evidence.

6 The effect of waiting for treatment

Michael Donmall and Tim Millar

This chapter considers the effects of waiting for treatment and whether drug users are more or less likely to take up a treatment offer, or remain engaged in treatment, if they are put on a waiting list. The possible effect of waiting for treatment is considered alongside a range of other factors. The surprising conclusion is that while several factors, most notably the treatment agency itself, influence whether or not a treatment offer is taken up and whether clients are then retained in treatment, waiting times do not in themselves exert a notable influence on these outcomes. However, it is suggested that waiting times may well influence clients' decisions to seek treatment in the first place.

Background

Throughout the 1990s there were long waiting times for drug misuse treatment at both community-based and in-patient services, depending on local policy, the availability of local treatment options and the extent of resources (DH 1996; NTA 2002a).

Given the public health imperative to engage drug users in treatment, the lack of treatment capacity to meet apparent levels of demand became a key concern. Reducing the number of drug misusers denied immediate access to appropriate treatment was a major objective in the government's 1998–2007 Drug Strategy (HM Government 1998). By 2003–4, the National Treatment Agency for Substance Misuse (NTA) had set waiting targets of from two to three weeks, depending on treatment modality, and waiting times were identified as one of four Key Performance Indicators for drug misuse services (NTA 2002a). These have since been revised on a regular basis (most recently NTA 2006a) and subject to detailed routine scrutiny and reporting at a local and national level.

There is evidence that waiting for treatment can have a direct effect on whether clients continue to pursue treatment and also on their subsequent experience of treatment. Compared to immediate access, a wait of only five to eight weeks has been reported to discourage as many as half of applicants for methadone maintenance treatment and to increase substantially the risk of in-treatment drug use, treatment expulsion and non-completion

(Bell *et al.* 1994). Among applicants to a cocaine treatment programme, longer delays between initial phone contact and the scheduled intake appointment were associated with lower attendance rates, waiting time being the only significant predictor of uptake among a selection of social and other drug-related variables (Festinger *et al.* 1995). Longer waits have also been observed to be associated with a greater likelihood of engaging in drug-related crime (Brown *et al.* 1989).

Long waiting times may also discourage clients from seeking treatment in the first place: the Audit Commission suggested that 'lengthy waiting lists can drive clients away', citing one area with a five-month waiting time for a community drug service appointment in which 'only one in every three clients offered an appointment, ever attended' (Audit Commission 2002). When users have been asked about their reasons for not seeking help, long waiting lists have been among the most frequently mentioned deterrents (ISDD 1989; Wilson 1992; Fountain *et al.* 2000). Clients have reported that, while on a waiting list, their interest in entering treatment decreased and their views about its effectiveness became more pessimistic (Brown *et al.* 1989). However, the period of pre-treatment wait has been reported to be associated with stable patterns of substance use, at least for those who eventually make it into a treatment programme (Best *et al.* 2002).

The evidence is thus equivocal. Some studies have found no association between waiting for treatment and whether clients are subsequently retained in treatment (Addenbrooke and Rathod 1990). Some have found no association between direct admission and treatment retention (Dennis *et al.* 1994). Influential factors may be the length of time waiting and the case mix of samples.

In response to concern about the effects of waiting times, the Department of Health commissioned the University of Manchester team to undertake a study of waiting times for drug misuse treatment in England, with the following aims:

- to ascertain the status of waiting lists for drug misuse treatment in England;
- to investigate if waiting had an impact on whether clients took up the offer of, and were retained in, treatment;
- to study the effects that waiting had on clients themselves.

The investigation focused on treatment for opiate use, specifically out-patient methadone prescribing and in-patient detoxification. Four related studies were undertaken:

Study 1: A national survey of drug services to identify, quantify and describe factors that affect waiting lists and their management

Study 2: A prospective study of the effects of waiting times on treatment uptake

Study 3: A retrospective study of the effects on treatment retention
Study 4: A qualitative study of user perspectives on the effect of waiting for treatment

NHS Research Ethics Approval for the research was granted by the North West Regional Multi-Centre Research Ethics Committee (MREC) in January 2001. Preliminary interviews were undertaken with an opportunistic sample of agency managers across England and the themes that emerged from this formed the basis of the national survey.

National survey of drug services (Study 1)

The survey was designed to identify factors that influence waiting lists for drug treatment, to ascertain the then current practice in managing waiting lists, and to quantify waiting times for treatment services in England. As this was prior to the development of the National Drug Treatment Monitoring System (NDTMS), a list of all known drug treatment services in England was compiled from Drug Misuse Database contacts, local intelligence and lists held by SCODA (Standing Conference on Drug Abuse – now called DrugScope). During December 2000 and January 2001, a postal questionnaire was sent to each of the 643 services identified on that list. Those services found to offer community-based treatment for opiate users formed the sampling frame for Studies 2 and 3.

Agency sample

A total of 322 services (50 per cent) provided responses to the survey. Respondent agencies appeared to be broadly representative of service provision in England: 36 per cent were from the statutory sector and 56 per cent were voluntary sector organisations, these proportions being very similar to those observed in SCODA's 1997 census of drug services in England and Wales (37 per cent statutory sector, 58 per cent voluntary sector). Comparison of respondent and non-respondent agencies, based on the SCODA service directory and telephone follow-up of non-respondents, suggested that they provided similar types of intervention, although respondents were more likely to provide arrest referral (37 per cent vs. 22 per cent), less likely to provide prison-based services (15 per cent vs. 39 per cent) and slightly less likely to provide prescribing (37 per cent vs. 43 per cent) or in-patient opiate detoxification (27 per cent vs. 33 per cent).

A total of 126 agencies (43 per cent), comprising 153 individual treatment units, provided substitute prescribing with methadone and/or in-patient detoxification for opiate users. Most (62 per cent) of this group were community drug, or drug and alcohol services, 15 per cent were in-patient opiate detoxification units and the remainder provided GP liaison, residential rehabilitation with in-house treatment, young people's drug services or were specialist units within a primary care team. A quarter (25 per cent) had 4.5 whole-time-equivalent (WTE) clinical workers or fewer, a quarter had 11 or more. Just under one-half (45 per cent) reported a staffing shortfall in relation to level of funding – the number of vacant posts ranging from 0.5 to 6 WTEs. Services appeared to be making full use of their financial resources: just under one-half (45 per cent) reported that their annual prescribing budget was usually overspent and a further 46 per cent that it was usually spent up to its limit.

Service caseloads ranged from six to 1,200 clients, with a mean of 209. A mean average of 76 per cent of the caseload were opiate users. Services received a mean of thirty-three referrals per month, although one-half received twenty-five or fewer. Self- or GP referrals were the most common routes into treatment. It is noteworthy that, despite concerns expressed in preliminary interviews about increasing pressure on services resulting from new criminal justice referral initiatives, at the time of the survey arrest referral accounted for less than 5 per cent of new clients at responding services.

The assessment procedure at this time, following referral and before start of treatment, typically involved an initial keyworker assessment and commonly (48 per cent) a subsequent clinical assessment. Services reported substantial client attrition following referral, the mean estimated dropout rate between referral and assessment being 25 per cent and as much as 40 per cent among 15 per cent of services. The mean estimated dropout rate between assessment and commencement of treatment was lower at 13 per cent, although 5 per cent of services estimated that dropout rates exceeded 30 per cent.

Waiting lists and their management

Most services (66 per cent) reported that they currently had a waiting list for access to treatment, with a mean of forty-five clients waiting for treatment at the time of the survey (2000–1). Hence, there were almost 7,000 clients waiting for treatment at the 153 participating services at this time.

Service policies varied in relation to their referral and assessment procedures. Consequently clients 'waited' at different points in the system: 47 per cent reported that waiting lists comprised those still waiting for an assessment and 25 per cent that they comprised those already assessed and waiting for treatment.

Most services (77 per cent) indicated that they operated some form of referral prioritisation. Waiting times for priority referrals were short, 50 per cent of services reporting that the usual wait between referral and start of treatment was one week or less. The groups most commonly fast-tracked into treatment were pregnant users (prioritised by 95 per cent of services), those with serious physical health problems (81 per cent), those with serious mental health problems (78 per cent) and those from families where there were child protection concerns (73 per cent). A significant minority (43 per cent) of services suggested that 'priority' referrals had increased over the previous three years and preliminary interviews highlighted concern that an increasing number of 'priority' clients were leading to increased waiting times for non-priority groups.

Non-priority clients waited up to one year between referral and assessment, although the median wait was four weeks and the mean eight weeks and most (75 per cent) reported waits of ten weeks or less. After assessment, non-priority clients waited up to thirty weeks for treatment to commence, the mean wait being four weeks and the median two weeks. The mean waiting time between referral and starting treatment was estimated to be twelve weeks, with a median wait of eight weeks.

Services most commonly (41 per cent) identified a lack of clinical staff as the main 'blockage' in their treatment system. This was sometimes viewed as the only relevant factor, although more often a combination of resource and capacity issues was identified: '[An] extra one doctor session and 0.5 nurse session would eliminate the list, plus an increase in the prescribing budget.'

Twelve per cent of respondents indicated that constrained prescribing budgets were a contributory factor and 18 per cent that a lack of shared care prescribing was leading to congestion within the specialist prescribing service because stable clients could not be transferred to GP care. Patchy shared care coverage caused some clients to be treated much more quickly than others:

> The waiting list is primarily based on whether a client comes from an area where GP shared care is available. If shared care *is* available then generally waiting lists are low. If it is not then these clients must be seen within our central prescribing service, which is presently at full capacity.

In order to deal with this congestion, most agencies (67 per cent) attempted to arrange interim GP prescribing for clients waiting for treatment, although with varying degrees of success.

The related problems of staffing shortfalls due to long-term sick leave and difficulty in recruiting experienced drug workers were also mentioned. One-fifth (19 per cent) of respondents indicated that staff caseloads were at full capacity and the same proportion suggested that demand for treatment was increasing, explaining this in terms of increasing prevalence, seasonal variation in demand (an influx of clients wishing to be drug-free for Christmas) and changes in catchment area.

Both residential and community-based services (13 per cent) highlighted a shortage of in-patient places (or 'beds'), the latter suggesting that clients waiting for in-patient treatment were leading to congestion in the service. However, 'beds' within the independent sector were reported to be standing empty whilst clients waited for funding decisions or court proceedings to be resolved.

While nearly two-thirds of services (59 per cent) routinely employed measures to manage their waiting lists, more than one in three did not. However, almost half (44 per cent) reported that they wrote to clients to check that they still wanted treatment, and one in five (20 per cent) attempted to increase service throughput by reviewing current caseload and discharging clients, either via planned departure or by 'defaulting' those who missed appointments or failed to comply with treatment. Very few (7 per cent) screened their waiting lists to ensure that only 'appropriate' clients were held on the list.

Treatment uptake and treatment retention (Studies 2 and 3)

These stages of the project were designed to ascertain the effect of waiting times on treatment uptake and retention in treatment. A 'prospective' study (Study 2), between July 2001 and March 2002, focused on treatment uptake: treatment agencies were asked to track clients from the point of referral to the start of prescribing to ascertain what proportion accepted an eventual offer of treatment. A 'retrospective' study (Study 3), between October 2001 and May 2002, focused on retention: data were gathered from agency records in order to ascertain how long clients had remained in treatment.

The intention was to compare uptake and retention rates for agencies with short (0–4 weeks) and long (9–20 weeks) waiting times. These limits were chosen to reflect the then current suggested maximum treatment waiting time target of four weeks and the pragmatic need to exclude services with waits in excess of twenty weeks in order to complete prospective data collection within the research schedule. This avoided the difficulties inherent in measuring the wait between referral and the start of treatment at the client level since, as many clients drop out before a treatment place is offered, their waiting time for treatment cannot be measured. Agencies with waits within these ranges were identified via the national survey and a random sample was selected from each list. Unfortunately, during data collection, waits increased in five of the seven 'short wait' agencies and decreased in two of the eight 'long wait' agencies, rendering the original design unworkable. Instead, analyses were undertaken at the individual client level.

Prospective treatment uptake study

A total of 1,053 clients met the study's inclusion criteria and were included in the prospective data analysis. Many of these clients (483) lost contact before commencing treatment, the bulk (83 per cent) dropping out between referral and assessment. Of those who attended assessment, 85 per cent actually entered treatment. The waiting time between initial referral and assessment therefore appears to be the most critical in engaging the client in the treatment process. From Study 1 (2000–1 survey), this waiting period was shown to be substantial. Indeed, clients not offered an immediate assessment waited as long as twenty-nine days (median) between referral and assessment, with a mean wait of forty-two days. The uptake study focused on factors that predicted whether an assessment appointment was attended. After exclusions due to missing data etc., the sample consisted of 876 clients, 569 who attended their assessment appointment, and 307 who failed to do so.

Relevant data were collected by agencies at different points in the referral process, usually minimal at referral and more extensive, including drug use and treatment history, at assessment. Primary analysis utilised those items collected at referral and included all sample clients. Secondary analysis utilised a wider set of data items, excluding clients from agencies only collecting the full data set at assessment. Multivariate models were used to examine the effect of each variable, independent of the other factors measured, and the agency attended was included as a variable in the models so as to take account of the study's 'nested' design. Variables were included in the models if they were thought to be important confounders, irrespective of whether univariate analysis suggested that they were associated with attending assessment. Analysis erred on the side of caution in this respect rather than searching for a simple, parsimonious, but potentially misleading, model.

The primary analysis ($n=782$) included gender, age (quinary group), ethnic group, referral source, agency attended, and waiting time between referral and assessment appointment. Of these, only age ($\chi^2=36.36$, 7 d.f., p<0.001), referral source ($\chi^2=13.43$, 4 d.f., p<0.01) and agency attended ($\chi^2=59.52$, 13 d.f., p<0.001) were found to have a statistically significant and independent association with assessment uptake. Waiting time was not associated with whether or not participants took up their assessment appointment. As age increased, so did the probability that participants would attend their assessment: for example, those aged 30–34 years were over three times more likely to attend their appointment than those aged 20–24 years (adjusted odds ratio 3.2). Compared to clients referred from other drug services (the reference category), those who self-referred were more likely to attend assessment (adjusted odds ratio 1.3) and those referred from other sources were less likely to do so (adjusted odds ratio 0.6). The strongest effect, by far, was for the agency attended: clients were seven times more likely to attend assessments at some agencies than at others.

The secondary level analysis included the following additional items: drugs used in the last four weeks, frequency of drug use, whether injected, age of first opiate use, duration of opiate use, months opiate-free in the last five years, and previous treatment experience. Six agencies were excluded from this analysis because they had very little data for the clients who were not assessed, leaving a sample of 298 clients who attended for assessment and 125 who failed to attend ($n=423$). Of these additional items, only previous treatment experience was found to be independently associated with uptake, such that those with previous experience were almost twice as likely to attend assessment.

To summarise, the prospective study found that, of the variables considered, only four independently predicted whether clients took up the offer of an assessment appointment: age; referral source; previous experience of treatment; and agency attended. The wait between referral and assessment did not have a significant effect and the agency itself exerted by far the strongest effect.

Retrospective treatment retention study

The study of treatment retention was based on a sample of 761 clients. Although the same agencies were recruited for both the retrospective retention and prospective uptake studies, the client samples were different. All of the clients had started treatment at least six months prior to the data collection period. Almost all (667, 88 per cent) had attended the first assessment appointment that they were offered, waiting a median average of 26 days (mean 48 days) between referral and the first assessment date offered them. There was a median average wait of 58 days (mean 86 days) between referral and starting a methadone prescription: 23 per cent of participants fell into the study's original 'short wait' category and 37 per cent the 'long wait' category, but these categories were not considered further in the analysis described below.

As with the study of uptake, logistic regression models were used to explore the effect of a variety of explanatory variables on treatment retention at three and six months. The results for three-month retention are discussed in light of the retention policy promoted at the time. The agency attended was again included in the regression model in order to account for the study's 'nested' design. In addition, the regression considered the independent effect of the following variables on treatment retention at three months: gender, age, ethnic group, duration of use, referral source, whether methadone consumption was supervised, daily or other pick-up of prescribed substitute drugs, use of alcohol and waiting time.

Referral source exerted a statistically significant independent effect (χ^2=16.5, 4 d.f., p=0.002): self-referred clients were more than three times (adjusted odds) as likely to remain in treatment for three months as those referred from other drug services (the reference category). Methadone pick-up regimes exerted an effect (χ^2=19.17, 2 d.f., p<0.001) such that those required to pick up their methadone on a daily basis for some of the treatment period were more likely to remain in treatment after three months than clients who were never, or were continuously, assigned to daily pick-up. Supervised consumption exerted an effect (χ^2=8.77, 2 d.f., p=0.013) such that those assigned to continuous supervision were three times less likely to remain in treatment than those never supervised. It is plausible that the more 'difficult' clients might be assigned to these regimes and this may explain this effect. It is also possible that these particular intensive interventions reflect a higher level of 'care and attention' from certain agencies. Duration of opiate use, that is, length of time since first use of opiates, was positively associated with treatment retention (χ^2=6.27, 1 d.f., p=0.012) as was problematic use of alcohol (χ^2=4.55, 1 d.f., p=0.033), alcohol users being twice as likely to remain in treatment. Once again, the strongest observed effect related to the agency attended (χ^2=76.98, 15 d.f., p<0.001): participants attending the agency with the best retention at three months were over ten times more likely to remain in treatment than those attending the reference agency.

To summarise, as with the analysis of treatment (assessment) uptake, waiting times did not exert a statistically significant independent effect on whether clients remained in treatment; the strongest effect was associated with the treatment agency itself.

Client perspectives on waiting for treatment (Study 4)

During April and May 2002 a series of fifteen semi-structured interviews was undertaken with clients who were currently waiting for drug treatment at four agencies in north-west England. These case studies were designed to explore their views about, and experiences of, being placed on a waiting list for methadone prescribing.

Most accepted that they would have to wait for a methadone prescription, but identified the need to discuss their situation with a keyworker in order to get advice as to how best to cope whilst waiting: 'even if you're not scripted, just someone to come to talk to and advise you on how you can help yourself 'til you get scripted' (24-year-old female heroin user).

Some indicated that they would find waiting easier if the service provided clearer expectations of how long they might be waiting. Others indicated that they had lost faith in the system on learning that the wait was longer than they had initially been told. Clearly, it is desirable for services to provide accurate information to clients in order to manage their expectations. 'I thought it was 6–12 weeks but now [a member of staff] has just said it's 12–15 weeks before you get a keyworker and that peed me off more that what I was' (31-year-old male heroin user). 'People don't understand what it's like [and] how difficult it is to wait' (21-year-old female heroin user).

Many were frustrated at the lack of contact with treatment services whilst waiting and some felt it necessary to chase up the service to find out what was happening. Again, better communication regarding their progress on the waiting list was often all that they asked for: 'they should have got in contact with me a lot more than what they have done . . . to keep me informed of what's happening' (39-year-old male heroin user); 'just let me know what's happening and send me a letter every now and again to let me know if I've jumped up the queue a bit' (38-year-old male heroin user); 'write to you, even if it's just once a month, to let you know how far you've moved down the waiting list' (24-year-old female heroin user).

Support from partners and/or family apparently helped to sustain motivation to enter treatment, especially where the treatment service had not offered interim support: 'a crutch for me at that time and her [his girlfriend] just being there for me was enough' (37-year-old male heroin user).

Notably, a substantial minority indicated that their drug use had increased whilst awaiting treatment. However, where provided, interim prescribing had helped others to reduce illicit use and criminal activity. Nonetheless, it was suggested that interim doses prescribed by GPs were often insufficient, so that clients 'topped up' their prescribed methadone whist waiting to enter specialist treatment: 'in the morning when I wake up I'm withdrawing so I know I need a bit more than I'm getting' (35-year-old male heroin user).

Many felt the need to find alternative activities to fill the time usually spent financing, buying and using illicit drugs; some felt that attending a day centre or drop-in service would have helped in this respect: 'when you've been into drugs as long as I have the only thing that fills your day is looking for drugs, getting the money, so once you stop doing that you've got so much time on your hands and it's so easy just to fall back into the drugs then' (35-year-old male heroin user).

There was clear resentment at arrest-referred clients being 'fast-tracked' into treatment; indeed a small number indicated that they knew people who had behaved so as to be arrested in order to secure faster access to treatment, and one interviewee had actually considered trying this: 'you need to get into trouble with the police and then they'll let you in . . . it's ridiculous that if I got into trouble with the police then I'd jump the queue' (38-year-old male heroin user); 'feel like going shoplifting just to get myself arrested . . . why not . . . I won't get in any real trouble 'cos I've got no prior convictions' (24-year-old female heroin user).

Perhaps the most important observation was that clients' *perceptions* of waiting times were an important factor that influenced their decision on whether to seek help. Many of those interviewed indicated that they had friends who were discouraged from approaching treatment services because they thought they would have to wait a long time for treatment: 'everyone thinks you'll be hanging around for months for a prescription' (28-year-old male heroin user).

Conclusions

It is clearly desirable that the wait from referral to treatment should be as short as possible in any health care setting both to encourage participation in the treatment process and to increase the chances of positive outcomes. In the case of drug misuse and related behavioural health problems, the importance of short waiting times is even more acute as presentation for treatment may coincide with readiness for change at a particular time or under particular circumstances. It is widely believed, and borne out by qualitative components reported in this study, that long waiting times can act as a disincentive both in terms of willingness to present in the first place, and willingness to persist in waiting for treatment post-referral. These drivers, along with the observation of widespread long waiting times for drug misuse treatment at the time, led to the need for, and focus of, this 'outcome of waiting lists' study.

Unexpectedly, given the policy emphasis on the need to reduce waiting times (NTA 2002a, 2006a), the study found no direct influence of waiting times on either uptake of treatment assessment or retention in treatment once it had started. Clients who had already made the decision to seek help were not deterred by waiting times, once they had made this decision.

This research therefore challenges the intrinsic value of focusing on waiting times as a measure of quality of service provision, in terms of uptake and retention in treatment. Other factors have been shown to influence these outcomes, so waiting times should be considered in the context of wider aspects of the organisation of drug treatment services. Reducing waiting times is not, in itself, sufficiently effective in ameliorating treatment attrition.

Of course, drug misuse treatment operates within a distinct public health and community safety context in which encouraging more drug users to engage in effective treatment is seen to be highly desirable. Treatment only has the chance to be effective if clients successfully engage with the process of presentation and assessment, and are then equipped to persist in waiting for treatment, should this be necessary. Any factors that increase client attrition in these early stages of treatment engagement will therefore act counter to the intention of effective treatment. It is essential to clarify which factors might influence treatment attrition and at what point they do so.

It is important to note that reductions in times of waiting for treatment may have other potentially important effects, such that any lack of effect on uptake and retention does not negate the value of reductions in waiting times. We have developed the concept of 'waiting reputations' which may have a profound and highly localised effect on whether or not people seek help for their drug-related problems in the first place. Most drug users have a limited choice of services to which they can present for help in any one locale. Elements of this study have indicated that many people may be discouraged from seeking treatment at all due to their perception of how long they will have to wait. In preliminary interviews agency managers spoke of 'referral apathy', and clients supported this: 'I know people who have just not bothered coming in the first place . . . [they think] it's a complete waste of time 'cos of the waiting list.' 'Even before I came, people were telling me it's the worst time, you're gonna be waiting weeks and weeks.' This observation is further supported by findings from the Audit Commission: 'Lengthy waiting lists can drive clients away . . . local agencies can be deterred from making onward referrals . . . because they knew they would simply be put on a waiting list' (Audit Commission 2002). In this respect it is very encouraging to note that waiting times for drug treatment have been markedly reduced in the past few years.

It should be highly significant to both policy and practice agendas that the most important factor observed to influence attrition in this study, as in others (e.g. Millar *et al.* 2003), was the agency itself. Variation in agency practices apparently contributes significantly to treatment success, at least in terms of uptake and short-term retention. This can be encapsulated as follows: clients at some agencies are encouraged to feel that it is worth the wait for treatment and, once treatment has started, some agencies are very much better than others at keeping their clients in treatment. Although this may be considered unsurprising (and anecdotally confirmed many times over), its importance here lies in the fact that this *agency effect*, on which there has been rather little focus in policy directives, is a much more significant driver of effectiveness than the 'waiting effect' on which there has been a substantial policy focus.

Clients themselves described agencies in terms of their accessibility, the level of support that was offered to them and previous positive experience of the treatment service: '. . . they've always took me back'. Some services offered interim support, a drop-in service, or merely the opportunity to pop in and talk: '. . . if things are getting too much or I'm feeling down I can come in and have a chin-wag with them and that's a good thing'. Some clients felt unsupported during their wait for treatment. In this respect, frustration about lack of contact between referral and assessment was a factor that was often mentioned. If agencies were better able to maintain contact '. . . at least they [clients] would know something is happening and that they're not just left on the waiting list'. Simple routine procedures, such as writing to clients on a regular basis to update them about their progress on the waiting list, could go a long way to addressing this type of frustration. In some agencies, clients lost their place on the waiting list if they failed to attend their assessment appointment. While it is understandable that services wish to encourage attendance, this response perhaps implies a failure to properly understand the sometimes chaotic nature of clients' lifestyles, and was viewed, by clients, as unsympathetic. A more flexible, sympathetic and understanding response would be more productive in encouraging individual clients to take up a treatment offer and might have the effect of improving services' reputations with their target audience.

Widespread differences in treatment practices have been identified here and elsewhere (e.g. Stewart *et al.* 2000), but the precise components of agency practice that bring about this positive and effective engagement remain to be clarified. It is apparent from the national survey of waiting lists that there was considerable variation in agency practice with respect to organisation and management of client flow through the treatment system at the time of the study. Furthermore, based on fieldwork experience in this and other studies, it is quite clear that some services provide a welcoming, positive and supportive environment from the moment of reception and through assessment, treatment and/or onward referral, whilst others, frankly, do not. In the light of these findings, the focus should surely shift towards a better understanding of 'agency effects' and urgent efforts should be made to identify and encourage good practice.

7 Early exit: estimating and explaining early exit from drug treatment

Polly Radcliffe and Alex Stevens

There has been a huge increase in recent years in the number of people being assessed for structured drug treatment. The National Treatment Agency for Substance Misuse (NTA) estimated a 113 per cent increase between 1998 and 2006 (NTA 2006b), and the number of drug users 'in contact with treatment' by 2006/7 was thought to be 195,000, compared to 85,000 in 1998, exceeding the NTA target to double the number of those in treatment. These figures represent an impressive effort to increase the impact of drug treatment in reducing the individual and social harms of dependent drug use.

However, there is evidence that a high proportion of dependent drug users who have made contact with drug treatment agencies in tiers 3 and 4[1] have not gone on to engage in treatment, even when they had been assessed and offered a place in a treatment programme. Others begin treatment but drop out within a month, therefore not satisfying the NTA *Models of Care* guidelines, which recommend that services should aim to retain clients for twelve weeks of 'case management' in order to maximise the potential benefits of treatment (NTA 2006a).

A more recent focus of policy on drug treatment is to increase its quality and effectiveness. One of the indicators for the new government target to 'reduce the harm caused by alcohol and drugs' is the number of drug users who are recorded as being in *effective* treatment (HM Government 2008). The rate of retention in treatment is clearly a gauge of both quality and effectiveness of treatment and our research speaks to this issue.

The available research on retention has tended to look at the predictors of retention over several months but has highlighted that a large proportion of those who drop out do so in the first few days and weeks of treatment. This chapter describes a study which examined the phenomenon of early exit from drug treatment. By early exit, we mean leaving treatment between assessment and thirty days in treatment. We have examined two stages of early exit: between assessment and treatment entry; and between entry and thirty days in treatment.

Early exit represents a potential waste of opportunities and resources, because time and money that are invested in initial contacts and assessment are lost when people do not go on into treatment. Although some drug users may benefit from a brief assessment or may only be seeking a short period in treatment to tide them over a difficult patch in their lives (or a difficulty in getting hold of their drugs of choice), leaving treatment early may also represent a missed opportunity for drug users to access and receive the help that they may need in order to achieve their own aims of reducing their drug use and improving their health.

It is clear that there is attrition at each stage of the process, between referral and assessment, between assessment and treatment and within the first month of treatment, that different factors may contribute to causing dropout at different stages, and that there is a need to look at different ways of maintaining clients in services at these points of contact.

US and English research in this area has focused on longer-term retention than this study of early exit (Beynon *et al.* 2006; DeLeon and Jainchill 1986; Joe *et al.* 1998; Maglione *et al.* 2000; Millar *et al.* 2004; Peters *et al.* 1999). Beynon *et al.*'s and Millar *et al.*'s studies of retention, conducted in the north-west of England, suggest that the populations most likely to drop out of drug treatment are:

- young people;
- men;
- primary stimulant users;
- people referred from the criminal justice system.

Research on the effects of waiting time for treatment is less clear, with some evidence that it does not affect retention once treatment has started, but may be associated with higher rates of dropout between assessment and treatment entry (Donmall *et al.* 2005; Strang *et al.* 2004).

However, both US and English research (including Chapter 6 by Donmall and Millar in this volume) suggests that it is the characteristics of services rather than of service users which are more important in terms of influencing retention over several months. Some staff and agencies are also better than others at retaining clients (Cartwright *et al.* 1996; Fiorentine *et al.* 1999; Millar *et al.* 2004; Project MATCH Research Group 1998).

Our study tested whether service user characteristics are important in influencing early exit. It also examined the differences in early exit between agencies and suggests why some agencies may have higher dropout rates than others.

Research aims and methods

The aims of the project were:

1 To provide an estimate of the rates of early exit from tier 3 and tier 4 drug treatment services in two regions of England – one provincial and one metropolitan.

2   To identify the characteristics of those dependent drug users who are most likely to exit early.
3   To provide information on why drug users leave early.
4   To make recommendations on how rates of early exit can be reduced.

The study adopted a comparative approach using two sources of data:

- Quantitative data from the National Drug Treatment Monitoring System (NDTMS) from three Drug Action Team areas for 2005/6. This dataset includes over 2,500 people. It is supplemented by analysis of casefile data from participating agencies.
- Qualitative data from interviews with sixteen staff and fifty-three service users in these areas, supplemented by discussion with other staff and service users in meetings and a focus group.

Service users were randomly sampled from drug treatment services in three English Drug Action Team areas, two metropolitan and one provincial. Thirty-nine of the interviewees were men, fourteen were women. The age range of the interviewees was between 19 and 50 years old. Forty of the interviewees were White British, four were Black British, five were of Mixed Heritage, two were Irish, one was Asian British and one was a Traveller. These services were providing various forms of outpatient treatment, including opiate substitution prescriptions, day services and structured counselling. Recruitment was carried out via the treatment service records of clients who had dropped out of treatment before the three months recommended as optimal by the NTA and who had given consent for their records to be viewed. We also used snowball sampling from interviewees to identify other potential respondents (Atkinson and Flint 2001).

The quantitative data provided information on service user characteristics, which was analysed using bivariate and multivariate (logistic regression and hierarchical linear modelling) methods. The qualitative data were analysed using the adaptive coding approach (Layder 1998). This uses existing theory and knowledge to inform the development of new concepts from the data. The different analyses were compared and contrasted in order to improve the reliability of our interpretation through within- and between-method triangulation (Fielding and Fielding 1986).

Key findings

In the quantitative data from NDTMS, we found that 24.5 per cent of the sample exited between assessment and thirty days in treatment. Over two-thirds of these early dropouts occurred between assessment and treatment entry.

We found very wide differences in the rates of early exit at different agencies. For example, in analysis of agency casefile data, the proportion of clients who dropped out before thirty days in treatment varied from 12 per cent to 75 per cent between different agencies. This may have been affected by differences in recording practices, but other research, including the NTORS study, has also suggested wide variability in performance between agencies (Best 2004).

The characteristics of service users which were associated in multivariate analysis (using hierarchical linear modelling) with a greater likelihood of early exit between assessment and thirty days in treatment were:

- Being younger (a person who was 25 years old was 2.15 times more likely to drop out early than a person who was 30 years).
- Being homeless (people of no fixed abode were 1.37 times more likely to drop out early than people who had some housing).
- Not being a current injector at assessment (people who reported not injecting were 1.49 times more likely to drop out early than injectors).

In bivariate analysis, early dropout was more common among people who were male, of white ethnicity, primary stimulant users, those referred from the criminal justice system and those who entered a non-prescription service. But the influence of these variables was not statistically significant when taking into account the influence of age, homelessness and injecting status (Stevens *et al.* 2008).

Injecting drug users in their late twenties and thirties who are seeking prescription treatment can be seen as the traditional client group for drug services. Our quantitative findings support our qualitative finding that drug users who do not belong to this traditional service user group often find drug services off-putting. This was the case for this woman in her fifties who had sought treatment for her problem use of prescription drugs:

> It's quite frightening sometimes as well, especially when I was on medication prescribed by the doctor, you think, you're an ordinary person and all of a sudden you're put in a world in a waiting room with heavy drug users as well, who can just take your bag because they want the money.

Several ex-clients told us that they perceived drug treatment to be for a typical group of – mostly male – heroin injectors, whom some referred to as 'junkies' (Radcliffe and Stevens 2008). Some people who had dropped out early had done so because they did not wish to be associated with this group – for example this young woman who had sought treatment for her problem cannabis use:

> I don't want anyone to see me and say, 'oh, look', because then they start making assumptions, 'is she a smackhead?' you know.

Drug treatment tends to be offered during office hours at central locations. Some of our interviewees reported that these places and times did not fit with their working hours, as in the following example from a man in his thirties:

> It seems like you're trapped when you get on your script because like work-wise you've got to worry about making the chemist everyday. Making your appointments to get tested and everything.
>
> (Keith)

Our interview data indicate in addition that the nine-to-five opening times of many drug treatment services are a particular problem for those who work at night, including sex workers, or those who live and work far from treatment settings. It might be possible to attract and retain a wider group of problematic drug users if more use were made of mainstream health care settings and techniques from other fields. For example, GP surgeries are not associated with the 'junkie' identity, are located in every neighbourhood, and can provide opiate substitution services that are at least as successful as specialist services (Gossop *et al.* 2003; Lewis and Bellis 2001). In the field of mental health, assertive outreach (i.e. the provision of intensive, multi-disciplinary support which works with people in their own environment) has been used to expand the engagement of people who are in need of treatment. It seems to have been successful in engaging people with more severe problems than those engaged in existing community mental health services (Schneider *et al.* 2006).

Our qualitative research suggests that drug treatment staff often use the concept of the unmotivated, chaotic drug user to explain why people leave early from drug treatment. We suggest, in contrast, that the notion of chaotic drug users often refers to people whose work and patterns of activity do not coincide with the nine-to-five opening hours of many drug treatment services, or who want different services than agencies are offering. Therefore we suggest that more drug users would be able to engage with services if services adapted to their needs. Our findings also suggest that, as motivation is mutable and can be developed or damaged by the quality and type of treatment offered (Stevens *et al.* 2006), treatment services should make use of existing methods to enhance motivation in the early stages of treatment. These methods include motivational interviewing (W. R. Miller *et al.* 2002), contingency management (NICE 2007b) and node-link mapping (D. D. Simpson *et al.* 1997), although their use does not guarantee success (Donovan *et al.* 2001).

NTA guidance on retention has also mentioned techniques such as sending handwritten, personalised letters to people who are at risk of dropout, or making individualised, motivational phone calls to them (Aas 2005). In our interviews, it seemed that techniques for enhancing early motivation and engagement were not widely used in the areas we sampled. Some staff did refer to 'getting the basics right' by providing a warm welcome and a supportive environment for people who approach drug treatment. Client interviewees talked about the importance of the personal attention that treatment staff did (or did not) give them.

Drug treatment services can also contribute to early exit by not publicising their services and waiting times, leaving other drug users' conventional wisdom as the main source of information for people considering treatment entry. This can discourage people from approaching treatment agencies in the first place. It may also lead to clashes between expectations and reality when people do enter treatment, which some interviewees reported as contributing to their dropping out.

Although waiting times were not associated with dropping out of treatment in our quantitative data, several of our interviewees reported that long waiting times and assessment processes which they perceived as bureaucratic deterred them from contacting and staying with treatment agencies. The emphasis in the 2008 Drug Strategy on developing a more 'personalised approach' to treatment services so as to respond to individual circumstances (HM Government 2008: 29) supports through policy our qualitative findings that service users are more likely to stay in treatment when they feel that someone has a personal interest in their wellbeing.

Many of the people who dropped out early in our study were primary users of crack cocaine. Additional efforts to engage crack users in treatment could include rapid intake into treatment by staff who are knowledgeable about crack, as well as services such as relaxation techniques, cognitive behavioural therapy, complementary therapies, longer opening hours and the provision of food and transport, although there has been little evaluation of the outcomes of such service enhancements (Arnull *et al.* 2007; Bird 2006). From our data, it seems that additional efforts, including help in accessing housing and welfare benefits, are also needed to help homeless drug users to stay in treatment.

Clashes of expectation and reality of services can also happen when people cannot get the service they have come into treatment to get (such as residential rehabilitation or buprenorphine prescription). Some interviewees reported that they dropped out because these services, which they had said they wanted at assessment, were not provided when they entered treatment. These findings imply that drug services should do more to publicise and describe their services to drug users. Commissioners of drug treatment services may wish to consider how services can best meet the expressed desires of drug users for more flexibility in prescribing (including the availability of buprenorphine) and for easier access to residential treatment.

Specific obstacles which affect many women with drug problems include lack of childcare and the fear of their children being taken away from them into local authority care. We found that existing recommendations to provide greater support to women in treatment, including women-only spaces, choice of gender of the treatment worker, providing transport and childcare, and varying opening times (Becker and Duffy 2002; Marsh *et al.* 2000) were not widely implemented in the sampled areas. We did not find that women were more likely than men to drop out early but it seems that such measures would help treatment services to improve retention of women. While the explicit priority of the 2008 Drug Strategy of encouraging the provision of 'family-friendly' treatment services is to be welcomed, we are cautious because its intention of targeting parents whose drug use may put their children at risk for 'early intervention and support' risks further stigmatising substance-misusing parents and/or making them less likely to access treatment services or disclose their substance misuse. In addition we recommend that women's particular experience of exploitation and violence in drug markets is adequately taken into account in the planning of services.

The 2008 Drug Strategy states that 'too many drug users relapse, do not complete treatment programmes, or stay in treatment for too long before re-establishing their lives' (HM Government 2008: 29). Our recommendations – that drug treatment services are available at flexible times, that more services are offered in mainstream health settings and that service users are offered help in accessing housing and welfare benefits – support this emphasis on the reintegration of drug users into communities. The recognition in the 2008 Drug Strategy that the problems associated with dependent drug use are linked to greater structural issues of poverty and social exclusion is import-ant. Our research findings provide evidence for measures to re-include dependent drug users for the benefit of their health and wellbeing and that of the communities in which they live.

Acknowledgements

We would like to thank the participating drug services and interviewees for their contribution to this research. We thank Beryl Poole for her specialist advice, and Isabel Kessler, Neil Hunt and Melony Sanders for their work on the project. All errors and opinions are however the responsibility of the authors.

Note

1 Tier 3 includes non-residential structured treatment, including prescribing, daycare, structured counselling and day programmes. Tier 4 includes residential programmes.

8 Barriers to the effective treatment of injecting drug users

Joanne Neale, Christine Godfrey, Steve Parrott, Laura Sheard and Charlotte Tompkins

Introduction

Drug injection causes a diverse range of health harms and is associated with high levels of criminality, family disruption and neighbourhood disorder. The provision of treatment services for drug users is, however, known to reduce drug injecting, the sharing of injecting equipment, health risks, criminal activity and drug misuse more generally (Gossop 2006; Amato *et al.* 2007; Connock *et al.* 2007; NICE 2007a). Furthermore, every pound spent on drug treatment in the UK saves the state £9.50 in costs relating to crime and health care (Godfrey *et al.* 2004). Given the effectiveness of drug treatment, injecting drug users (IDUs) require easy access to services. This chapter explores the extent to which English drug policy has been successful in achieving this by investigating the barriers IDUs encounter when they try to access support. It concludes by reviewing the findings in light of *Drugs: Protecting Families and Communities. The 2008 Drug Strategy.*

Policy background

In 1998, New Labour produced *Tackling Drugs to Build a Better Britain: The Government's Ten Year Strategy for Tackling Drugs Misuse.*[1] This document emphasised the importance of getting more problem drug users into treatment and, to this end, advocated specific support for young people, ethnic minorities, and women and their babies. Accurate information, advice and practical help were to be given to avoid drug-related health problems; appropriate links would be made with accommodation, education and employment services; an integrated, effective and efficient response would be offered to drug users with mental health problems; and arrangements for drug-misusing prisoners would be coherent, focused and linked to community provision.

By the time the *Updated Drug Strategy 2002* was published, Labour was claiming that significant progress had been made. In particular, more drug users were entering treatment and waiting periods were down – developments enabled by the establishment of the National Treatment Agency for Substance

Misuse (NTA) in 2001.[2] Also, more drug users were being moved out of the criminal justice system and into treatment – a change facilitated by investment in a range of criminal justice programmes, such as arrest referral schemes, Drug Treatment and Testing Orders and drug testing of arrestees. Alongside this, progress2work had just been launched with the aim of helping recovering drug users to find and sustain paid employment.

Despite these encouraging developments, the *Updated Drug Strategy* recognised that further work was required. Accordingly, investment in additional treatment services was promised so that more drug users could be treated per year and maximum waiting times from referral to receipt of treatment would be reduced. There was also a commitment to providing new services for crack and cocaine users and more targeted support for women, minority groups, homeless drug users, and those involved in prostitution or begging. The number of primary care professionals working with drug users was to increase and extra training and accreditation were to be developed to augment the drug treatment workforce. Equally, more referrals to treatment from the criminal justice system, extra treatment places within prisons, and better continuity of treatment for prisoners leaving custody were pledged.

According to the 2004 drug strategy progress report, *Tackling Drugs: Changing Lives. Keeping Communities Safe from Drugs*, 54 per cent more drug users were in treatment than in 1998; waiting times for treatment were down by 72 per cent compared with 2001; the drug treatment workforce was 50 per cent larger than in 2002; there was better and more accessible treatment for crack and cocaine users than ever before; drug treatment services were available in all prisons; and the Drug Interventions Programme was taking advantage of every opportunity to direct drug-misusing offenders out of crime and into treatment. Continued investment in drug treatment services – including better support with housing, finance, new skills and job opportunities – was promised, along with enhanced efforts to assist drug users who were women, parents, homeless, working as prostitutes, caught in the criminal justice system, from black and minority ethnic (BME) groups, or who had mental health problems.

The research literature

In recent years, English drug policy has clearly committed itself to ensuring that effective drug treatment – broadly defined to encompass medical and non-medical interventions that might reduce the health and social harms caused by drug use – is available promptly to all who need it. However, the difficulties of achieving this and the need for further work have been openly acknowledged. To increase understanding of such issues, a review of published literature on the barriers IDUs encounter when accessing services was undertaken by the present authors. Surprisingly little UK research was identified but international work showed that problems related to both structural and individual factors.

The main structural barrier to help-seeking identified by the review was insufficient service provision (Metsch and McCoy 1999; Wood *et al.* 2002; Freund and Hawkins 2004), but this was compounded by poor information about treatment availability which meant that injectors did not always know about the full range of provision available to them (Carroll and Rounsaville 1992; Swift and Copeland 1996). Other structural barriers included bureaucratic hurdles, such as too much 'red tape' (McCollum and Trepper 1995); long waiting lists (Drumm *et al.* 2003; Carr *et al.* 2008); limited opening hours (Wood *et al.* 2002); lack of childcare (McCollum and Trepper 1995); stigmatising, negative or unsympathetic staff attitudes (Copeland 1997; Chakrapani *et al.* 2008); and strict appointment times (Metsch and McCoy 1999).

In terms of individual factors, women (Swift and Copeland 1996), members of some BME groups (Wood *et al.* 2005), homeless people (Deck and Carlson 2004), prisoners (Staton *et al.* 2001) and those living in rural areas (Deck and Carlson 2004) were all encountering problems when trying to secure support. Drug-using parents were reluctant to engage with services because they did not want to be separated from their children (Sterk *et al.* 2000) or feared losing custody of them if their ability to care was questioned (MacMaster 2005). Beyond this, some injectors did not want help because they did not see their drug use as a problem (Carroll and Rounsaville 1992), did not like the support on offer (Drumm *et al.* 2003) or did not feel that appropriate treatment was available (Digiusto and Treloar 2007). Others were too ashamed, embarrassed or guilty about their drug-taking (McCollum and Trepper 1995) or too concerned about confidentiality (Weiss *et al.* 1993) to approach professionals.

Although the international literature provides much valuable information on treatment barriers, it fails to generate a clear understanding of why injectors in England are not accessing services. Accordingly, a study of barriers to the effective treatment of IDUs, which also explored the barriers encountered by particular sub-groups of IDUs, was undertaken. The fieldwork, which took place in 2005–6, involved in-depth interviews with a demographically mixed group of seventy-five injectors who were recruited from needle exchange services located in inner-city, urban and rural areas of West Yorkshire, England.[3]

Findings from a qualitative study of seventy-five injectors

Barriers encountered

Insufficient services and support

Injectors in the study often reported that services – particularly needle exchanges and drug treatment within the criminal justice system – had become easier to access in recent years. Despite this, a clear desire for more services – especially local services – was evident. Most consistently, injectors wanted more prescribing services (both specialist community prescribing services and general practitioners who were willing to prescribe). However, they also highlighted a need for more counsellors (in the community and in prisons); more residential detoxification and rehabilitation services (especially those that accepted children, provided some medication and were not too regimented); more needle exchanges; more drop-in services; and more outreach services.

In addition, many injectors wanted services to provide routine access to a broader range of support. This included informal advice and information; financial assistance in travelling to agencies; access to prescribed medications other than methadone (such as buprenorphine, dihydrocodeine and benzo-diazepines); information and leaflets (on drugs, drug-related health problems and where to get help); assistance with housing, education, and job-seeking; diversionary leisure activities; and complementary therapies. Finally, a number of individuals wanted more support for injectors who successfully kept out of the criminal justice system:

> I think there should be more help for people who don't want to be a criminal . . . I feel like the badder you are, the more help you get. . . . Because everything relates to 'Well have you got a probation worker?', 'No. Oh well, you can't have that service then.'
>
> (Female, 36 years)

Lack of information and ineligibility for support

The interviews revealed that some injectors were not receiving support because they did not know that particular services (drop-in, outreach, stimulant workers, counselling and residential services) existed or were ignorant of their local availability or how they were delivered. Additionally, a number of IDUs had encountered problems obtaining help because they had been deemed ineligible. This had sometimes occurred because they had been banned or suspended from services – usually for missing appointments or abusing their medication. Others were unable to obtain housing and state benefits because they were not classed as 'in priority need', were too young, or did not qualify as a British citizen.

Waiting

Having to wait for drug treatment (particularly substitute medication or a place in a residential unit) was also an important barrier to securing support. Injectors routinely argued that those who wanted help should receive this immediately – otherwise they would continue using drugs and committing crime. Being made to wait could also result in lost enthusiasm and motivation for help-seeking. Equally, those waiting could be sent to prison, move out of the area, overdose, or even die before treatment was received:

> I don't see why you should have to wait six weeks just to see a doctor and get medication. I think if you really, really want to get off of it [drugs], they should help you to see that doctor a lot quicker. Because anything could happen in that six weeks . . . I could have a drugs overdose or drop dead, could end up in prison, anything.
>
> (Male, 30 years)

Another form of waiting that deterred service use was 'hanging around' in agencies in order to be seen by a service worker. Waiting in drug services where drug dealing or violence might occur was stressful; waiting for lengthy periods at housing services and in courts was difficult for those experiencing withdrawal symptoms; and waiting to collect methadone in a pharmacy could be embarrassing.

Appointments and bureaucracy

Having to attend inflexible pre-arranged appointments at services also constituted a major barrier to accessing support. This was mainly because injectors' lives tended to be busy and full of competing priorities. For example, obtaining money and buying drugs were often deemed more urgent than visiting agencies – particularly if withdrawal symptoms were anticipated:

> You're not gonna go and sit in housing advice at nine o'clock in the morning if you're rattling [withdrawing]. . . . You're gonna be out getting money together or scoring and making sure you're not poorly.
>
> (Female, 31 years)

Additionally, many participants had so many appointments that they found it stressful trying to manage them all. Clashes between engagements at drug agencies, jobcentres, housing services, criminal justice services and social services were all reported, but were seldom treated sympathetically by service providers.

The bureaucracy associated with accessing services was a further barrier identified. For example, injectors wanting substitute medication often had to present at agencies for consecutive days or weeks to prove that they were committed to being treated. Others felt that the lines of responsibility between agencies were so confused that nobody was actually taking responsibility for them.

Shame and stigma

Many injectors also reported that they were reluctant to seek help because they were ashamed or embarrassed about their drug use and this was exacerbated by the negative service provider attitudes they encountered. Thus IDUs often reported that professionals were judgemental and looked down on them; were abrupt and had little or no interaction with them; treated them differently from other customers or patients; assumed that they were untrustworthy; perceived their problems to be self-inflicted; did not listen to them; and even refused to help them. One woman explained:

> People won't go [to the hospital] until they are nearly dead, because you get treated so badly. So if there was somewhere you could go, where you are going to be treated like a decent human being, then as soon as you have got something that is not right, you are going to go straightaway and get it sorted.
>
> (Female, 48 years)

Travel

Travel represented a further barrier to accessing support, particularly when injectors were engaged with multiple agencies or living in a rural area. Sometimes there was insufficient time to get between services; on other occasions, suitable travel connections were not available. In particular, travel was difficult for those without access to private transport; those without money for public transport or taxis; and those with health problems (particularly mobility problems). Additionally, travel to an agency could be difficult or impossible if individuals were experiencing withdrawal symptoms and felt physically tired or unwell.

Fear

Fear of encountering other drug users and dealers in waiting rooms was another factor preventing IDUs from attending services. Some stated that this was because they would be tempted to use drugs if they met old drug-using acquaintances. Others wanted to maintain distance between themselves and the drug-using world. Some individuals did not want anyone to find out about their drug use because they were afraid of upsetting or causing shame to family members or were anxious that their children would be taken into care. Additionally, some individuals were afraid of particular types of treatment, especially methadone and group work, or particular types of services, especially dentists. Finally, a few individuals were reluctant to seek help because they were frightened of the withdrawal symptoms they might experience or because they felt that they did not know how to live their lives without using drugs.

Disliking or not wanting treatment

A number of participants also described being unwilling to use services because they did not like the treatment or support on offer. In respect of substitute medication, some did not want to be prescribed methadone because they considered that it was highly addictive, produced more severe withdrawal symptoms than heroin, had negative effects on the body, and did not actually prevent heroin use. Others did not want to be prescribed buprenorphine because they had previously had negative experiences of it or had heard negative things about it. In contrast, some injectors were reluctant to receive psychiatric help, counselling, general emotional support, or alternative therapies because they thought that they were ineffective. Finally, several injectors argued that some people did not use drug treatment services because they simply did not want to stop using drugs.

Barriers experienced by particular groups of injectors[4]

Female injectors

Overall, there was little evidence that women experienced any gender-specific problems in accessing services. For example, women did not argue that services were male-dominated or failed to cater for females' needs. Being pregnant and having children could negatively affect their service use, but similar difficulties relating to parenting were also discussed by some men.

Injectors with children

Many injectors reported that being a parent had at some point deterred their use of services. Most importantly, this was because they were afraid that social services would take their children into care. In addition, a number of parents had missed appointments because they had had nobody to look after infants and did not want to take them to services. Others reported that it was difficult for them to access residential services because contact with children (and other family) was not permitted. Despite this, having children was not always a barrier to accessing support since some services had crèches and some injectors had good informal childcare, managed their appointments around childcare, or took their children with them to appointments.

BME injectors

Whilst every effort was made to include BME injectors in the study, only nine could be identified and therefore very limited conclusions can be drawn from the data. Of these nine individuals, two (both Eastern European) did not speak English and were interviewed with the help of an interpreter. Both discussed problems relating to their lack of British citizenship and indicated that language had been a major barrier when attempting to access drug services, pharmacies, social services and the jobcentre. In addition, two other BME injectors reported that they had encountered racism at services. The remaining five identified no specific barriers relating to their ethnic origin.

Stimulant injectors

Stimulant injectors repeatedly emphasised that they needed more help with their problems than was currently available. Although some had received advice, counselling and alternative therapies, they often felt that drug services were focused on helping heroin users and did not cater for, or understand, their particular needs:

> People that are running the agency here, they just seem to be more up front with heroin and just want to deal with heroin problems. Amphetamines are like not much doing.
>
> (Male, 33 years)

A key barrier reported by stimulant users was the lack of suitable prescribed substitute medication.[5] They also explained that paranoia and depression often deterred them from help-seeking, and complained that there were limited opportunities for counselling. Amphetamine users additionally described problems making and keeping appointments, given that they often failed to remember dates and times and were frequently too tired to attend, especially when trying to reduce or stop their use:

> Me on amphetamines . . . I have got a memory like a sieve . . . I don't even know whether I am coming or going half the time . . . I just miss one appointment and it [treatment] stops.
>
> (Male, 28 years)

Homeless injectors

Being homeless often prevented injectors from using services. Reasons for this included difficulties remembering appointments; not being able to register with a doctor or pharmacy without an address; never being in one place for long enough to receive help; not knowing where to go for assistance; and not having an address to which appointments could be posted:

> Not having a fixed abode, you can't have your next appointment mailed to you . . . I have gone for my appointment and they have gone, 'Well, we couldn't tell you, couldn't let you know, your appointment has been changed.'
>
> (Male, 34 years)

Many homeless injectors reported a Catch-22 situation whereby they could not receive help with their drug problems because they did not have stable housing yet they could not secure stable housing because of their drug problems. One key element in this vicious circle was the difficulty of obtaining assistance from housing services. Housing staff were perceived as particularly unsympathetic, whilst withdrawal symptoms made long waits in housing offices impossible. Furthermore, homeless injectors could not afford deposits to secure private tenancies.

Injectors with mental health problems

Depression, anxiety, paranoia and other mental health issues could all prevent injectors from seeking support. A minority reported being so depressed that they could not leave their house. Others stated that their paranoia (about wasting staff time, missing appointments, being forcibly detained for hospital treatment, and having their mental health problems documented in their medical records) stopped them from engaging with services. Not being ready to talk about their psychological difficulties and feeling unable to open up to others also prevented some injectors from securing help.

Those whose mental health problems were most severe sometimes found that they could only obtain suitable support from specialist psychiatric services. Others were accessing counselling from drug agencies but felt that they were not 'getting anywhere'. Some commented that drug workers were insufficiently skilled and experienced in mental health issues or too pressed for time to explore psychological problems effectively with them. In consequence, these injectors terminated counselling sessions or failed to attend their appointments.

Injectors with physical health problems

A number of participants were suffering from physical health problems directly related to their injecting – such as Hepatitis B or C, DVT, blood clots and abscesses. These individuals reported mobility problems due to swollen or painful legs, wheelchair use and leg amputations. As a result, they found it difficult to attend appointments or collect their substitute medication:

> I have got two open abscesses at the moment and I have got two blood clots in my right leg and two in my left leg. So, it don't make it easy for me getting about.
>
> (Male, 30 years)

In addition, mobility problems negatively impacted on other areas of their lives, including opportunities to access training or secure employment, especially manual work.

Injectors seeking paid employment

Injectors in the study often identified difficulties attending employment services and securing a job because they had so many other commitments, including probation and social work appointments. As this man explained:

When have I got time to look for work? ... I couldn't do owt [anything] during week because I have got contact [formal contact with a child in care] and it is a court order that we have got to keep going. ... So I couldn't look for work during afternoon. ... When I went to court last Monday, they gave me a curfew seven [p.m.] to seven [a.m.]. That means I can't work nights.

(Male, 38 years)

In addition, injectors reported that jobcentre staff regularly told them that there were no jobs available, especially if they had a criminal record. Staying in contact with the jobcentre was particularly problematic for those who did not have a fixed address or access to a telephone. Moreover, even if injectors did use employment services, there were other barriers to obtaining paid work. These included poor health, limited skills and experience, and the stigma of being a drug user. Despite this, many injectors wanted to work but believed that this would only be possible if they hid their drug use from employment services and potential employers.

Injectors in the criminal justice system

Injectors frequently argued that those in contact with the criminal justice system had easier access to treatment and support than those who were law-abiding. This, they stated, was because criminal justice programmes provided rapid access to prescribed drugs and a wide range of interesting diversionary classes and groups. In fact, positive perceptions of the services received within the criminal justice system sometimes appeared to affect treatment-seeking behaviour. For example, a small number of injectors stated that they had committed crime because they would then be more likely to obtain help with their drug problems.

Many injectors also saw prison as a positive opportunity to secure treatment quickly. In this regard, they praised the recent expansion of prison drug services, including needs assessments; drug-free wings; methadone and buprenorphine prescribing; maintenance prescribing; supplementary support/complementary therapies; and buprenorphine on release. Despite this, they still complained about the inconsistent and restrictive nature of prison-based treatments, the lack of support available for mental health problems, and hostile prison staff attitudes. Injectors generally reported that continuity of treatment between prison and the community had improved in recent years but argued that this was still haphazard and unreliable. Indeed, some complained that they had been drug-free whilst in prison but had since reused drugs because they had been unable to secure treatment on their release.

Some implications for policy in light of the new ten-year Drug Strategy

The study's findings are now discussed in light of *Drugs: Protecting Families and Communities. The 2008 Drug Strategy*. According to the new strategy, the number of people in contact with drug treatment services has more than doubled since 1998 and the average national waiting time has been reduced to less than two and a half weeks. Improving treatment access remains a key policy goal, although the emphasis has now shifted towards better treatment outcomes. Recognition within the new strategy that progress has been made but further work is required is broadly supported by IDUs in the study, who reported that treatment services were now easier to access than in previous years but that barriers persisted and waiting times remained problematic.

Our research showed that IDUs were failing to access support for a variety of reasons, including the absolute lack of services and not liking the treatment on offer. It is therefore encouraging that the new strategy promises to broaden the range of evidence-based treatments available – including innovative treatments such as injectable heroin and methadone – and is committed to further efforts to meet the housing, education, training and employment needs of those successfully completing treatment. The extension of interventions throughout the criminal justice system – including better continuity of care on release from prison – is also to be welcomed. However, we note that detail regarding how services, and which particular types of service, will be expanded is lacking from the proposals.

As with earlier policy documents, the 2008 strategy recognises that some groups of drug users are likely to require targeted support. Indeed, young people, women, crack or poly-drug users, particular BME or other minority communities, sex workers, parents with dependent children, drug users with mental health problems and those with complex needs are all mentioned. This is a potentially valuable corrective to access problems but our research indicates a need for caution. First, there are other groups – for example, stimulant injectors or injectors with physical health problems – who also require more support but are not mentioned. Second, some groups – such as women – may not be quite as marginalised from services as is perhaps presumed. Third, individuals within targeted groups do not necessarily encounter barriers when accessing support; for example, many parents have good childcare arrangements and attend services without difficulty. Fourth, in a world of insufficient provision, prioritising some groups (such as offenders) over others can have unintended negative consequences (such as individuals deliberately committing crime).

Importantly, our study revealed that it is necessary to see each drug user as an individual in his or her own right. So, it is not possible to assume that injector A will encounter barrier B at service C. Rather the barriers encountered depend on the particular needs, circumstances and psychological states of mind of an injector at a particular moment in time. In view of this, we welcome the new drug strategy's proposal to provide more tailored and personalised support, including the piloting of individual budgets. Similarly, we value the continued associations made between drug use and the broader concept of social exclusion – thus highlighting that the government fully recognises the complex web of interacting and mutually reinforcing personal and social problems that individual drug users frequently experience.

Given their often complex needs, it is not surprising that the daily lives of the IDUs interviewed involved high levels of contact with a diverse range of services. Yet, dealing with many agencies was often stressful for them. The new strategy's objective of improving joint working – including better links between prison- and community-based services – is therefore good news. In particular, better information sharing between services might reduce some of the unnecessary bureaucracy about which IDUs complained. Equally, joint working might enable lines of accountability between agencies to be clarified so that drug users do not fall through service gaps. It is unfortunate, however, that the new strategy does not consider how this collaboration might be achieved at the local level. It is also worrying that no consideration appears to have been given to how linking benefit receipt to participation in drug treatment might compromise therapeutic relationships, particularly if drug workers are required to tell jobcentre staff that clients have failed to attend appointments.

A common problem of access identified in the study and in previous research was professionals' negative attitudes towards IDUs. It seems reasonable to assume that injectors would be more willing to ask for support if service providers were less judgemental of them. The new drug strategy does not explicitly discuss stigma. Nonetheless, the need to integrate those with drug problems within mainstream services is emphasised. Equally, there is continued commitment to developing a competent substance misuse workforce through better training for generic and specialist practitioners and for those working within the criminal justice system. Such measures should begin to improve the standard of service delivered to this often unpopular and marginalised client group. Disappointingly, though, no strategies for tackling the reluctance of employers to recruit former drug users are identified.

Ultimately, many of the changes that might improve IDUs' access to services require additional resources. Yet, at the time the new strategy was launched, every indication was that public spending on drug services would not be increasing, except within prisons. This inevitably constrains how much improvement in access can actually be achieved. Despite this, our findings suggest that some barriers to treatment might, with a little thought and creativity, be removed at little or no extra cost. For example, service providers could be more welcoming of drug users; they could remove any unnecessary agency bureaucracy; they could be more flexible about appointment times; they could publicise their work more widely; they could review waiting room arrangements to help those who wish to preserve some anonymity; they could assist drug users in planning their travel to appointments; and they could reduce drug users' fears of attending services by providing them with greater information about what to expect. Whilst not perfect, such changes could be implemented relatively quickly in some services and would be likely to be highly valued by many IDUs.

Acknowledgements

The authors wish to thank: the seventy-five injectors who gave up their time to be involved; staff working at the three participating needle exchanges who facilitated access to the study participants; and Katy Harris, Toni Tattersall and Karen Stewart for transcribing the interviews.

Notes

1 This strategy focused mainly on England, with similar but separate strategies developed for Wales, Scotland and Northern Ireland.
2 The NTA's 2002 document *Models of Care for the Treatment of Adult Drug Misusers* (updated in 2006) set out an expectation that each local region would offer drug users a full range of services, including: non-substance misuse specific (or generic) services; low threshold open access drug misuse services; structured community-based specialist drug misuse services; and residential substance misuse specific services.
3 The research also explored how barriers varied between service types; the particular circumstances in which barriers did/did not prevent IDUs from accessing help; possible ways of removing barriers to the effective treatment of IDUs; the costs of IDUs not entering treatment; and the costs of removing barriers to IDU treatment. These additional components are reported elsewhere (Neale *et al.* 2006, 2007, 2008; Tompkins *et al.* 2007).
4 Because of the relatively small sub-group sample sizes, findings should be treated cautiously. The smallest sub-group (n=9) was BME injectors. Details regarding the numbers of participants in the other sub-groups can be found in Neale *et al.* (2006).
5 Only one participant had been prescribed dextroamphetamine.

9 Prescribing injectable opiates for the treatment of opiate dependence

Nicola Metrebian, Louise Sell, William Shanahan, Tom Carnwath, Ron Alcorn, Sue Ruben, Mani Mehdikhani and Gerry V. Stimson

Providing injectable opiates such as methadone and pharmaceutical heroin (diamorphine) for the treatment of opiate dependence has been a distinctive feature of the British System's response to drug problems for nearly fifty years. Until recently, the United Kingdom was the only country to prescribe pharmaceutical heroin for opiate dependence and the only country to prescribe injectable methadone ampoules, with the exception of a few patients in Switzerland. While oral methadone is the standard form of maintenance substitution treatment and is effective for most heroin users entering treatment, substitution treatment with injectable opiates has been part of the UK's drug treatment options since the 1960s, albeit on a small scale.

Injectable opiate treatment (or IOT) is a controversial area that has produced much debate over the decades. With growing international interest in heroin treatment, trials of heroin treatment have been undertaken, or are in the process of being undertaken, all around the world. As international research evidence for the effectiveness of heroin treatment has accrued since the late 1990s, the UK has re-evaluated injectable opiate treatment. From 2001, national policy began to change as the government recognized the potential contribution of injectable opiate treatment. As a result, new clinical guidelines for injectable opiate treatment were devised, new pilot supervised injecting clinics were established and a national trial of injectable opiate treatment was begun. More recently, injectable opiate treatment has been included in the 2008 government Drug Strategy. This chapter outlines the history of injectable opiate treatment in the UK, describes the changing practice of, and policy for, this treatment option, and discusses the growing international research evidence. In addition, a recent study funded by the Department of Health to assess the feasibility of conducting a trial of injectable methadone treatment is described.

History of injectable opiate treatment in the UK

In 1926, the Departmental Committee on Morphine and Heroin Addiction (the Rolleston Committee) legitimized the prescribing of heroin and other opiates for the treatment of opiate dependence in the UK in certain circumstances: when patients were being gradually withdrawn from the drug, and when 'after every effort has been made for the cure of the addiction' the patient was 'capable of leading a useful and fairly normal life so long as he takes a certain non-progressive quantity, usually small, of the drug of addiction and ceases to be able to do so, when the regular allowance is withdrawn' (Ministry of Health 1926).

The latter form of treatment was interpreted to mean that the prescribing of heroin was legitimate medical practice and became known as *the British System*, and posed clinical questions about drug treatment which are still being debated today. What constitutes 'every effort' to cure the opiate-dependent patient; what criteria are to be used to assess which patients are 'capable of leading a useful and fairly normal life'; what is the appropriate dose of heroin to be prescribed and for how long should a patient be maintained on heroin?

Up until the 1960s, there were only small numbers of known heroin users in the UK, many of whom were in the medical and allied professions and dependent on morphine or pethidine. As such, there was little medical or political interest in their treatment. This changed in the early 1960s when a growing number of young hedonistic heroin users in London sought prescriptions of heroin from NHS general practitioners. One psychiatrist in private practice attracted a great many users by her eccentric and generous prescribing of heroin and cocaine. As a result of Home Office concern, the Interdepartmental Committee on Drug Addiction (the Brain Committee) was reconvened in 1964 (having met previously in 1961) to offer the government advice on how to deal with the new situation. In its report, the committee made three main recommendations: that supplies of heroin should be restricted, that a notification system of addicts be established, and that special drug treatment centres should be established (Ministry of Health and Scottish Home and Health Department 1965). Legislation requiring doctors to have a licence to prescribe heroin for the treatment of opiate dependence followed these recommendations.

Licences to prescribe heroin were generally only given to consultant psychiatrists working in the new drug clinics set up in 1968, or to junior doctors working under them. From the early 1970s, doctors at the clinics became uncomfortable prescribing heroin and started to shift patients onto methadone. At first, they moved patients onto injectable methadone ampoules and then to oral methadone. However, by the mid-1970s some clinics were beginning to introduce a policy that only oral methadone would be available for new patients. By the late 1970s, the prescribing of heroin and injectable methadone had virtually ceased (Stimson and Oppenheimer 1982).

While a national debate on the proposed benefits and harms of heroin prescribing started many decades ago in the 1970s, it was reinvigorated in 1995 with many countries considering whether to prescribe heroin. Providing a medical prescription of heroin to opiate-dependent drug users has been seen in some countries as a way of solving the 'heroin problem' with potential benefits to individuals and to society (Mattick *et al.* 1998). In 1992, Australia launched a number of research studies looking at the feasibility of prescribing heroin (Bammer *et al.* 1999). This work and the UK's experience of prescribing heroin have led to much international interest in this treatment. Randomized controlled trials of heroin have been completed in Switzerland (Perneger *et al.* 1998), the Netherlands (van den Brink *et al.* 2003), Germany (Haasen *et al.* 2007), Spain (March *et al.* 2006) and Canada (Bammer *et al.* 1999; Fischer *et al.* 2002, 2007).

Any doctor in the UK can prescribe methadone ampoules for injection. Methadone ampoules were first prescribed in the UK in the 1970s, in part as a way to move patients away from heroin (Mitcheson 1994). Prescribing injectable methadone was back on the agenda in the 1980s as a possible harm reduction measure to help attract injecting drug users into treatment. Faced with prescribing an injectable opiate, methadone has been the drug of choice for the majority of doctors (Strang and Sheridan 1997; Sarfraz and Alcorn 1999; Carnwath 2003), due to the longer duration of action and its more accepted medical status. However, many drug users have argued that given the option between injectable methadone and diamorphine, diamorphine would be their drug of choice (Sell *et al.* 2001).

The lack of research evidence for the effectiveness of prescribing injectable opiates in the UK has encouraged much debate on the advantages and disadvantages of injectable opiate treatment. Some clinicians argue that prescribing injectable opiates enhances treatment attraction and retention for this group and is effective in reducing health, social and crime problems (Strang and Gossop 1994). Moreover, those advocating injectable opiate treatment argue that drug users unable or unwilling to stop injecting will be less likely to use illicit drugs if provided with injectable heroin. However, there are concerns about the desirability of facilitating continued injecting, due to the risk of blood-borne infection (HCV, HBV and HIV), increased risk of overdose and other injection-related health problems. In addition, some have argued that prescribing drugs for injection will encourage dependence and be less likely to motivate behaviour change. Most of the debate has centred around the drug – diamorphine – rather than on injectable routes of administration. Injectable methadone ampoules are more readily prescribed and have attracted far less controversy.

Up until 2001, there was no national policy on treatment using injectable opiates and no treatment guidelines. Before 1999, doctors were advised to prescribe oral methadone and not to prescribe injectable opiates except in consultation with specialist treatment services (DHSS 1984; Department of Health, Scottish Home and Health Department and Welsh Office 1991). However, the Department of Health in their 1999 guidelines for the clinical management of drug dependence (DH 1999a), while discouraging doctors from prescribing injectable opiate treatment, recognized that there was a view that a few long-term injectors might benefit from receiving injectable methadone. They suggested that with the availability of injectable methadone there is little clinical indication for prescribing diamorphine.

Extent and nature of injectable opiate treatment in the UK

In 1995, the majority (97 per cent) of NHS opiate prescriptions for the treatment of opiate dependence in England and Wales were for methadone (Strang *et al.* 1996); 2 per cent were for heroin and 1 per cent for buprenorphine. Ten years later, methadone continues to account for the majority of prescriptions (83 per cent), with an increase in the proportion of prescriptions for buprenorphine (16 per cent) (Strang *et al.* 2007). In contrast, the practice of prescribing injectable opiate substitution treatment for opiate dependence has been steadily diminishing. Prescriptions for methadone ampoules have significantly reduced from 9.3 per cent of all methadone prescriptions in England and Wales in 1995 (Strang *et al.* 1996), to 1.85 per cent of all methadone prescriptions in 2005 (Strang *et al.* 2007). Moreover, prescriptions for heroin have gone down from 1.6 per cent of opiate prescriptions in 1995 (Strang *et al.* 1996), to 0.3 per cent in 2005 (Strang *et al.* 2007). Thus, whilst the proportions of opiate prescriptions for methadone and buprenorphine have remained fairly stable, the proportion of opiate prescriptions for injectable opiates (heroin and methadone ampoules) in the UK has proportionally diminished, with few new patients commencing this form of treatment. It is estimated that in 2000 there were forty-six doctors prescribing heroin to approximately 480 patients and that doctors had inherited most of these patients from other doctors (Metrebian *et al.* 2002).

Until recently[1] there has been no consensus on clinical eligibility for receiving injectable opiate treatment or how treatment should be delivered: for example, what dose, how the drug should be dispensed and for how long the treatment should be provided. While most doctors who prescribed heroin agreed that the criteria for treatment should include a long injecting history and failure to respond to more conventional treatment, other criteria varied (Metrebian *et al.* 2007). Prescribing heroin was generally reserved for the few, as a treatment of last resort for those who did not respond sufficiently well to other treatments and had a long history of injecting (Metrebian *et al.* 2007). However, there was also a significant minority of patients who had been prescribed heroin despite never previously receiving oral methadone (Metrebian *et al.* 2006). This suggests some doctors were prescribing heroin as a first line treatment. Drug users were probably more likely to receive injectable methadone ampoules than injectable diamorphine ampoules, if they were to be prescribed an injectable opiate. At one large clinic in north-west England, the majority of those receiving injectable opiates were receiving a prescription for injectable methadone (Sell and Zador 2004). Moreover, it was clinic practice to try to stabilize patients on methadone ampoules initially rather than to prescribe diamorphine (Sell *et al.* 2001). A number of patients had been initiated onto a heroin prescription due to intolerance with receiving a prescription for injectable methadone (Metrebian *et al.* 2007).

In the UK, injectable opiate treatment has been dispensed for unsupervised consumption at home usually on a daily basis by a community pharmacist (Sell *et al.* 2001; Metrebian *et al.* 2002). Regular supervision of injecting was rare. The lack of supervised consumption for prescribed heroin sets the UK apart from other countries recently undertaking trials to examine its effectiveness (Uchtenhagen *et al.* 1998; van den Brink *et al.* 2003) (in these countries, heroin is taken daily under supervision throughout the duration of treatment). The lack of supervised consumption has been thought to increase the likelihood of diversion of prescriptions onto the illicit street market and was reported by doctors as a reason for not prescribing heroin due to concerns around the opportunity for diversion of prescriptions with 'take home' unsupervised doses. In 2003, national guidance on injectable opiate treatment recommended that this treatment should only be delivered under supervision.

Growing body of evidence for injectable opiate treatment

The prescription of injectable preparations should be based on evidence of their cost-effectiveness over conventional oral methadone treatment. While this treatment modality has been one of the UK treatment options for drug dependence, this evidence has not existed. In 1996, the Department of Health review of drug treatment services in England (DH 1996) noted the necessity for controlled studies to examine the effectiveness of prescribing injectable methadone in the UK, and the 1999 *Drug Misuse and Dependence: Guidelines on Clinical Management* (DH 1999a) recognized the need for research in this area to 'guide rational clinical practice'.

Only a few studies have been conducted in the UK, and they are mostly either clinicians' views or small observational studies with small sample sizes (Battersby *et al.* 1992; McCusker and Davies 1996; Metrebian *et al.* 1998, 2001; C. Ford and Ryrie 1999). The only trials of injectable opiate treatment conducted in the UK were either undertaken decades previously to examine the effectiveness of heroin treatment, but had provided inconclusive results (Hartnoll *et al.* 1980), or had been conducted with a relatively small sample size examining the effectiveness of injectable methadone treatment (Strang *et al.* 2000b).

Outside the UK, there have been a number of randomized controlled trials of heroin treatment conducted in Europe (van den Brink *et al.* 2003; March *et al.* 2006; Haasen *et al.* 2007 and Perneger *et al.* 1998). In Switzerland, Professor Uchtenhagen and colleagues carried out a large cohort study of injectable heroin treatment (Uchtenhagen *et al.* 1998). Whilst its findings were limited by it not being a randomized controlled trial, it paved the way for other countries to conduct more rigorous scientific research trials. All the trials have found positive results.

In Geneva, forty-six long-term dependent heroin users were randomized to either receive a prescription for injectable heroin or be put on a waiting list where most received oral methadone (Perneger *et al.* 1998). After six months, the heroin group showed significant reductions in illicit heroin use and criminal behaviour and significant improvements in psychological health and social functioning, compared with those on the waiting list. In the Dutch heroin trial (van den Brink *et al.* 2003) patients continued to receive methadone and in addition were given prescribed heroin. Those in the heroin arms of the trial were compared with patients who received the standard maintenance treatment of oral methadone. Two randomized controlled trials were conducted, comparing (a) the co-prescription of inhalable heroin with oral methadone, and (b) the co-prescription of injectable heroin with oral methadone. Patients in trial 1 were randomly allocated to receive (a) oral methadone for twelve months, or (b) methadone and inhalable heroin for twelve months, or (c) methadone for six months followed by methadone and inhalable heroin for six months. Patients in trial 2 were randomly allocated to receive either (a) methadone for twelve months, or (b) methadone and injectable heroin for twelve months. All groups were followed up for a further six months.

This trial recruited patients who were already in methadone treatment programmes but who were doing badly and were defined as chronic, treatment-resistant heroin addicts. The primary outcome measure was at least a 40 per cent improvement in physical health, mental health, or social functioning, and no increase in substance misuse and no deterioration of 40 per cent or more in any area. Patients with this outcome were called 'responders'. At twelve months, in trial 1, 87 per cent of the methadone group had completed treatment, compared to 68 per cent of the co-prescribed inhalable heroin group. In trial 2, 85 per cent of the methadone group had completed treatment, compared to 72 per cent of the co-prescribed injectable heroin group. However, patients receiving injectable heroin were able to switch to receive inhalable heroin; 33 per cent made this switch. After twelve months, 48 per cent of patients in the co-prescribed inhalable heroin group were 'responders', compared to 25 per cent in the methadone group. Similarly, 57 per cent of patients in the co-prescribed injectable heroin group were 'responders', compared to 32 per cent in the methadone group. Two months after discontinuation of the co-prescribed inhalable heroin treatment, the majority of 'responders' had deteriorated considerably.

The Spanish trial took place in Granada (March *et al.* 2006). Sixty-two opioid-dependent people were randomly assigned to either supervised injected heroin or oral methadone and followed up for nine months. The study found no differences in retention rates but both groups improved. Those receiving heroin showed great improvements in health, risk behaviour, reduction of street heroin use or involvement in crime.

The German trial (Haasen *et al.* 2007) was undertaken with 1,015 people who were either (a) receiving methadone treatment and continuing to inject heroin, or (b) heroin-dependent but not in treatment. Participants were randomized to receive either injectable heroin or oral methadone for twelve months at seven treatment sites. Two response criteria – improvement of physical and/or mental health and decrease in illicit drug use – were evaluated in an intention-to-treat analysis. Retention was higher in the heroin group than in the oral methadone group (67 per cent vs. 40 per cent) and the heroin group showed a significantly greater response on both health and reduction of illicit drug use primary outcome measures (80 per cent vs. 74 per cent; 69 per cent vs. 55 per cent). A two-year follow-up of heroin-treated patients enrolled in the German heroin trial (Verthein *et al.* 2008) found that 82 per cent of patients remaining in treatment at one year were retained at two years. In addition, the benefits in health, drug use and criminal activity seen in the first twelve months of heroin treatment were maintained over two years, and social benefits continued to improve the longer patients stayed in treatment.

While all these studies provide evidence for improved outcomes with heroin treatment and suggest heroin treatment has great potential, how far their results are generalizable to the UK is unknown. The trials were conducted in different locations with different social and economic situations, and different available treatment options, and used different target populations, and different outcome measures, and the treatments themselves varied. A recent Cochrane review concluded that it is difficult to come to a conclusion about the effectiveness of heroin prescribing because of the heterogeneity of these studies, in particular the 'non comparability of outcomes' (i.e. they have different outcome measures) (Ferri *et al.* 2006). Furthermore, the results of studies were sometimes in disagreement with each other and this was explained by differences between rules within treatment groups. There is still no evidence of the effectiveness of injectable methadone.

Feasibility study for a future trial of injectable methadone treatment

In 2001, the Department of Health funded the authors to assess the feasibility of conducting a national multi-centre randomized controlled trial to compare the outcomes and costs of offering and prescribing injectable versus oral methadone to opiate-dependent injecting drug users (Metrebian *et al.* 2003). The objectives of the study included: assessing the feasibility of recruiting and randomizing a selected group of opiate-dependent injecting drug users; assessing the feasibility of procedures for trial co-ordination, collection and monitoring of data; assessing clinic staffs' compliance with the study protocol; and assessing the feasibility of implementing supervised injectable methadone treatment within an oral methadone maintenance service.

The study was designed to replicate the proposed research design of a proposed national multi-centre trial but on a small scale. Consenting participants were allocated to receive either the offer and prescription of injectable methadone (IM) or oral methadone only (OM) (control) by an unequal 3:2 (oral:injectable methadone) randomization, stratified by centre. To avoid possible biases in group allocation, all randomization of participants was carried out independently of the treatment. An unequal randomization was used to reduce the numbers of participants allocated to injectable methadone treatment and thus reduce the treatment costs for participating sites. Compared to oral methadone, the drug and dispensing costs are higher for injectable methadone. This randomization ratio is small enough to make it a realistic option without needing a much bigger sample size or losing too much statistical power. Primary outcome measures included (a) rate of eligible participants presenting to treatment, (b) proportion of eligible participants who agree to be randomized, (c) proportion of eligible participants who are successfully enrolled into and retained in the study, and (d) proportion of study participants followed up at two and six months. Secondary outcome measures included (a) completeness of data obtained, and (b) clinic staffs' compliance with the study protocol.

Opioid-dependent drug users enrolled at five established UK drug treatment centres were screened for potential eligibility. Sites were chosen on the basis that they had established methadone programmes and clinicians experienced in providing both oral and injectable treatments. Drug users from three of the five sites were further assessed to confirm eligibility and invited to participate in the pilot trial. The study aimed to recruit between forty and sixty participants within the normal pattern of patient recruitment, at the rate of fourteen to twenty per site over four months. Eligibility criteria were based on current clinical practice and recommendations in *Drug Misuse and Dependence: Guidelines on Clinical Management* (DH 1999a). Eligible participants had to be between 21 and 70 years old and requesting a new episode of treatment. They had to be currently injecting and opioid-dependent, have a minimum of three years' self-reported opioid injecting and have been injecting for nine months of the previous year, and self-report injecting opiates at least once a day in the last four weeks. In addition, they had to be able to inject intramuscularly or intravenously in the arm and they had to have had verifiable former oral methadone treatment for at least six months. Individuals were excluded if (a) they had a history of infective endocarditis, (b) they were receiving anti-coagulant treatment, (c) they had severe mental illness assessed by mental state examination, (d) they were pregnant or lactating, and (e) they had a history of violence in the clinic. Ethical approval was obtained from relevant local ethics committees.

Structured interviews of participants were conducted at baseline, two months after randomization and six months after randomization. Frequency of contact with other agencies and professionals was measured in interviews with participants. Trial participants' injecting sites were examined by clinical staff on a monthly basis. Self-reported drug use was corroborated against urinalysis results. Urine samples were collected for testing. Data were collected on the resources used by each participant in treatment, including the amount of methadone dispensed per patient over the period of the trial, the involvement of site staff in observed supervised consumption of methadone and of community pharmacists in the dispensing of methadone, and on the time input of site staff in the treatment of each patient. Follow-up assessments were conducted at two and six months by independent interviewers.

The trial aimed to evaluate current clinical practice. Apart from the requirements of the trial clinic protocols, participants were subject to and offered usual treatment in a usual setting. To maintain some uniformity, but allowing enough flexibility to encourage recruitment and enhance generalizability, treatments were delivered against agreed trial clinic protocols which set minimum standards for treatment delivery. To ensure and monitor treatment compliance with prescribed medication, for the first three months in treatment, oral methadone was dispensed and observed at either the drug clinic or a community pharmacy (Site 2). Between Monday and Friday, injectable methadone was taken under the supervision of medical staff at the drug clinic. Weekend doses of oral and injectable methadone were dispensed on Friday for unsupervised consumption at home. Participants were expected to return their used ampoules to the drug treatment centre. Batch numbers for ampoules were recorded by dispensing pharmacists. After three months in treatment, oral and injectable methadone were dispensed daily from the clinic (Sites 1, 2 and 3) or community pharmacy (Site 2) for unsupervised consumption at home.

Over the seven-month recruitment period, of 933 opiate-dependent drug users seen routinely at the five clinics, 903 (91 per cent) were screened for potential eligibility for the trial [765 (95 per cent) at the three participating sites and 138 (74 per cent) at the two additional study sites] (see Figure 9.1). Eleven per cent of those screened were identified as potentially eligible for the study (12 per cent of opiate-dependent drug users screened at the three participating sites, and 9 per cent of opiate-dependent drug users screened at the two additional sites). Participants were potentially eligible if they replied 'yes' or 'don't know' to questions on eligibility criteria and 'no' and 'don't know' to questions on ineligibility criteria. Thus participants would be not eligible only if they replied 'no' to questions on eligibility criteria and 'yes' to questions on ineligibility criteria. The option of 'don't know' was added to allow staff conducting the assessment to use the limited information they had at a first assessment without the need to spend time trying to gather more information. The majority of those found not to be potentially eligible had either failed to meet the eligibility criterion around injecting or had not previously received oral methadone treatment (continuously for at least six months) (see Table 9.1).

As shown in Figure 9.1, at the three treatment centres participating in the trial, 43 per cent (27/63) of potentially eligible participants (who were asked) were interested in participating in the trial. It had not been possible to ask

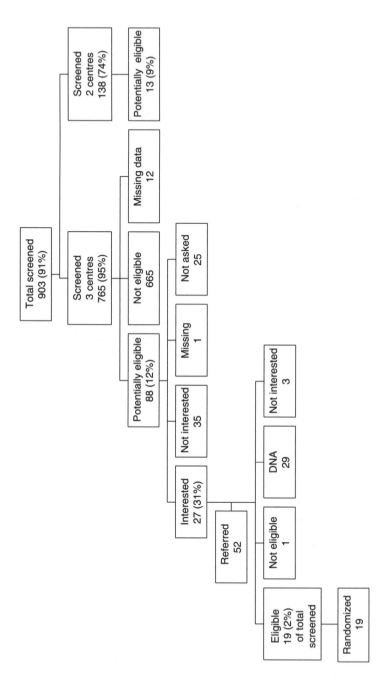

Figure 9.1 Patient screening and recruitment.

Table 9.1 Proportion fulfilling eligibility criteria for the trial (five participating sites) (*N*=903)

Eligibility criteria	Yes % (n)	No % (n)	D/k % (n)
Aged between 21 and 70	95 (861)	4 (37)	1 (5)
Opioid-dependent	86 (781)	12 (108)	2 (14)
Currently injecting opiates (injecting at least once a day in the last 4 weeks)	37 (335)	60 (541)	3 (27)
Injecting for 9/12 months of the previous year	33 (296)	60 (543)	7 (64)
Injecting for a minimum of 3 years	31 (284)	59 (532)	10 (87)
Able to inject IM or IV in the arm	49 (445)	32 (285)	19 (173)
Previously received oral methadone treatment (continuously for at least 6 months)	32 (291)	54 (486)	14 (126)

Ineligibility criteria	Yes % (n)	No % (n)	D/k % (n)
History of infective endocarditis	1 (10)	68 (616)	31 (227)
Receiving anti-coagulant treatment	2 (20)	73 (660)	25 (223)
Current active severe mental illness	7 (62)	73 (655)	21 (186)
If female, pregnant or lactating (n=224)	2 (20)	18 (158)	4 (46)
History of violence in treatment	2 (14)	72 (649)	27 (240)

	Yes	No	Missing data
Those meeting all eligibility criteria	101	790	12

participants from Site 2 if they were interested as they had been screened retrospectively but they were all referred for a full assessment (25).[1] Fifty-six per cent (35/63) of potentially eligible participants (who were asked) were not interested in participating in the trial. Reasons for not wanting to participate in the trial were not recorded. However, nursing staff from Sites 1 and 3 suggested that potentially eligible participants often requested to receive oral methadone detoxification and did not wish to receive injectable methadone. Two participants requested diamorphine.

(NB: At Site 2, all individuals presenting to treatment/on the treatment waiting list were screened retrospectively using information recorded at the time the patient was first assessed. If potentially eligible, these participants were asked to attend for a full assessment.)

Of fifty-two participants referred for a full assessment, nineteen (37 per cent) were found to be eligible. Nineteen participants were randomized to the trial; 2 per cent (19/765) of participants screened and 22 per cent (19/88) of potentially eligible participants. The recruitment rate for the three sites was 2.7 per month (just below one per month per site). Of the nineteen participants randomized, eleven were allocated to receive oral methadone and eight to receive injectable methadone. One patient allocated to injectable methadone chose to receive oral methadone. Two participants unhappy with their treatment allocation of oral methadone dropped out immediately after randomization. One patient allocated to receive injectable methadone failed to attend for treatment. Sixteen participants were successfully enrolled onto the trial and fourteen participants were successfully followed up at two months. One patient was withdrawn from the trial by treatment centre staff on health grounds. Twelve participants were followed up at six months (63 per cent; 12/19).

The majority of participants attended for supervision every day throughout the first three months in treatment. Nursing staff recorded that it took participants between five and fifteen minutes to inject. All participants returned their used ampoules with the exception of one patient who failed to return all his ampoules on two days. No serious adverse events were recorded. One patient receiving injectable methadone developed a minor rash around the injecting site.

The findings suggest that this study was unable to recruit and successfully enrol onto the trial a sufficient number of opiate-dependent drug users. Similar low recruitment rates had been reported in previous studies using similar eligibility criteria (Metrebian *et al.* 1998; Strang *et al.* 2000b). Only a relatively small number (11 per cent) of opiate-dependent drug users were found to be 'potentially eligible'. The majority had failed to meet the eligibility criteria on items concerning injecting or had not previously received oral methadone treatment continuously for six months (Table 9.1). This suggests that the target population of opiate-dependent drug users make up approximately 10–12 per cent of those presenting to treatment. It may be possible that a greater number are already receiving oral methadone treatment at specialist drug clinics or are presenting to GPs or private doctors.

Of those potentially eligible (who were asked) at the three sites, 43 per cent were interested in participating in the study. This rate of interest is comparable with other randomized controlled trials conducted outside the substance misuse field where a wide variation in ranges can occur: from 2 to 3 per cent to more than 60 per cent (Andrew Nunn personal communication). The majority of participants presenting for treatment wanted to receive oral methadone detoxification.

The authors concluded that a trial should be undertaken with a similar design but with modified eligibility criteria that follow the new guidance on injectable opiate treatment (NTA 2003) but allow for an increase in the numbers recruited – by recruiting participants from existing clients of drug treatment services.

Beginnings of renewed interest

In 2002, the potential contribution of injectable opiate prescribing to the treatment of opiate dependence was recognized by the government in their *Updated Drug Strategy* (Home Office 2002). They called for injectable heroin treatment to be expanded to all those with a clinical need for it, under strict medical supervision. Furthermore, the need for research to evaluate heroin prescribing treatment was recommended by the House of Commons Home Affairs Committee in 2002. Following this, the National Treatment Agency (NTA) convened an expert committee to produce new guidance on injectable opiate treatment (NTA 2003). Recommendations were made for patient eligibility criteria and service delivery. The guidance recommended that injectable opiate treatment should be a second line treatment for patients not responding to oral substitution treatment delivered under optimal conditions (e.g. optimized oral methadone) and that it should be offered in services that can provide supervised consumption (at least initially). It also recommended the potential advantages of delivering injectable opiate treatment under 'European style' supervised injecting clinics. The guidance also recognized that there was a small number of patients already receiving injectable opiate treatment under the old 'British System' and suggested that these patients might continue to receive it in the same manner if found to be benefiting from it.

As a result of government calls, in 2004, funds were made available from the Home Office and National Treatment Agency for the establishment of new pilot supervised injecting clinics providing both injectable heroin and injectable methadone treatment under strict daily supervision. In parallel, a research grant from a national charity (Action on Addiction) and the Big Lottery was awarded to the Institute of Psychiatry to conduct a multi-site randomized controlled trial to assess the safety, efficacy and cost-effectiveness of injectable methadone and injectable heroin compared to optimized oral methadone (RIOTT – Randomized Injectable Opioid Treatment Trial; Lintzeris *et al.* 2006). The trial was to be conducted within these new pilot supervised injecting clinics to examine the role of injectable methadone and injectable heroin treatment delivered under the conditions identified in the new UK national guidance (NTA 2003). Specifically, the key question to be addressed was whether efforts should be made to optimize conventional oral maintenance treatment (e.g. encouraging high doses, supervised dosing, psychosocial interventions, and regular attendance) for long-term opiate-dependent patients who, despite receiving conventional oral maintenance treatment, continue not to benefit, in order to reduce regular illicit heroin use, or whether such patients should be treated with injected methadone or injected heroin in newly developed supervised injecting clinics. The trial began in 2005 with the aim of recruiting 150 clients to be randomized to receive either injectable heroin, injectable methadone or optimized oral methadone at three new supervised injecting clinics established in London, Darlington and Brighton.

All doses of injectable methadone and heroin are supervised by medical staff on-site. There are no take-home doses. Results are expected in the summer of 2009.

Further support for injectable opiate treatment can be found in the new 'clinical guidelines' – the UK guidelines on clinical management of drug misuse and dependence (DH 2007). The guidelines, written for all doctors, but especially those providing pharmacological interventions for drug misusers, acknowledge that there is a small section of the treatment population who, despite receiving oral opioid maintenance treatment, fail to make progress and continue to be involved in high levels of injecting drug misuse. They suggest some of these patients may benefit from receiving optimal oral maintenance treatment, while others may benefit from injectable maintenance treatment. However, they state that injectable opiate treatment 'is a second-line treatment that should only be considered when optimized oral methadone and buprenorphine maintenance treatment are available and are found not to be suitable or, after proper trial, fail to deliver the expected benefit' (DH 2007). They stipulate that patients should only be considered for injectable opioid prescribing in line with the eight key principles that were outlined in the NTA guidance (NTA 2003). In addition, they recognize the potential of the new pilot supervised injecting clinics.

Most recently, the government's new Drug Strategy *Drugs: Protecting Families and Communities* (HM Government 2008) has announced that, subject to findings of the RIOTT trial, they would support injectable opiate treatment, identifying it as part of a range of treatment options for opiate dependence, and would roll out this treatment to more clients with a clinical need for it:

- On treatment, we will . . . use all emerging and all available evidence to make sure we are supporting the treatment that is most effective, targeted on the right users – with abstinence-based treatment for some, drug-replacement over time for others, and innovative treatments including injectable heroin and methadone where they have been proved to work and reduce crime.

  (HM Government 2008: 6).

- We will build on new evidence of what works and maximize the range of approaches used, including by: rolling out the prescription of injectable heroin and methadone to clients who do not respond to other forms of treatment, subject to the findings, due in 2009, of pilots exploring the use of this type of treatment.

  (HM Government 2008: 30)

In conclusion, while overt policy formation has changed the nature of this treatment, to what extent is, as yet, still unclear. Certainly injectable opiate treatment is now considered to be a real option in the range of treatments available to the specialist clinician. There is now national guidance on its role, and on who should receive it and when it should be delivered. Two questions remain unanswered: is it more effective than optimized oral maintenance treatment, and how should it be delivered? The first question will be answered with the findings of the RIOTT trial. The second relates to what model(s) of service delivery should be adopted and this is likely to be determined in the course of the next few years.

Note

1 In 2003 the National Treatment Agency for Substance Misuse (NTA) issued guidance on prescribing heroin and injectable methadone (NTA 2003).

10 Cognitive behaviour therapy for opiate misusers in methadone maintenance treatment

Christos Kouimtsidis and Colin Drummond on behalf of the UKCBTMM project group

Introduction

The mainstay of opiate addiction treatment is substitution therapy with opioid agonists, particularly methadone and buprenorphine (NICE 2007c). There is evidence that psychosocial interventions used as adjunctive treatment in methadone maintenance programmes are important in determining clinical outcome (NTA 2006a). Cognitive behaviour therapy (CBT) has been the most widely studied of these.

However, recent clinical guidelines from the National Institute of Healthcare and Clinical Effectiveness (NICE 2007b) call into question the value of CBT in methadone treatment, based on a meta-analysis of the evidence. NICE recommends that CBT should not be used routinely as a first line intervention in this context. The guidelines point to greater evidence of efficacy of family interventions based on CBT principles and contingency management (CM) in opioid treatment.

This conclusion is controversial for a number of reasons. First, family therapy and CM have not been studied in a UK context in methadone treatment: all of the evidence so far is from the USA. So there is no guarantee that similar levels of effectiveness will be found if applied in the UK. Second, the UK treatment workforce has greater experience and training in CBT than in family therapy and CM is not routinely used in a UK setting. Nevertheless, CM is one element of CBT and elsewhere the NICE guidelines point to the need to identify high risk situations and explore alternative coping strategies with clients, which are core components of CBT.

Although management of psychiatric comorbidity was not specifically covered by these guidelines, it is suggested by the guidelines that CBT 'should be considered for co-morbid disorders such as anxiety and depression for people who misuse cannabis, cocaine and opiates' and the reader is referred further to the guidelines for the management of the relevant comorbid disorders (NICE 2007b). CBT is an important component of treatment for a range of comorbid psychiatric disorders. Therefore we feel that different CBT techniques and applications will still have an important place in the management of opiate misusers in methadone treatment.

The research project described here aimed to study the implementation, effectiveness and cost-effectiveness of CBT in the context of methadone maintenance treatment (UKCBTMM; Drummond *et al.* 2004). The results were considered within the wider evidence base that informed the NICE guidelines and the Drug Strategy. In addition, we believe that the research findings presented here can inform the implementation process of the guidelines and highlight important areas of concern. We aim to demonstrate that pragmatic research can provide very important information beyond evidence clinical efficacy studies might generate.

Previous research on CBT in methadone treatment

In 1999, the service provision and overall organization of service delivery were different from how they are currently. At that time, the UK government's anti-drugs strategy (HM Government 1998) and *Our Healthier Nation* (DH 1998b) had recognized the need to provide effective and accessible treatments to enable drug misusers to overcome their drug problems and improve their health and social functioning. However, the report of the *Task Force to Review Services for Drug Misusers* (DH 1996) identified the paucity of quality research on effectiveness of treatment, particularly that conducted in the UK and particularly in relation to counselling services. Since then, major changes have taken place, some of them based on research findings generated by the Drugs Misuse Research Initiative programme.

CBT had been evaluated as an adjunct to methadone maintenance treatment (MMT). Woody *et al.* (1983) compared intensive CBT, supportive-expressive psychotherapy (SE), both including a basic drug counselling approach, versus basic drug counselling (DC) alone in the context of MMT. At twelve months follow-up, both CBT and SE had better outcomes in terms of drug use, criminality, employment and psychological symptoms. However, there were no significant differences between CBT and SE. In a subsequent study using a similar design but where the interventions were matched for therapeutic input, SE was still found to be superior to DC at six months follow-up (Woody *et al.* 1995), suggesting that the type of therapy was more important than amount of therapist contact.

Only a few studies have examined the cost-effectiveness of CBT. McLellan *et al.* (1993) compared 'minimum methadone services' (MMS – with minimal counselling input) with 'standard methadone services' (SMS – including regular CBT sessions) and 'extended methadone services' (EMS – including CBT plus a range of professional and vocational input). At six months follow-up, there was a 'dose–response' relationship between amount of therapy and outcome. In a later follow-up of the McLellan *et al.* (1993) cohort, Kraft *et al.* (1997) found that, while the dose–response relationship between the three treatments persisted at one year, the intermediate intensity SMS was more cost-effective than the other two therapies. A study by Avants *et al.* (1999) found no difference between twice-weekly CBT and a more intensive five-day-a-week day programme. This suggested a divergence between efficacy and cost-effectiveness and supports an intermediate intensity approach.

Our study was designed principally to assess the effectiveness and cost-effectiveness of CBT in MMT, in contrast to most of the previous studies, which have been concerned mainly with efficacy. A key priority identified by the Task Force (DH 1996) was the need for greater evidence of effectiveness to guide rational commissioning of services, including evaluation of different counselling approaches. To that end, this study had certain key features designed to assess cost-effectiveness and maximize its generalizability throughout the NHS drug treatment system. This was a pragmatic multicentre randomized controlled trial in which the control condition (MMT) was as close as possible to the usual treatment approach in UK clinics, whilst incorporating a degree of standardization and exclusion of some patients, necessary to protect internal validity. Therapists were drawn from existing clinic staff and were trained to deliver the CBT intervention. Further, the CBT was deliberately adjunctive to standard MMT. Thus, while the trial aimed to compare treatments of different intensities, the cost-effectiveness analysis and the treatment process measures allowed conclusions to be drawn about the value of adding CBT to standard treatment.

Methodological issues in designing the UKCBTMM trial

As discussed above, no randomized controlled trial of CBT in MMT has been conducted in the UK NHS setting. As a result, this study encountered several practical problems, which could be attributed with some confidence to the major differences between UK and US treatment philosophies and service provision.

The sample size and power calculation of this study were based on the closest similar US project by Woody *et al.* (1995). This study examined the effect sizes of each subscale composite score of the Addiction Severity Index (ASI) (Kokkevi and Hartgers 1995). In terms of the mean drug use composite score (ASI), an effect size of 0.46 (medium effect size) was found. However this was a small, single-site efficacy study and we believed that an effect size of 0.3 would be more likely in a multicentre trial of psychotherapy. With $p < 0.05$, power = 0.8, using a two-tailed test, we estimated that we would require a followed-up sample size of approximately 90 in each group (180 in total). With a follow-up rate of 80 per cent, we would require an initial sample of approximately 220 (110 per group).

We planned to screen 600 clients and recruit 220 (37 per cent) into the trial over a twelve-month period based on previous similar published US studies. However, both the proportion of eligible clients and the number willing to enter the trial were considerably lower than previous published research had suggested. We found an eligibility rate of 40 per cent (eligible/screened) (instead of 73 per cent) and were only able to recruit sixty, which is a screen conversion rate of 7 per cent (instead of 37 per cent).

There are several possible reasons why these rates were lower than we had anticipated. It became clear during the study that there were some major differences between the UK and US study samples of drug users in treatment, not least the greater level of accessibility of methadone treatment available in the UK, compared with the limited availability and barriers limiting access to drug treatment for US drug users. Within the US services, there is an expectation of behaviour change (compared with some of the harm reduction aims in the UK) and a culture of adjunctive psychological treatments to complement the methadone maintenance programme. Clients are expected to attend group and individual therapy as part of their programme. This is different from the culture dominant in most UK treatment services, where psychological services are relatively rare and there are few sanctions in place for non-compliance with the basic keyworking appointments.

The low screen conversion rates we found were influenced by three main factors affecting (i) eligibility, (ii) ability to approach eligible clients, and (iii) interest in participation. The main reasons for ineligibility were due to low dose of methadone (<30 mg, 29 per cent), clients not being engaged in treatment sufficiently for the study (28 per cent), and living in unstable housing (24 per cent). Since this study was completed, some of those problems have now been reduced. For example, the national average dosage of prescribed methadone for maintenance in 2005 had increased to 56.7 mg from a much lower level at the time of our study (Commission for Healthcare Audit and Inspection 2006).

The researchers were unable to approach about a third (38 per cent; 128/338) of eligible clients because many had been discharged or dropped out of treatment. These reasons mainly reflect again the harm minimization, low threshold and high turnover of patients within UK services.

The main reason reported by the eligible clients for non-participation (25 per cent) was that they were not willing to take part in a research project or more specifically because they were currently working and they did not have the time to attend the therapy appointments.

Nevertheless, we believe that, as this was a pragmatic trial of implementation of CBT in a UK methadone treatment setting, it provides important lessons for wider implementation of this approach. There are clearly many barriers to the implementation of CBT in this setting and our study points to caution in applying research evidence on the effectiveness of psychological interventions conducted solely in US settings to the UK NHS.

Methodology

Trial design

The study was a pragmatic, multicentre randomized controlled, parallel group design comparing standard MMT plus CBT with standard MMT alone. Outcome assessments were undertaken at one year with an interim assessment at six months. The main aim of the study was to evaluate the effectiveness and cost-effectiveness of CBT as an adjunct to MMT as it was offered within typical NHS services. Outcome was assessed in terms of addiction severity (primary outcomes were the percentage of days abstinent and mean daily level of illicit opiate use) and health economic measures. The study had several secondary aims which were important in clarifying implementation aspects: interaction between certain subject characteristics and treatment type to identify treatment-specific prognostic variables for outcome; the process of change in relation to effects on cognitive schema, coping, self-efficacy and expectancies; and the influence of the quality of counselling and therapist influences on treatment outcome.

All subjects received standard MMT. This comprised regular, at a minimum, fortnightly appointments with a keyworker in an outpatient drug treatment clinic according to a purpose-designed manual, and the prescription of oral methadone linctus (within a clinical range of 30 mg to 140 mg per day) (DH 1999a). An MMT manual was developed, given to all study MMT keyworkers, who were trained in its use. Each keyworking session aimed to last on average thirty minutes. The keyworking focused on identifying specific needs and delivering concrete services rather than dealing with psychological processes.

Subjects allocated to the CBT group received individual CBT sessions delivered by trained CBT therapists in addition to the standard MMT. Each session aimed to last fifty minutes and took place in the same clinic location as the patient's appointment with the keyworker. CBT sessions consisted of a maximum of twenty-four sessions conducted over a maximum period of six months. The sessions were based on an individual case formulation with twelve sessions as the minimum 'dose' of CBT required in all patients. In practice, sessions were planned to take place approximately on a weekly basis. CBT sessions were conducted according to a CBT treatment manual, which was specially developed for this trial by members of the project group.

The CBT therapists were recruited from existing staff from participating sites and they underwent an intensive two-week (ten working days) programme of training before the intervention phase of the trial. This was run as two separate week-long training sessions, a period of one month apart, during which time the trainees were expected to practise their skills with test cases from their clinic. The training programme included instruction on the principles of CBT, its application to addiction and clinical practice. Methods used included didactic training, role-play, case simulation, scenarios for discussion and video examples. The programme included an overview of the process of therapy outlining the main techniques and their order of application, methods of engaging patients, developing case formulations, using cognitive and behavioural techniques, role-play of blocks to therapy, and techniques to effect progress in therapy. The subsequent weekly supervision sessions aimed to consolidate and aid the application of knowledge to the therapeutic setting. This supervision was offered by experienced CBT therapists.

Following completion of training, therapists were required to practise therapy with existing clients, under supervision, and submit tape-recorded sessions for blind accreditation by two independent assessors.

The quality of CBT counselling was assessed using the Cognitive Therapy Scale (CTS – Young and Beck 1980), which comprises two subscales, one that measures the skills of cognitive therapists and one that measures general interpersonal and relationship factors in therapy. We also used the Cognitive Behaviour Therapy Rating Scale (CBTRS – Carroll 1998a) to assess adherence to the manual. Both instruments were rated by the supervisor after having listened to a therapist's tape to rate the session. These measures were also used by two independent expert raters to assess therapist skill and the application of CBT. In addition, the therapists completed the second related measure, the CBT Therapist Checklist (CBTTC – Carroll 1998b), after each session to self-rate their skills for each aspect of CBT. Once completed, this form was used during supervision to assist in skill development.

CBT therapist characteristics and experience of training

In total, eighty-two clinicians were recruited to take part in the study: thirty-one recruited to deliver the CBT therapy and fifty-one the MMT intervention. In order to assess the training package and evaluate the experience of the staff trained for CBT, before the end of the trial we asked them to complete a questionnaire about their professional background, training, accreditation, supervision and after-study experiences: twenty out of thirty-one therapists responded.

The professional statuses of those recruited to be trained as CBT therapists were as follows: community psychiatric nurses (14); drug workers (8); psychologists (3); psychiatrists (specialist registrars) (2); social workers (3); and university lecturer in psychology (1). Three of the drug workers had a qualification in counselling, two were graduates and three of them had neither of these qualifications. Some of the recruited staff (8/20) had some experience in generic CBT as part of their professional training and eleven out of fourteen had training or experience in other types of psychological interventions (motivational interviewing, HIV counselling, psychodynamic therapy and solution-focused therapy). The mean clinical experience of the staff in addictions treatment was 5.75 years (0.5–20). Fourteen found the training offered better than expected, and five as expected. Two found that it was not focused enough on how to engage clients and how to practise the techniques. Several people commented that they would have preferred a longer period of training.

Of the thirty-one recruited to deliver CBT, over half (55 per cent) dropped out of the study either because they did not want to continue (9) or they moved on to other jobs or positions (8). Of the fourteen retained at the start of study recruitment, eleven (79 per cent) reached accreditation to deliver CBT therapy, two were partially accredited (almost all the skills required and the supervisor felt that they would reach accreditation once they were allocated a study client) and one did not reach accreditation. Nine of the eleven fully accredited therapists were allocated at least one study client, as were both partially accredited therapists.

After the end of the trial, we also conducted four focus groups for the accredited therapists (two groups for the North sites, one for London sites and one for South sites). Eleven out of thirteen therapists participated. The groups discussed in more detail the findings of the questionnaire survey. The group participants emphasized the importance of longer training and the importance of having easy access to supervision from the early stages of accreditation. All the participants reported that they continued to use in their everyday clinical practice the CBT principles and/or specific techniques after the end of their participation in the trial. Nine of them had used all aspects of CBT and most had used the CBT manual as a reference tool to inform their everyday clinical practice. Six people had continued with further CBT training after the end of the trial.

We used relatively low eligibility criteria of previous experience for recruitment of therapists compared to previous US research (where therapists were usually PhD psychologists or experienced CBT therapists from centres of excellence). Very few had previous CBT training and most needed a significant level of supervision in addition to their training before reaching the accreditation standard. Although this could have had an adverse effect on the effectiveness of the intervention offered, this was a pragmatic study. We believe therefore that the results of implementation of a CBT intervention in this study provide a reasonable picture of what would be likely to happen in the typical NHS clinical setting if this approach were to be implemented nationally, and thus help to inform discussion of the required investment in the workforce.

The CBT manual

CBT was offered according to a purposely developed manual. This manual brought together the two main CBT treatment models in addiction, the Relapse Prevention model of Marlatt and Gordon (1985) and the Cognitive Therapy model of Beck *et al.* (1993), and it largely followed the session format described by Carroll (1998a, 1998b). Whilst these two models shared the same theoretical principles and concepts (such as identification of high risk situations and coping skills training), they had differences in relation to therapeutic emphasis and delivery methods. The model used in this study was expanded later to include information on how to apply it to different types of substance misuse within different types of services (Kouimtsidis *et al.* 2007).

The first part of the manual described in detail the cognitive and behavioural techniques and provided advice on how and when to apply them. This was followed by a step-by-step approach to assessment and case formulation. This was a major difference compared to previous manuals. Case formulation is a dynamic therapy hypothesis that should be shared with the client, should be reviewed regularly to incorporate new understanding of the patient's problem, and should determine the therapy plan. In this way, although therapy is highly structured, it can be flexible and tailored to a patient's needs (Kouimtsidis *et al.* 2007).

The core of the manual followed the format of a step-by-step treatment planner and consisted of core and elective topics. The order of topics and the choice of elective topics were determined by the formulation. This approach allowed therapists to pay attention to comorbidity issues common in opioid misuse and to improve coordination of the client's care, and was in line with national guidelines for comorbidity management (DH 2002).

Eight core topics covered issues which were fundamental to addiction from a cognitive perspective. Twelve elective topics covered issues of mental health comorbidity, multiple substance dependence and common aspects and problems encountered during treatment (Table 10.1).

Main study results

As discussed above, the study had limited statistical power to detect treatment effects due to lower recruitment than anticipated. Therefore the results should be interpreted with caution. The small sample size increases the risk for a type II error (i.e. a significant difference is not detected). In such a case the effect size of the comparisons can give an indication as to whether the differences might have reached significance in a bigger sample. Although there were not any significant differences detected between the two groups for any of the outcome variables, the CBT group was doing better overall and the

Table 10.1 List of core and elective topics in the CBT manual

Core topics	Elective topics
Identifying and dealing with stimulus conditions	Depression and anxiety
	Anger and impulse control
Refusal skills/assertiveness	Alcohol misuse
All-purpose coping plan	Methadone maintenance compliance
Seemingly irrelevant decisions	Risk behaviours/injecting behaviours
Problem solving	Coping with crisis
Adapting lifestyle (changes)	Compulsive criminal behaviour
Boredom/emptiness and bereavement	Relationship problems
Termination	Employment/job seeking
	Sleep management
	Childcare
	Dealing with common problems

effect sizes were within the predicted range based on earlier studies, indicating, as discussed above, that those differences might have reached significance with a larger sample. This has allowed the UKCBTMM study to be incorporated into a subsequent meta-analysis of comparable clinical trials, including the NICE psychosocial guidelines.

We conducted two types of analysis: an intention-to-treat analysis, where all participants allocated in the groups were included (independently of their engagement with the intervention or not); and a per protocol analysis where only those engaged with the intervention were included in the analysis. Intention-to-treat analysis is in favour of the null hypothesis, therefore reducing the probability that differences would reach significance.

Intention-to-treat analysis

An increase in the percentage of days abstinent (PDA) from illicit heroin was found in both treatment groups at six months, with a greater increase in the CBT group (16 per cent vs. 9 per cent) and a standardized effect size difference of 0.28. At twelve months, there was a further increase in number of days abstinent from heroin in both groups (22.9 per cent vs. 16.9 per cent: CBT vs. MMT), compared to 100 per cent using heroin at baseline.

Per protocol analysis

As with the intention-to-treat analysis, there was a greater increase in PDA from heroin at six months in the CBT group (24 per cent) than in the MMT group (7 per cent). Once again, although this difference was not statistically significant, there was a larger standardized effect size (0.61). There was a greater increase in abstinence from heroin for both groups at twelve months and the difference was sustained in favour of the CBT group, with an effect size difference of 0.50.

Economic evaluation

For both groups, there was a decrease in the use of health services in the first six months after treatment but some increase in use after this time. Both groups however had fewer days in hospital in the year after treatment than in the year before treatment. The results for crime, however, were less clear. The CBT group had fewer income-generating crimes in the year after treatment. The levels in the MMT group were low at baseline but seem to vary across the period. For both groups there was an estimated annual resource saving. For the intervention group, these resource savings compared to the study treatment costs were in the ratio of 15:1, whereas for the control group the ratio of resource consequences to treatment was 14:1. In monetary terms, combining the treatment and resource consequences suggests a net resource saving per client of £8,421 for the CBT group and a saving of £1,607 for the control group. Comparing the two treatments yields an incremental net saving of £6,814 per client for CBT compared to control.

The overall result does not clearly favour one treatment over another, although the large numerator suggests that the savings from CBT and MMT are on average outweighing the small loss of health status. These results indicate that CBT is cost-saving compared to standard MMT alone.

In addition to the limited statistical power discussed above, there was another problem affecting the interpretation of the study results. The number of CBT sessions attended was lower than anticipated. Of the twenty-nine clients randomized to receive CBT, eighteen (62 per cent) attended at least one CBT session, with a mean of 2.6, and a median of four sessions. It is therefore difficult to attribute the results found to CBT exposure. Equally it would be premature to conclude that CBT is ineffective in opioid misusers. It is possible that larger differences in outcome would be associated with higher exposure to CBT. Due to the small number of participants, a dose–response analysis was not possible.

The relatively limited number of sessions attended could be an indication of a major difficulty in engaging patients in a structured therapy of this type in a UK NHS drug treatment setting. This, in conjunction with the small screen conversion rate (7 per cent of those screened were recruited), could indicate that if CBT was offered as a routine treatment in the NHS drug treatment services for opioid misusers, it would be taken up by only a minority of the total population of patients. We believe, though, that many patients were unwilling to take part in the CBT possibly because the clinical culture that the patients were used to was one with limited or no psychological therapy and relatively low expectations about the client's engagement and compliance with treatment. If the services had psychological interventions as a routine treatment and they were better resourced to provide more intensive interventions in general, it is possible that patients would be more willing to engage in, and obtain benefit from, CBT and other psychological interventions. Further, if contingency management was applied to attendance at CBT sessions, this might have increased engagement in CBT.

Conclusions

We have already presented the limited direct findings of this study and discussed extensively the factors affecting those findings. As this was the first pragmatic study of the topic in the UK, there were several indirect findings associated with the execution of the research project that provided important information about (i) clinical services and their ability to incorporate structured psychosocial interventions; (ii) important components for the development of psychosocial services such as training needs, methods and appropriate treatment planners; and (iii) gaps in research infrastructure.

- Services offering assertive intervention with patients seen in primary care were unable to recruit patients for the study.
- Services offering on-site methadone dispensing and booked keyworker appointments, compared to open appointments/drop-in, were better able to recruit patients and to accommodate the study.

The above two factors could be considered indicators of the minimum structure that a service should have in order to be able to provide structured psychosocial interventions.

These recruitment problems could be seen as indicators of future problems that implementation of NICE guidelines for psychosocial interventions might encounter as they could affect implementation of any structured psychosocial interventions, such as CM and cognitive behavioural family interventions, within tertiary substitution prescribing services. These findings may also have relevance in the implementation of the NICE guidelines with other treatment groups such as primary stimulant users or cannabis users (where CBT has strong supportive evidence), and CBT applied to psychiatric comorbidity in drug misusers.

These findings support the notion that it is necessary to promote and establish a psychologically friendly environment before proceeding to offer more specific psychological interventions. To this effect it is more appropriate for a stepped care type of approach to be introduced. It would make sense if at the base of this approach is the well established and effective substitution treatment. At a second stage structured keyworking should be offered to all patients. Keyworking would incorporate the principles of CBT, collaborative approach and positive reinforcement, as advised by the NICE guidelines. In this way the recommended change of treatment philosophy would be achieved (NICE 2007b). Then other structured psychological interventions could be added for selected groups of patients. The study experience suggests that those changes would be more effective and easier to implement if they could follow the principle of cohesion rather than that of fragmentation which seems to be followed at the moment. The concept of substitute prescribing should be expanded, rather than deconstructed to its minimum components of signing 'a script' by 'a doctor', keyworking, and structured psychological interventions offered by different providers with minimum liaison and service coordination.

- Training for CBT can be brief and effective. Staff can develop therapy skills which are improved with clinical experience and maintained over time.
- Regular supervision is a crucial factor for the engagement and successful work of CBT therapists. Difficulty in identifying suitable supervisors and access to supervision sessions had an aversive effect on therapists' motivation and confidence to deliver the CBT intervention.
- Brief and practical treatment planners are helpful as an everyday therapy tool.

- High turnover of staff and high caseload had an adverse effect on staff's involvement with the study.

It seems that the dilemma between quantity and quality is far more real than it was anticipated to be. Cost-effective treatment is not the same as cheap treatment. Investment in staff numbers, appropriate training and availability of psychological therapy supervision are essential prerequisites to achieve quality treatment. This is now even more important as initial targets of accessibility and increased numbers in treatment have been achieved. The challenge now is to put the patient at the centre of our practice and policy and improve the quality of active treatment offered rather than just reduce the harm to society.

Acknowledgements

We would like to thank the many therapists, keyworkers, consultant psychiatrists, administrators, CBT supervisors, and not least the patients for giving generously of their time and taking part in this study. We thank also in particular: Selma Shirazi, David Mosley, Jo Moloney and Steve Chamberlain; Professor A.T. Beck for his comments on the manual; and Professor A.T. McLellan who provided advice on the design of the project.

The UKCBTMM project group

Professor Colin Drummond, National Addiction Centre, Institute of Psychiatry, King's College London. UKCBTMM Principal Investigator

Dr Christos Kouimtsidis, Department of Addictive Behaviour, St George's Hospital Medical School, University of London. Investigator, Lead Author of CBT Manual and CBT Trainer, CBT Supervisor

Dr Martina Reynolds, Department of Addictive Behaviour, St George's Hospital Medical School, University of London (now Department of Human Sciences, Brunel University). Investigator, Lead Author of CBT Manual and CBT Therapist

Professor Ian Russell, Institute of Medical and Social Care Research, University of Wales, Bangor. Investigator, Trial Methodology and Lead Statistician

Professor Christine Godfrey, Department of Health Sciences and Centre for Health Economics, University of York. Investigator, Lead Health Economist

Ms Monica McCusker, Department of Addictive Behaviour, St George's Hospital Medical School, University of London. Investigator, Trial Co-coordinator and Research Assistant

Mr Simon Coulton, York Trials Unit, Department of Health Sciences, University of York. Investigator, Trial Statistician

Mr Steve Parrott, Centre for Health Economics, University of York. Investigator, Trial Health Economist

Dr Paul Davis, Camden and Islington Substance Misuse Service, C&I NHS Trust, London. Investigator, CBT Trainer, Supervisor, Clinical Lead (North London) and Contributor to Manual

Professor Nick Tarrier, Academic Division of Clinical Psychology, University of Manchester. Investigator, Contributor to CBT Manual and CBT Trainer

Dr Douglas Turkington, Department of Psychiatry, University of Newcastle upon Tyne. Investigator, Contributor to CBT Manual and CBT Trainer

Dr Louise Sell, Manchester, Bolton, Salford and Trafford Substance Misuse Directorate, BST Mental Health NHS Trust, Manchester. Investigator, Clinical Lead – Greater Manchester sites and Contributor to CBT Manual

Dr John Merrill, Manchester, Bolton, Salford and Trafford Substance Misuse Directorate, BST Mental Health NHS Trust, Manchester. Investigator, Clinical Lead – Greater Manchester (2000)

Dr Hugh Williams, Substance Misuse Service, South Downs Health NHS Trust, Brighton and Hove. Investigator, Clinical Lead – Brighton

Dr Mohammed Abou-Saleh, Department of Addictive Behaviour, St George's Hospital Medical School, University of London. Investigator, Clinical Lead (South London)

Professor Hamid Ghodse, Department of Addictive Behaviour, St George's Hospital Medical School, University of London, Investigator, Clinical Lead (South London)

Dr Sally Porter, St George's Hospital Medical School (now at South London and Maudsley NHS Trust), London. Investigator, Clinical Lead (South London)

Ms Rebecca Daw, Department of Addictive Behaviour, St George's Hospital Medical School, University of London (now Clinical Psychology course, University of Coventry). Research Assistant (South)

Mr Nigel Fyles, Manchester, Bolton, Salford and Trafford Substance Misuse Directorate, BST Mental Health NHS Trust, Manchester. Research Assistant (North)

Mr Sam Keating, Department of Addictive Behaviour, St George's Hospital Medical School, University of London. Research Assistant (South)

Ms Anne Moloney, Department of Clinical Psychology, School of Psychiatry and Behavioural Sciences, University of Manchester. Research Assistant (North)

Ms Kate Pryce, Department of Clinical Psychology, Addictions Directorate, South London and Maudsley Trust. Research Assistant (South)

Mr Mani Mehdikhani, Neurorehabilitation Unit, Lancashire Teaching Hospitals NHS Trust, Preston. Research Assistant (North)

Mr Ben Barnaby, Department of Addictive Behaviour, St George's Hospital Medical School, University of London (now Clinical Psychology course, University College, University of London). Research Assistant (South)

Dr Jack Leach, Wigan and Leigh Substance Misuse Service, 5 Boroughs Partnership NHS Trust, Warrington. Clinical Lead – Greater Manchester sites (2002–3)

Dr Sue Ruben, Liverpool Substance Misuse Service, Mersey Care NHS Trust, Liverpool. Clinical Lead – Liverpool site (2002)

11 Involving service users in efforts to improve the quality of drug misuse services

Michael J. Crawford, Sue Patterson, Kostas Agath and Tim Weaver

User involvement (UI) has been promoted as a means of improving the quality of health and social care services across Europe and North America over the last thirty years (E. Bates 1983; Crawford *et al.* 2004). In several countries, policies aimed at promoting user involvement are underpinned by legislation requiring service providers to involve people who use services in the decisions they make. In England and Wales, providers of state-funded health and social care, including drug misuse services, have a statutory requirement to involve users when planning changes to the services (Home Office 2002).

User involvement has also been promoted as a means of improving the quality of drug misuse services (NTA 2002b). It has been argued that UI has the potential to improve uptake and retention in services (Randall and DrugScope 2002; Fountain *et al.* 2003). However, concerns have been expressed that, relative to other areas of health care, drug misuse services have been slow to involve service users (Southwell 2002; Schulte *et al.* 2007). In this chapter, we discuss the context in which user involvement in drug misuse services has developed and summarise findings from research which has explored factors that appear to promote and hinder this process. The implications of these findings for future service developments are also discussed.

The focus of the chapter is on 'top-down' efforts made by professionals to engage users in planning, commissioning and delivering services. We have not attempted to provide an account of other important aspects of user involvement, such as advocacy and political activism, and do not seek to address the 'bottom-up' involvement sought by user movements. While engagement of users in planning their own care may also be defined as user involvement, this form of individual involvement is also beyond the scope of this chapter.

Aspirations and evidence

User involvement in public health services has been promoted both as a 'means to an end' and as an 'end in itself'. It has been argued that, as current and potential service users pay for the services they receive, they have a right to contribute to how they are run (HM Government 1990). From this perspective, user involvement is seen as having an inherent value through enhancing democracy and accountability. User involvement has also been promoted as a means of achieving other aims, including:

- To improve service quality. User involvement is seen as a means of capturing the expertise of people who have used services in order to try to ensure they are delivered in an effective manner (NHS Executive 1999; Coulter 2002).
- To obtain public support for provider-led changes. It is argued that by consulting service users support can be obtained for decisions that may otherwise be unpopular (Hildebrandt 1994; S. Harrison and Mort 1998).
- To improve public perceptions of health care. Opinion polls repeatedly show that health care is one of the top priorities of the electorate in most countries. In this context, increasing levels of public satisfaction with health care services is likely to be a government priority (Ham and Alberti 2002).
- As a means of promoting wellbeing and reducing social exclusion. It is argued that user involvement has a therapeutic value as it may help improve the self-esteem and wellbeing of those service users who take part in the process (Barnes and Wistow 1994).

Attempts to examine whether UI is effective in achieving these aims have been limited and the available evidence is mixed. Surveys of service commissioners and providers suggest that many people who have been involved in this process believe that it can improve service quality (Checkoway *et al.* 1984; S. Harrison *et al.* 2002; Crawford *et al.* 2003). In contrast, retrospective examination of records from UI initiatives has revealed that many suggestions made by service users do not lead to change (Richardson and Bray 1987; Milewa 1997). Systematic reviews examining the outcomes of UI have concluded that the changes to services have been made following consultation with service users but that the impact of these changes on the effects and cost-effectiveness of services has not been examined (Crawford *et al.* 2002).

User involvement in drug misuse services

While user involvement in the development and delivery of services was reported outside of the UK from the late 1980s (e.g. Grund *et al.* 1992; Kerr *et al.* 2001), it was still largely absent in Britain a decade later. In England, interviews with service users and providers in 2001–3 suggested that one in six service providers did not involve users at all (Schulte *et al.* 2007). In response to concerns that drug misuse services were failing to involve service users, the National Treatment Agency (NTA), which oversees substance misuse services in the UK, provided guidance and financial support to services in an effort to stimulate user involvement (NTA 2002b, 2006c). This guidance, which was primarily aimed at commissioners of services, stated that UI was an essential part of efforts to improve the quality of drug misuse services, and also emphasised users' 'right to become involved in activities that affect their health and well-being'.

In the next section of this chapter we discuss findings and recommendations from recent studies and reports of user involvement in drug misuse services, including those from a multi-method evaluation of UI in drug misuse services in England which we conducted in 2006. This study involved a survey of service commissioners, providers and users in a representative sample of treatment services covering a third of the population of England, and six case studies, in which interviews and focus groups explored participants' experiences of user involvement in the development of drug treatment services (Patterson *et al.* 2009a, 2009b). We received completed surveys from 45 (90 per cent) commissioning agencies, 21 (42 per cent) NHS Trusts, 32 (64 per cent) voluntary sector organisations and 17 (49 per cent) out of 35 service user group representatives that we tried to contact. In-depth interviews were conducted with 139 stakeholders in the six case study sites. The project was commissioned as part of the UK Department of Health Policy Research Programme DMRI.

Methods of involvement

Methods for involving users of drug misuse services in service development are listed in Table 11.1. Responses to our survey identified ongoing contacts with individual service users, consultation with user groups and surveys as the three most common methods used to involve users. We found evidence to suggest that some service providers may have placed too great an emphasis on user groups as the solitary involvement strategy. While some user groups were

Table 11.1 Methods for involving service users in the development and delivery of drug misuse services

Type of method	Examples
Time-limited methods	User surveys Focus groups Action research, including user-led research User Focused Monitoring
Ad hoc methods	Feedback via staff members Feedback from services users via complaints, suggestion boxes, etc. Informal contacts between individual service users and managers

Ongoing consultation	Support for setting up and running user groups
	    (managers may attend user group meetings or invite user group
	    members onto existing committees)
	Employment of a User Involvement coordinator
	Newsletters, websites, and other forms of information sharing

Service delivery	Volunteer programmes Employment of service users

able to act as a point of contact for service users who wanted to make a contribution to local service developments, others had been set up without a clear aim, and reliance on one or two active members meant that groups were difficult to sustain once these members moved on (Patterson *et al.* 2009c). Surveys generally aimed to measure levels of satisfaction with existing services. A minority of service providers reported using more intensive methods for trying to capture service user views, such as User Focused Monitoring in which service users are trained to administer and analyse data from interviews with other service users (Rose 1998). One-quarter of health care providers told us that service users were involved in interviewing for new members of staff. Less than one-fifth of service providers reported employing service users in a voluntary or paid capacity to deliver services.

Two-thirds of the service providers who responded to the survey stated that they provided financial or other resources to support UI. Most frequently, such support was provided through reimbursing travel and other expenses incurred by service users carrying out UI activities, training and mentoring, and financial support to enable users to attend conferences. Approximately one-third of service providers reported paying service users, in cash or with vouchers, for participation in service activities.

Factors that hinder user involvement in drug misuse services

Most of the factors that appear to hinder involvement of service users in the development of drug misuse services have also been extensively reported in other areas of health and social care (see Table 11.2). In our study,

Table 11.2 Barriers to successful involvement of service users

General factors (seen in other areas of health and social care)	
Culture	Tokenism and lack of commitment
	Service resistance
	Perceived inability of users to participate
Organisational structure	Governance arrangements
	Bureaucratic processes
	Confidentiality
Other factors	Funding
	Limited interest of service users
	Complexity of service provision
	Skills and experience of service users

Factors of special significance in drug misuse services
Distrust and stigma
Illegality of drug use
Impact of dependence on drugs
Efforts to develop drug-free lifestyle
Diversity among users of drug
    misuse services

respondents' accounts demonstrated that UI was shaped by complex inter-related influences. Many of these, including organisational complexity, funding, time and lack of organisational expertise, have also been widely reported in other contexts (McGrath and Grant 1992; D. Rutter *et al.* 2004; Daykin *et al.* 2007). Across sites, stakeholders also emphasised a number of factors which appear to be particularly salient to the drug treatment field and these are discussed below.

Stigmatisation of drug users

Prejudice and stigma related to drug use were an invidious and pervasive influence on UI. Users reported experiencing discrimination in the community, within treatment services, and as participants in UI activities. Commissioners and managers frequently confirmed this, describing colleagues' assumptions regarding the perceived inability of users to participate in 'sophisticated' forums and contribute to complex processes deemed to require specialist skills. These assumptions were said to create discomfort for those facilitating UI. Some of the service providers we interviewed told us that colleagues felt uncomfortable engaging service users. They said that this discomfort related to assumptions about drug use and people who use drugs. These included beliefs about the 'self-inflicted' nature of drug dependence and the view that this negated users' right to contribute to service development. These findings are supported by the experiences of others who have highlighted the impact that stigmatisation and a 'culture of blame' play in preventing successful user involvement in this field (Garrett and Foster 2005).

Diversity of users of drug misuse services

A common theme across respondent groups was the heterogeneity of the user population and the potential challenges this represents to UI. Differences included those: (a) between current and ex-drug users; (b) between people using different primary drugs; and (c) among people with different perceptions about the rightful focus of user involvement, i.e. political activism or service development. Some of the service providers that we interviewed raised concerns about exposure of people in treatment to people who were current drug users. For many drug service users, one of their aims may be to have less contact with people who are still using drugs. Clinicians expressed concerns that participation in UI might undermine this aim by increasing the contact they had with people who were still using drugs. Others have also highlighted how the diversity of users of drug misuse services can lead to tensions and in-fighting (GLADA 2005). In contrast, some service users saw the diversity of people with experience of using drug misuse services as one of the strengths of user groups.

The complexity of service provision

While the complexity of services and changes in the organisation of services have been identified as barriers to involvement in other contexts (D. Rutter *et al.* 2004), this issue appears to be particularly salient in the context of substance misuse services in Britain. Much of the effort to develop UI in drug misuse services in recent years has taken place at the level of commissioning agencies. However, commissioning agencies typically have relationships with multiple providers of services located within both the voluntary and public sectors. This means that service users wanting to make a contribution to service developments may need to develop links with several different organisations involved in commissioning and delivery of services. The mixed economy of service provision, together with the range of treatment modalities and models implemented within and across services, makes the establishment of consistent mechanisms for UI a more challenging task. In most areas, public sector drug misuse services are provided by Mental Health Trusts. In some areas, separate methods for involving users of drug services and general mental health services did not exist, and where this was the case, users of drug services stated that shared UI fora may fail to take account of the views of users of drug misuse services.

Factors that promote user involvement in drug misuse services

Factors that promote UI in the development and delivery of drug misuse services also have much in common with those reported in other contexts. These include the commitment of senior staff, dedicated budgets for supporting ongoing UI activities and clear methods for providing feedback which make it clear how the views of service users have influenced change. Participating in structured meetings governed by unfamiliar procedures meant that, in order to play a sustained role, service users needed training and support.

Clear aims

Aims which are unclear can raise expectations which cannot be fulfilled and leave service users unsure about the value of their contribution (Garrett and Foster 2005). The recommendation of ADFAM (2001), a UK charity that works with families of drug users, seems a sound one: 'Don't ask for views if you can't or won't do anything with them – make it clear what you can change and can't.'

Clear feedback

The service users we interviewed often wondered what happened to feedback they provided to services and if any action was taken in response to their contribution to service developments. They suggested that more feedback regarding outcomes would increase the likelihood of further participation. Case studies of UI in the development of services in other health care settings have concluded that service users need to see change resulting from their work if effective user involvement is to be sustained (Ovretveit and Davies 1988; Todd *et al.* 2000).

Combining several different methods

As a recent report on drug user involvement in London concluded: 'drug users are a diverse group with different needs, expectations and skills. Therefore it's unlikely that there is a single approach that would support them to be involved and enthusiastic about participating in public life' (GLADA 2005). Recognition of the diverse backgrounds of service users and the often intermittent pattern of contact with services highlights the need to combine ongoing methods for involvement with time-limited methods. Surveys are relatively inexpensive to conduct and, while response rates may be poor, they may still be used to generate information about deficits in service provision and areas of concern to service users. Other time-limited methods, such as focus groups and participatory action research, have also been used to good effect in the development of drug misuse services. For instance, McFarlane and Thomson (1998) set up a focus group of prisoners to try to identify steps that could be taken to improve drug service provision in a local prison. Findings from the focus group were used to help design an information pack for prisoners and led to a proposal to set up a drug-free wing with regular voluntary drug testing. In their account of a participatory action research project, Coupland and Maher (2005) describe how collaborative research conducted by workers from a university department in Melbourne, Australia with service users and providers helped to develop insights into reasons why young intravenous drug users do not engage with existing services. The authors conclude that peer workers had privileged access to drug users and were able to obtain sensitive data that may have been withheld from researchers or service providers.

Resources

Our findings demonstrated wide variation in the extent to which service commissioners and providers fund and otherwise resource user involvement. In addition to helping to sustain the contribution of service users to improve the effectiveness of services, funding may also be seen by users as an important sign that service providers value the work they do (GLADA 2005).

Training

Our findings support previous commentary emphasising the importance of ensuring access to relevant training for service users, which is seen as crucial to development of effective UI. However, it seems that in the drug misuse arena specific skill-focused training, for example in relation to meeting processes and procedures, ought to be delivered within a framework encompassing the rationale and objectives of UI. In this context, shared training in which multiple stakeholders participated was seen to provide opportunities for open communication and development of reciprocal understanding and respect that would engender further involvement. It is important that purpose, structure and content of training for service users be negotiated.

What has UI in drug misuse services achieved?

Service commissioners, providers and users who participated in our study described a range of changes which user involvement had contributed to or hastened. The most frequently reported related to the development of UI, such as increased representation of users on committees, employment of UI workers and development of user groups (Patterson *et al.* 2009a). Nearly half of service commissioners also reported changes to service opening hours and the development of mobile services. Others described expansion of prescribing options (for example, the inclusion of subutex and changes to dosing regimens), alterations to injecting paraphernalia provided to service users, and introduction of new services, such as structured day care. These findings, together with other published reports in this field, suggest that involvement of service users can lead to changes in the configuration and range of services that are provided. However, as with other areas of health care, the impact of these changes on the effects and cost-effectiveness of services is largely unknown.

The future of UI in the development of drug misuse services

One of the main findings from our interviews with commissioners and providers of drug misuse services was that most do not see UI as integral to achieving other policy objectives. For instance, in recent years service commissioners in England have been required to take steps to increase the number of people accessing treatment services (Home Office 2002). However, none of the service commissioners and providers we interviewed linked UI with efforts aimed at achieving this target. While service providers were able to describe examples where users' views contributed to changes in service delivery, the impact of these changes on numbers accessing services or being engaged in treatment is not known. It is therefore not surprising that many service providers see UI as being an 'additional requirement' placed on them rather than a means of achieving their main service objectives (Patterson *et al.* 2009b).

We believe that future research and development initiatives need to examine the impact of user involvement. Whilst assessing the contribution of user involvement to changes in service outcomes is a complex task (Smith 1998), the successful application of case study methods to evaluate the impact of consumer involvement in the commercial sector suggests that it is possible (e.g. Weiser 1995; Magidson and Brandyberry 2001). It seems particularly important to examine the impact of user involvement on perceived service quality and the links between UI-led developments and the attainment of other policy goals such as retention in treatment.

One area where examining the impact of UI on service-level outcomes may be particularly productive is through employing users of drug misuse services in delivering services. In general mental health services, evidence suggests that some services, such as case management, are at least as effective when delivered by former service users, and that levels of satisfaction with care delivered by former users may be higher than those delivered by health care professionals (E. L. Simpson and House 2002). In interviews with service users in northern England, Schulte and colleagues (Schulte *et al.* 2007) found greater support for UI through opportunities for voluntary and paid employment than through any other methods of UI. Evaluation of such schemes in the drug treatment field clearly has the potential to inform further development of UI and it merits stronger support than it currently receives.

However, in the absence of clear evidence about the impact of UI, it appears that the short- to medium-term future of UI in drug misuse services in England and Wales will continue to rely on the commitment of central government. In this regard the new drug treatment strategy is particularly significant (HM Government 2008). Whilst representatives of users of drug misuse services were involved in the development of this strategy, the absence of explicit reference to UI in the document is both surprising and disappointing. The strategy includes a commitment to deliver new approaches to social re-integration and picks up a longstanding request of service users that interventions need to address practical and social problems including training and employment. While not explicitly referred to in the strategy, the potential for drug users and service users to contribute to the development of changes to services and to public education aimed at preventing drug misuse is clear to see.

Findings from research conducted in this field suggest that the majority of commissioners and providers of drug services in England are making efforts to involve users and that this process appears to have had some impact on service delivery. However, user involvement is disparate and organisational expertise in UI is in the early stages of development. In this context, the ongoing commitment of central government seems crucial to effective UI. Given the planned devolution of drug strategy management from the NTA to regional authorities, we emphasise the importance of ensuring clarity in relation to UI leadership and accountability. The manner in which the NTA's responsibility for user involvement is transferred is likely to have a considerable bearing on the success of future efforts to involve service users. Policy and guidelines must provide a robust yet flexible framework to enable local implementation of UI and support its ongoing development.

12 Co-morbidity in treatment populations

Tim Weaver, Vikki Charles, Thomas Barnes and Peter Tyrer

Background

This chapter reviews the findings of a research study which measured the prevalence of mental illness and substance misuse co-morbidity (hereafter referred to as co-morbidity) in substance misuse and mental health treatment populations. The study was funded by the Drugs Misuse Research Initiative (DMRI) in 2000 and completed between 2001 and 2002. Although the chapter reports data collected seven years prior to the publication of this volume, we will argue that the findings are still relevant. First, the study has not been replicated and so still provides the best UK evidence about the epidemiology of co-morbidity in treatment populations. Second, while the study findings have had an influence on policy (which merits documentation), some key findings about the extent of non-psychotic mental illness within drug treatment populations have not been acted upon. Third, as we argue in the conclusions, a re-assessment of these findings is timely given the development of care co-ordination (see Chapter 5) and efforts to increase the capacity of services to provide psychosocial interventions.

Before describing the research in detail, let us review the scientific and policy context within which the research was commissioned and undertaken.

What is co-morbidity?

Co-morbidity describes the co-existence of two or more disorders. Within the substance misuse and mental health treatment fields, the term refers to patients who concurrently exhibit both a substance misuse and a mental health problem. Co-morbid clinical presentations may be 'multiple', and can include poly-substance use, misuse or dependence; include multiple psychiatric conditions; have different aetiologies; and be coupled with a range of social problems (V. Crawford and Crome 2001).

Drug policy in the late 1990s: what was the approach to co-morbidity?

In 1998 when the first ten-year Drug Strategy was published (HM Government 1998) there was growing concern about co-morbidity but little evidence about its extent and nature within the UK. Much of the concern, then as now, focused on the clinical management problems associated with substance use amongst patients of mental health services who had a psychotic mental illness, such as schizophrenia.

The 1998 Drug Strategy recognised the problem of co-morbidity from a drug treatment perspective. It included an aspiration to 'provide an integrated, effective and efficient response to people with drugs and mental health problems' (HM Government 1998). A key component of the ten-year Drug Strategy was the establishment of the National Treatment Agency (NTA) for Substance Misuse in 2001. In 2002, the NTA published *Models of Care* (MoC) which provided treatment agencies with practice guidance based on best available current evidence and a 'professional consensus of "what works best" ' (NTA 2002b).

By definition, the treatment needs of people with co-morbidity potentially fall within the remit of both mental health and substance misuse services. Indeed, MoC addressed the management of co-morbidity in terms of a 'cross-cutting issue'. MoC recognised the heterogeneity of co-morbid presentation and the difficulties of assessment, diagnosis and management. Acknowledging there was no robust UK evidence about the prevalence of co-morbidity within drug treatment settings, MoC mapped out the first specific responsibilities for drug treatment services in relation to co-morbid patient groups. This was expressed in terms of the development of collaborative working relationships with mental health services around the management of patients with psychosis. MoC anticipated that such patients would be in treatment with a Community Mental Health Team (CMHT) and be subject to management under the Care Programme Approach (CPA) (DH 1995, 1998a, 1999b). It was further assumed that the CMHT would be the lead agency and would be guided by separate DH guidance (DH 2002). Drug and alcohol services were seen to be agencies working with the mental health service and responsible for specific elements of the CPA care plan (NTA 2002b).

It was known that a range of co-morbid psychiatric disorders were associated with increased severity of substance misuse disorder (Brooner *et al.* 1997; Driessen *et al.* 1998) and poor substance misuse treatment outcome (Carey *et al.* 1991). However, MoC made little reference to the needs of drug treatment service patients with co-morbid affective disorders or personality disorder and had a clear focus on the needs of patients with psychosis.

Mental health service policy on co-morbidity

In contrast to the drug treatment field, co-morbidity had a central position in the minds of mental health policy makers during the 1990s who were concerned with the development of community care for people with psychotic disorders (DH 1999b). Concerns about co-morbidity in this population were generated by evidence from the USA. Research had shown that nearly half of all US patients with schizophrenia also experienced a substance misuse disorder at some time in their lives (Regier *et al.* 1990) and that the presence of either psychiatric or substance misuse disorder significantly increased the odds of the other also being present (Kessler *et al.* 1994).

In the UK, there was no comparable evidence that enabled policy makers to assess whether treatment services here faced the same challenges (Hall 1996; Weaver *et al.* 1999). The National Psychiatric Morbidity Survey published in the late 1990s (Jenkins *et al.* 1998) provided little data about co-morbidity (Farrell *et al.* 1998). Moreover, no evidence about concurrent psychiatric illness was provided by either the *British Crime Survey* – the main contemporary source of epidemiological data about drug use in the community (e.g. Ramsay and Partridge 1999) – or the embryonic drug treatment monitoring databases (Hickman *et al.* 1997).

Nevertheless, while the prevalence of co-morbidity was poorly described, emerging research evidence began to show that substance use amongst psychiatric patients was associated with increased admission (Haywood *et al.* 1995), violent behaviour (Scott *et al.* 1998; Swartz *et al.* 1998) and an increased risk of suicide and self-harm (Appleby *et al.* 1999a). Highly influential in the policy arena at this time was the growing public perception that people with severe mental illness and co-morbid substance misuse posed a risk to the general public. This was fuelled by a number of public inquiries into homicides committed by people with mental illness during the 1990s. Several high profile inquiries implicated co-morbidity as a precipitating factor while also highlighting the failings of services to effectively supervise such patients in the community (e.g. Heginbotham *et al.* 1994; Ritchie *et al.* 1994).

The subsequent commentary on the *Confidential Inquiry into Suicide and Homicide by People with Mental Illness* (J. Shaw *et al.* 1999) observed: 'there is repeated evidence that alcohol and drug misuse are among the main problems facing the development of safer services'. The report went on to recommend (in language echoed by subsequent policy and guidance) that, 'the problem of substance misuse is now in a central position in mental health services and cannot continue to be the domain of a distant specialty' (Appleby *et al.* 1999b). Despite lively debate about the inferences to be drawn from these homicide data, consensus was forming around this last point. For example, Taylor and Gunn (1999) sought to demonstrate the statistically remote possibility of being the homicide victim of someone with mental illness while also showing that the chances of this occurring had not been increased by the development of community care during the 1990s. Nevertheless, while providing necessary perspective to this debate they also commented:

> there is reluctance and probably even inability on the part of most services to provide for people with problems of substance misuse or personality disorder. Such people are now the most important challenge for the development of mental health services. People with personality disorders and/or problems of substance misuse (there is considerable

comorbidity between these disorders) form the majority of the broader category of people with mental disorder who kill others.

In direct response to these high profile cases and the debate that they generated, the UK government set out to introduce risk assessment and strengthened community supervision arrangements for mental health patients (NHSME 1994a, 1994b). These initiatives set the tone for a decade of community care reforms which introduced assertive outreach teams and early intervention services to supervise the most challenging mental health patients and maintain their compliance with treatment (DH 1999b, 2001, 2002).

Key research questions for the Drug Misuse Research Initiative

Hence, in the late 1990s, there was increasing concern about the challenge of managing co-morbidity. But this debate focused almost exclusively on patients with severe mental illness in the context of the development of community-based treatment for mental illness, rather than the expansion of drug treatment.

When the DMRI was launched, improvement in the management of co-morbidity was becoming an NHS priority. Although some of the clearest statements of this new priority were to emerge contemporaneously with the findings of the DMRI research (Banerjee *et al.* 2002; DH 2002; NTA 2002b), it was clear that research was required to inform a policy that was beginning to be shaped in an 'evidence vacuum'. Policy makers had little evidence about the current capacity of these services to manage co-morbidity and this severely hampered the identification of appropriate service delivery models (Weaver *et al.* 1999).

The Comorbidity of Substance Misuse and Mental Illness Collaborative Study (COSMIC)

The main aim of the COSMIC study was to estimate the prevalence of co-morbidity amongst current patients of NHS community drug and alcohol services and CMHTs. We also wanted to describe patterns of co-morbidity and assess treatment needs.

The study was conducted in two inner London boroughs and two provincial inner cities. Drug and alcohol teams in all areas offered structured, appointment-based services. The CMHTs were all consultant-led, multi-disciplinary teams which prioritised patients with severe and enduring mental illness in geographically defined catchment areas in accordance with contemporary CPA guidelines (DH 1999b).

In each site, we implemented a two-phase, cross-sectional survey. Phase I involved a complete census of each treatment population, collecting brief data about all patients assessed and allocated to a keyworker and psychiatrist/RMO on the census date. We obtained data about 1,645 substance misuse patients and 2,528 CMHT patients.

Phase II comprised an interview survey with patients drawn at random from these cases. We sampled 400 CMHT patients and 353 substance misuse patients, obtaining interviews with 282 from the CMHT sample (70.5 per cent) and 278 (78.8 per cent) from the substance misuse services (216 drug service patients, 62 alcohol services patients).

The interviews applied a common set of research instruments to both mental health and substance misuse populations. In brief, these comprised measures of psychopathology (Åsberg *et al.* 1978), depression (Montgomery and Åsberg 1979), anxiety (Tyrer *et al.* 1984), personality disorder (Tyrer 2000) and psychosis (McGuffin *et al.* 1991).

We measured drug use over the past year, associated problems, drug dependence (Gossop *et al.* 1995) and harmful alcohol use (Saunders *et al.* 1993). Problem drug use within the CMHT population was defined as self-reported drug-related problems in economic, domestic, social, legal or interpersonal domains. In addition to these main outcome measures, we used the Camberwell Assessment of Need (CAN) (Phelan *et al.* 1995) to assess the health and social care needs of subjects. We also asked keyworkers and care co-ordinators to report whether a range of pre-defined interventions were provided, needed or not needed by each patient.

Our main analysis involved calculation of the proportions of each treatment population with co-morbidity and the size of sub-populations defined in terms of differential psychiatric diagnosis and pattern of substance misuse. We also:

- compared research assessments with keyworkers' data provided about each patient to measure the proportions of co-morbid cases that had been identified by keyworkers;
- measured the type and severity of co-morbidity to assess the proportions of each treatment population with high or low potential for cross-referral;
- assessed levels of met and unmet need;
- compared the prevalence of co-morbidity in the London centre with the non-London centres.

Prevalence estimates are reported below and exact binomial 95 per cent confidence intervals (CI), included in Table 12.1. The statistical significance of observed differences in proportions was assessed using Pearson's chi-square or Fisher's exact tests. The statistical significance of difference between groups in the central tendency of continuous data was assessed using non-parametric Mann-Whitney U or Kruskall-Wallis tests.

Findings from drug and alcohol services

The drug services focused on opiate dependency and most of the drug service sample reported on lifetime opiate use (92.6 per cent, $n=200$). The majority of alcohol service patients reported harmful levels of alcohol use in the past year (91.9 per cent, $n=54$). However, severe poly-drug use was the norm in the drug service population and misuse of alcohol was a common complicating problem. Similarly, illicit or non-prescribed drug use was a complicating problem in the management of a substantial minority of alcohol patients.

Table 12.1 shows the main prevalence findings with confidence intervals. This shows that within the substance misuse populations, 74.5 per cent ($n=161$) of drug patients and 85.5 per cent ($n=53$) of alcohol patients had a past year psychiatric disorder. Psychotic disorders were present in 7.9 per cent ($n=17$) of drug patients and 19.4 per cent ($n=12$) of alcohol patients. Affective or anxiety disorders were identified in 67.6 per cent ($n=146$) of drug patients and 80.6 per cent ($n=50$) of alcohol patients. Personality disorders were present in 37 per cent ($n=80$) of drug patients and 53.2 per cent ($n=33$) of alcohol patients. There were no statistically significant differences in these prevalence findings between London and non-London centres.

Over a third of drug and alcohol patients (37.1 per cent, $n=103$) had a disorder in two or more psychiatric disorder types. For groups with psychotic disorders and personality disorders respectively, the vast majority of subjects were assessed as positive for a second disorder (27/29, 93 per cent and 98/113, 86.7 per cent respectively). Nearly three-quarters of subjects rated positive for a primary diagnosis of psychosis (21/29, 72 per cent) and also rated positive for affective/anxiety disorder *and* a personality disorder. Half (102/196, 52 per cent) of patients with an affective and/or anxiety disorder also rated positive for personality disorder and/or psychosis. Hence, co-morbidities were commonly 'multiple' rather than 'dual'.

All patients with psychotic disorder (i.e. 17 drug service patients, 7.9 per cent; 12 alcohol service patients, 19.4 per cent) exhibited 'complex care needs' and recorded CPRS scores (median: drug patients 22 (range 0–42), alcohol patients 32 (range 13–54) that were high relative even to CMHT patients with psychosis (median: 8, range 0–38). Hence all were likely to have high referral potential to CMHTs for CPA management. In reality, just over two-thirds of these patients ($n=20$, 69 per cent) were on a CMHT caseload. Most ($n=20$) were patients with psychotic disorders but there were six patients in this population with non-psychotic disorders. This latter figure represented a relatively small proportion of the additional 10–13 per cent in each treatment population who had severe depression *and* the sort of 'complex care needs' likely to make them candidates for CPA management.

Overall, in relation to the management of mental health problems we found that over a third of co-morbid patients (31.7 per cent, 68/214) had *no* contact with *any* health services specifically for their mental health problem. While many of the remaining patients reported mental health-related consultations

Table 12.1 Prevalence of co-morbidity. (1) Prevalence of psychiatric disorder in drug (*N*=216) and alcohol (*N*=62) service patients. (2) Prevalence of self-reported harmful alcohol, problem drug use and dependent drug use in the past year in Community Mental Health Teams (*N*=282)

	n	%	Exact binomial 95% confidence interval
DRUG SERVICE PATIENTS (*N*=216)			
Psychotic disorders	17	(7.9)	4.7 to 12.3
Schizophrenia	6	(2.8)	1.0 to 5.9
Manic depression/bipolar affective disorder	1	(0.5)	0.01 to 2.6
Non-specific psychosis	10	(4.6)	2.2 to 8.3
Personality disorder	80	(37.0)	30.6 to 43.9
Affective and/or anxiety disorder	146	(67.6)	60.9 to 73.8
Summary			
No disorder	55	(25.5)	19.8 to 31.8
Psychiatric disorder present	161	(74.5)	68.2 to 80.2
ALCOHOL SERVICE PATIENTS (*N*=62)			
Psychotic disorders	12	(19.4)	10.4 to 31.4
Schizophrenia	2	(3.2)	0.4 to 11.2
Manic depression/bipolar affective disorder	3	(4.8)	1.0 to 13.5
Non-specific psychosis	7	(11.3)	4.7 to 21.9
Personality disorder	33	(53.2)	40.1 to 66.0
Affective and/or anxiety disorder	50	(80.6)	68.6 to 89.6
Summary			
No disorder	9	(14.5)	6.9 to 25.8
Psychiatric disorder present	53	(85.5)	74.2 to 93.1
COMMUNITY MENTAL HEALTH TEAMS (*N*=282)			
Illicit drug use in the past year			
Problem drug use	84	(29.8)	24.5 to 35.5
*Frequency of reported use by drug type**			
Cannabis	71	(25.2)	20.2 to 30.7
Sedatives/tranquillisers	21	(7.4)	4.7 to 11.2
Crack cocaine	16	(5.7)	3.3 to 9.1
Heroin	11	(3.9)	2.0 to 6.9
Ecstasy	11	(3.9)	2.0 to 6.9
Amphetamines	9	(3.2)	1.5 to 6.0
Cocaine	8	(2.8)	1.2 to 5.5
Opiate substitutes	4	(1.4)	0.4 to 3.6
Dependent use of illicit or non-prescribed drugs			
Dependent (score of 7 or more on SDS)	47	(16.7)	12.5 to 21.5
Alcohol			
Abstinent	71	(25.2)	20.2 to 30.7
Non-harmful alcohol use in past year AUDIT < 8)	139	(49.3)	43.3 to 55.3
Harmful use (AUDIT ≥ 8)	72	(25.5)	20.5 to 31.0
Summary			
No harmful alcohol use or drug use reported	158	(56.0)	50.0 to 61.9
Harmful alcohol use or drug use reported	124	(44.0)	38.1 to 50.0

* Aggregation of sub-group may exceed group totals due to patients reporting poly-drug use. Use of LSD, ketamine, ritalin, steroids, amyl nitrite and magic mushrooms reported in < 1.1% of cases. No reported use of solvents, GHB, khat.

with GPs, in a quarter of co-morbid cases (26.6 per cent, 57/214) this appeared to be the only management intervention. Two out of five co-morbid patients (41.6 per cent, 89/214) reported consulting a psychiatrist about their mental health problems, while one in five (22 per cent, 48/214) reported contact with a psychiatrist in adult mental health services.

When we compared keyworker-reported co-morbidity with the relevant reference assessments obtained at interview, we found non-co-morbid patients were generally correctly identified as such by services (specificity >90 per cent). However, patients with psychiatric disorders were mostly unrecognised (sensitivity 20–35 per cent).

Findings from community mental health services

Three-quarters of the CMHT population had a psychotic disorder (76.6 per cent, $n=216$). Most of the remaining patients were assessed to have severe depression. The majority of CMHT patients (64.5 per cent, $n=182$) rated positive for more than one of the main disorder groups used in our primary analysis: psychosis, affective and/or anxiety disorder and personality disorder. Personality disorder was prevalent within the CMHT population with 39.4 per cent ($n=111$) assessed as having one or more personality disorder.

Harmful alcohol use was reported by 25.5 per cent of patients ($n=72$) while problem drug use was reported by 29.8 per cent ($n=84$). Drug dependency was identified in 16.7 per cent ($n=47$). Overall, 44 per cent ($n=124$) of CMHT patients reported past year problem drug use and/or harmful alcohol use. Hazardous and harmful alcohol use was strongly associated with problem drug use (patients reporting no drug use: 19 per cent; patients reporting problem drug use: 40.2 per cent; $x^2 1df = 13.7, p < 0.001$).

The prevalence of co-morbidity we observed in the CMHT population is higher than previously reported in comparable UK settings, a finding largely accounted for by levels of drug use that are significantly higher than previously observed (Menezes *et al.* 1996; Wright *et al.* 2000; P. J. Duke *et al.* 2001). Of the 84 (29.8 per cent) patients reporting past year problem drug use, more than half reported use of just one drug type ($n=51$, 18 per cent of all cases, 58 per cent of those reporting drug use). Most who reported single-drug use smoked cannabis ($n=41$, 14.5 per cent of all cases). Twenty-two patients (7.8 per cent) reported using cocaine, crack cocaine and/or opiates.

When compared to non-London centres, we found that a significantly higher proportion of CMHT patients from London centres reported problem drug use (42.1 per cent vs. 21.4 per cent, $x^2 1df = 13.9, p < 0.001$) and drug dependency (24.6 per cent vs. 11.3 per cent; $x^2 1df = 8.6, p = 0.005$). These differences remained significant after controlling for sex, ethnicity, age and other case-mix variables. However, there was no evidence of a difference in the prevalence of harmful alcohol use between centres.

Only 10 of the 47 patients (21.2 per cent) assessed to have dependent drug use received any drug-related intervention. Just 2.1 per cent (*n*=6) of CMHT patients were opiate-dependent. These patients would appear to have a high referral potential for statutory opiate-based drug treatment services, but only half (*n*=3) had contact with a specialist drug service. These were the only CMHT patients in contact with drug services. An additional eight patients (2.8 per cent of the sample) reported crack/cocaine or other stimulant dependence and may potentially qualify for referral to stimulant services (if available). Although significant additional numbers were cannabis-dependent, these patients were unlikely to meet referral criteria applied by routinely available drug services.

The population with potential for referral to alcohol services (defined by an AUDIT score >15) was 9.2 per cent (*n*=26). However, just two of these patients were allocated to a specialist alcohol service.

Less than one in five of co-morbid patients being managed without referral to a substance misuse service received specific drug- or alcohol-related interventions, such as motivational interviewing or health education/advice regarding harm minimisation through their mental health keyworkers.

When we compared care co-ordinator-reported co-morbidity with the relevant reference assessments obtained at interview, we found non-co-morbid patients were generally correctly identified as such by services (specificity > 90 per cent). CMHT patients reporting harmful alcohol use were mostly unrecognised (sensitivity 20–38 per cent), but in relation to patients reporting (any) drug use, care co-ordinators did achieve moderately good sensitivity (60 per cent).

The implications for policy

The COSMIC study provided new evidence about the prevalence and management of co-morbidity in the UK. However, certain study limitations should be acknowledged before the important implications for policy and service development are described.

- First, the study measured the prevalence of co-morbidity in current *treatment* populations. Our findings may not be generalisable to substance users or people with mental illness not in treatment.
- Second, the cross-sectional study precludes any assessment of the aetiology of co-morbidity.
- Third, some prevalence estimates lack precision due to the small sample sizes.
- Fourth, the COSMIC study represented an advance on previous single-centre studies but further investigation in more regions would be required before any definitive picture emerges about regional variation in prevalence.

Mental health services

Our findings show that co-morbidity of severe mental illness and substance misuse is highly prevalent in urban UK mental health settings. Indeed, co-morbid patients are shown to be a heterogeneous population and a core patient group for mental health services. Data about patterns of drug use showed that a relatively small proportion of co-morbid CMHT patients use the opiate or stimulant drugs which potentially make them appropriate and eligible for referral to specialist drug treatment.

Taken together these findings illustrate that emerging Department of Health policy on the management of co-morbidity has been largely correct to suggest that 'substance misuse is usual rather than exceptional amongst people with severe mental health problems' (DH 2002). Department of Health guidance has clearly prioritised the management of patients with psychosis and co-morbid substance misuse, although it also recognises the heterogeneity within co-morbid populations. It argues that the needs of both dependent and problematic users of a range of drugs (including alcohol) and populations with personality disorder should be met. The policy further acknowledges that some of these patients will not qualify, or will require specialist support from *both* mental health and substance misuse services, and that many will need to be managed within mental health services without referral.

Our study findings concerning the prevalence and heterogeneity of co-morbidity provide strong confirmation that practice within mental health services should continue to develop around a policy framework which has become known as 'mainstreaming' (DH 2002). Mainstreaming means that mental health services accept the lead responsibility for the management of patients with severe mental illness and co-morbid substance misuse, while at the same time establishing clearer working relationships with substance misuse services. The role of substance misuse services in this context is to provide specialist support in certain cases where this is appropriate, but also to provide 'consultancy' and training to mental health services in order to develop the competencies which mental health workers require to manage co-morbidity independently and without referral (DH 2002).

In the late 1990s, some centres of excellence in the USA developed and strongly promoted the idea of integrated treatment teams that combined mental health and substance misuse practitioners (Mueser *et al.* 1997; Drake *et al.* 1998; Mueser and Drake 2003). However, a Cochrane review first published in 1999 found no secure RCT data for the effectiveness of these teams (Ley *et al.* 1999), and was highly influential within the UK where commentators had already expressed doubts about the applicability of such approaches in UK settings (Hall and Farrell 1997; Johnson 1997; Weaver *et al.* 1999). Policy has strongly followed this sceptical line. Department of Health guidance published in 2002 clearly rebuts any notion that there was a case for developing integrated treatment teams. It states, 'integrated treatment . . . can be delivered in this country by existing mental health services following training and support from substance misuse services', and that 'new hybrid services' were not required. Instead guidance has stressed the key role of assertive outreach teams and early intervention services in managing 'dual diagnosis' (DH 2001, 2002). By contrast, today, US consensus-based guidelines place an emphasis on 'integrated treatment' while taking a somewhat more flexible approach to questions about the appropriate service context (Ziedonis *et al.* 2005).

Within the UK context, there remains a need to develop treatment interventions for psychotic patients with co-morbid substance misuse and to develop preventive strategies in view of the persistence of this co-morbidity once established. We are still at the early stage of explaining why substance misuse is so common in those with schizophrenia, and the conclusion that it 'alleviates dysphoria' (Gregg *et al.* 2007) is likely to account for a small part only. The COSMIC study found that a large proportion of co-morbid CMHT patients did not receive the specialist substance misuse intervention they required. There is no doubt that responding to this need represents a major challenge for mental health services and is only likely to be effective in the long term if supported in two key ways:

- First, for mainstreaming to work, mental health staff will need training to ensure that they have the core competencies required to manage co-morbid patients, e.g. the knowledge and skills required to take a detailed drug and alcohol history (Banerjee *et al.* 2002).
- Second, much more investment in research will be needed to assess the effectiveness of treatment programmes for co-morbidity within UK service contexts. In the USA, research has shown that, with appropriate psychological therapy and social support, motivation and engagement with substance misuse treatment can be established amongst patients with psychosis, and that when combined with case management and assertive outreach, engagement and retention in treatment and continuity of care can be enhanced (Ziedonis *et al.* 2005). One of the more promising lines of research in the UK involves applying motivational interviewing and cognitive behavioural therapy aimed at substance misuse behaviour in a CMHT treatment context (Barrowclough *et al.* 2001, 2003), and the results of a large pragmatic trial are awaited at the time of writing (Barrowclough *et al.* 2006).

Hence, there is an emerging UK consensus that it is most appropriate for mainstream mental health services to manage patients with psychosis and types of co-morbid substance misuse for which alternative services are not available (Banerjee *et al.* 2002; DH 2002; NTA 2002b).

Drug and alcohol service populations

The COSMIC study found that a majority of drug and alcohol patients experience mental health problems. While most co-morbid patients have affective and/or anxiety disorders, it was also common for patients to have a second concurrent psychiatric disorder and multiple substance misuse problems.

Patients with psychotic disorders represented a relatively small proportion of the treatment population but were an important group for the severity of their symptoms, high rates of other concurrent psychiatric disorders and the level of social need. We found that two-thirds of this group had contact with mental health services, though we have limited information about the adequacy of the interventions received. Drugs policy has focused extensively on this population and achieved consistency with the mental health guidance (described above). It has also pursued the operational objective of establishing joint management arrangements with mental health providers for patients with severe mental illness who come into contact with substance misuse services. The COSMIC study showed that the majority of drug and alcohol patients with psychotic disorders had contact with mental health services but there was still an unmet need for referral within this population.

Since these data were collected, the NTA has introduced a model of case management into UK drug treatment services known as 'care co-ordination' (NTA 2002b). Care co-ordination represents a key component of the co-ordinated drug strategy underpinning efforts to develop comprehensive local treatment systems (NTA 2002b). MoC originally identified drug misusers with 'severe mental health co-morbidity' (defined as schizophrenia, bipolar affective disorder or severe depression in the context of problem drug use) as a population in need of 'enhanced care co-ordination' on the grounds of the complexity of treatment needs and the requirement of co-ordinating management with mental health services. However, both the 2006 update of MoC (NTA 2006a) and the accompanying *Care Planning* guidance (NTA 2006d) removed reference to enhanced care co-ordination on the grounds that patients presented with a range of needs, 'from simple to highly complex, and this must be reflected in the care plan and the intensity of care co-ordination'. However, the primary responsibility of mental health services for the management of patients with severe mental illness was confirmed. Indeed this population was now referred to as subject to 'externally co-ordinated care' (NTA 2006a).

The focus on the joint management of populations with severe mental illness continues a historical focus on this population but also continues the relative lack of priority given to patients with non-psychotic mental illness and personality disorders. The COSMIC study showed that these disorders were prevalent in substance misuse treatment populations but frequently undetected and often not subject to intervention. As a basic minimum, this population should have access to specialist psychiatric assessment and the possibility of appropriate specialist intervention. Without effective pharmacological and psychotherapeutic interventions, these patients may experience poor substance misuse treatment outcomes (Brooner *et al.* 1997).

Guidance provided by MoC about the appropriate management of patients with non-psychotic mental illness and 'personality problems' was non-prescriptive and it was clear that interventions to meet needs in these areas 'may either be delivered by [drug treatment] keyworker as the main deliverer of care or delivered by others, in which case the care will be coordinated by the keyworker' (NTA 2006a).

Writing well before the COSMIC study was undertaken, Hall and Farrell (1997) argued that resources needed to be deployed so that substance misuse services could implement available evidence-based pharmacological and psychotherapeutic treatments for a much higher proportion of these patients. Policy has given relatively little emphasis to the management of these populations. However, recently published treatment guidelines have cited findings from the COSMIC study as justification for including clear guidance that in relation to anxiety, self-harm, bipolar disorder and depression, drug treatment services should implement 'specific psychological management in line with appropriate guidance, such as NICE and other psychiatric and drug misuse guidelines'. Treatment services now need to be given the resources to make this a reality.

Future directions

A feature of the policy debate about co-morbidity has been the much more extensive and focused attention which has been given to co-morbidity by mental health policy makers. The clear strategic treatment priorities outlined in the 1998 Drug Strategy (HM Government 1998), its 2002 update (Home Office 2002) and the new ten-year Drug Strategy published in 2008 (HM Government 2008) were the diversion into treatment of drug-using offenders and the development of services for crack and other stimulant drug users. Within this context, there was limited reference to co-morbidity. A commitment to the development of cross-agency collaboration and drug treatment services flexible enough to respond to 'complex needs, such as drug users with mental health problems' (HM Government 2008) failed to present any significant elaboration on the 1998 strategy (HM Government 1998) or MoC (NTA 2002b).

The scale and heterogeneity of need identified by the COSMIC study indicates the complexity of issues related to service development. Although strides have been made, the capacity of both mental health and substance misuse services to manage the spectrum of co-morbidity both independently and collaboratively needs to be further developed.

The COSMIC Study Group

Imperial College London: Tim Weaver, Vikki Charles, Zenobia Carnwath, Peter Madden, Adrian Renton, Gerry Stimson, Peter Tyrer, Thomas Barnes, Chris Bench and Susan Paterson
Turning Point, Brent: Chris Ford
Central and North West London Mental Health NHS Trust: Jonathon Greenside, Owen Bowden Jones and William Shanahan
Community Health Sheffield NHS Trust: Helen Bourne, Muhammad Z. Iqbal and Nicholas Seivewright
Nottingham Healthcare NHS Trust: Sylvia Cooper, Katina Anagostakis, Hugh Middleton and Neil Wright

13 Epidemiology of drug misuse and psychiatric comorbidity in primary care

Martin Frisher, Ilana Crome, Orsolina Martino, James Bashford and Peter Croft

Introduction

The concept of comorbid mental health problems and drug misuse has gained prominence in recent years. This is in part due to the closure of large psychiatric hospitals and the increasing prevalence of drug use in the community. The challenges involved in treating comorbid patients are increasingly being recognized, as are the consequences of comorbidity on crime, family relationships, self-harm, homelessness, poor medication compliance and re-hospitalization.

There are, however, considerable methodological difficulties in studying comorbidity. Definitions of comorbidity and criteria for diagnosis of mental illness and drug misuse differ and change over time. There are a multitude of different types of comorbidity and settings where it may be identified (Crome 1999), and 'many areas (of comorbidity) remain unexplored particularly relating to prevalence, course and treatment outcome in the United Kingdom' (V. Crawford and Crome 2001).

An important first step in developing a response for comorbid patients is determining the number of patients in the UK. Different types of comorbidity, depending on the time sequence and interactions between the two (or more) conditions, may present. For example, even a single experience with cannabis or LSD may lead to a psychiatric syndrome, while chronic drug misuse may exacerbate a pre-existing psychiatric syndrome. Conversely, a primary psychiatric disorder may lead to drug use for a variety of reasons, including low self-esteem (J. Taylor *et al.* 2006), or self-medication (Potvin *et al.* 2006). It has been hypothesized that the link between drug misuse and psychiatric conditions is mediated by dopamine. Many drugs enhance dopaminergic effects and these could 'aggravate or precipitate schizophrenic or manic psychosis while withdrawal from substances may be conducive to the development of depression in association with low dopamine' (Abou-Saleh 2004). Comorbidity may also be an expression of brain processes linked to fear, anxiety and other emotions (Chambers *et al.* 2006).

The only large-scale study investigating comorbidity in the UK is the National Psychiatric Morbidity Survey (Farrell *et al.* 1998). Three surveys conducted between 1996 and 1997 found that 2 per cent of the household population in the UK were classified as drug-dependent (on licit and illicit drugs) and were eight times as likely to have a psychiatric condition compared to the general population.

In the United States, prevalence estimates for dual diagnosis come from two large studies. The 1990 Epidemiological Catchment Area (Regier *et al.* 1990) found that 53 per cent of people who abuse drugs have at least one comorbid mental illness. In the 1994 National Comorbidity Survey (NCS) (Kessler *et al.* 1994) 48 per cent of the 8,098 people surveyed, between 15 and 54 years of age, reported a substance misuse disorder or psychiatric illness during their lifetime. A large-scale study of people diagnosed with mental illness in the USA found that 29 per cent had a lifetime history of either drug misuse or dependency (N. Miller *et al.* 1990).

The epidemiological studies give some indication of the overall prevalence of dual diagnosis but this covers a very wide spectrum of conditions. Furthermore, as they are cross-sectional, it is difficult to make inferences from them about causality or use them to identify groups with particular treatment needs. Prevalence rates also depend on factors such as the composition of the assessment team, the clinical situation in which the evaluation takes place and the severity of the disorders that contribute to dual diagnosis.

In this chapter, the General Practice Research Database (GPRD) is used to investigate comorbidity. Since 1994, the Secretary of State for Health has owned the database, and in 1999, the Medicines Control Agency (which became part of the Medicines and Healthcare Products Regulatory Agency in April 2003) took over management of the GPRD.

During the 1990s, the GPRD was instrumental in a number of important drug utilization and drug safety studies, for example in relation to oral contraceptives and venous thromboembolic disease. The GPRD has also been used to study a wide range of psychiatric conditions and medications, including schizophrenia, antidepressants and suicide, attention deficit disorder, alcoholism and eating disorders. Notable features of the GPRD are the training that GPs receive in entering data into the system as well as the regular validation checks that ensure the research data are of high quality. There have also been specific studies on the validity of psychiatric illness and drug abuse. Nevertheless, it has been noted that the '[UK] medical community has not fully appreciated the value of this extraordinary public health resource' (Jick 1997).

This chapter reports on the first national assessment of comorbidity in a specified health care setting. The first phase of the study described psychiatric and drug misuse comorbidity among 1.4 million patients treated in primary care in England and Wales from 1993 to 1998. The results of the first phase showed an increasing burden of comorbidity in primary care over the study period (Frisher *et al.* 2005). The second ongoing phase of the study extends the geographical frame of reference to include Scotland and Northern Ireland and examines the time period from 1996 to 2005.

Detailed diagnostic history is essential for managing comorbid patients (Crome 1999). The GPRD enables the study of patterns of diagnosed drug misuse in primary care and association with psychiatric comorbidity, prescribed medication and treatment outcomes.

Validity of the General Practice Research Database

The quality of GPRD data is routinely assessed (Hollowell 1997). Fifteen key indicators, deemed to be of importance to practices and researchers, are monitored every six weeks. Previous research has shown that the classification of psychosis, schizophrenia, affective psychosis and non-affective psychosis was accurate, the rate of misclassification was low and there were few cases that were not entered onto the database (Nazareth *et al.* 1993). The accuracy (sensitivity) of the computer categories for schizophrenia, non-affective psychosis and all non-organic psychoses was good (88–91 per cent) and compared favourably with psychiatric case registers. The psychosis verification study also examined prescription records, in order to determine whether patients with anti-psychotic medication were recorded as psychotic on the database, and found that fewer than 10 per cent of patients receiving anti-psychosis medication were not entered onto the database. Further examination of case notes revealed that misclassifications were often due to diagnostic uncertainty rather than incorrect computer entries.

In 1997, the rate of reported drug misusers/registered patients was 124/100,000 on the GPRD while the rate of reported drug misusers/population was 3/100,000 for the Regional Drug Misuse Database (RDMD) (Frisher *et al.* 2000). These findings provide assurance that the GPRD is not subject to under-reporting in relation to drug misuse.

Limitations of general practice data

Consultation data can only reflect those problems presented to health care. Other research methodologies would need to consider the proportion of drug misusers with co-existent mental illness who do not present to the health care services, e.g. criminal justice or social care agencies. However, the phrase 'dual diagnosis' implies that diagnoses have been made and thus it seems reasonable to study this problem at the point of first presentation to primary health care services, namely primary care. Furthermore, an objective of our study is to investigate the health care provided (consultations, prescriptions, referrals) and the GPRD is able to provide this information.

Annual comorbidity rate 1996–2005

Figure 13.1 illustrates the change in the annual comorbidity rate from 1996 to 2005. The 2005 rate was 70 per 100,000 patient years of exposure (PYE) (i.e. 0.7 per 1,000 patients). Although there was a fall in 2005, there is a significant

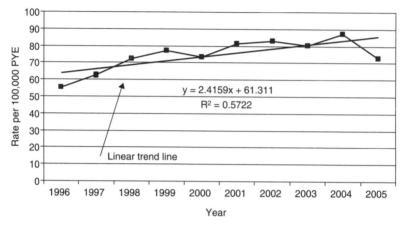

$$y = 2.4159x + 61.311$$
$$R^2 = 0.5722$$

Figure 13.1 Annual prevalence of comorbidity per 100,000 PYE, 1996–2005.

linear trend over the period. Although this rate may seem very low, it represents about 30,000 patients per year in the UK. The average annual increase is about 3 per cent. This means that there are about an extra thousand comorbid cases in UK general practice each year.

What Figure 13.1 does not tell us is how GPs regard these cases. Do they consider them as being 'different' from mono-morbid cases? Does their treatment differ? Are they considered to be more difficult cases? From the data reported here, it cannot be ascertained whether GPs consider these cases to be a distinct group of cases and, if they do, whether their approach differs. All we can say with certainty is that the number of comorbid cases is increasing. While the GPRD is limited in terms of these issues, the data do afford the opportunity to examine other aspects of comorbidity. From the data collected by GPs, it is possible to examine the different types of comorbidity.

Types of comorbidity

The term 'drug misuse' is used here as an overarching term for all diagnoses relating to substances, excluding nicotine and alcohol. The drug misuse codes were divided into three categories: (a) 'drug abuse'; (b) 'drug dependence/addiction'; and (c) 'licit drug problems'. This classification is necessary because it reflects the terms that GPs actually used and also because GPs tend not to code specific drugs of abuse. The data indicate that the drug-dependent cohort is substantially older than the drug abuse cohort. Licit drug abuse or dependence is the term used for medications prescribed by the GP and usually covers the class of drugs classified as 'benzodiazepines', which are prescribed for the 'short-term relief of severe anxiety' or for sleep disorders. Benzodiazepines include diazepam, alprazolam, bromazepam, nitrazepam, temazepam and lorazepam.

Psychiatric diagnoses are categorized into six main categories – psychosis, schizophrenia, paranoia, neurosis, personality disorders and other disorders. These categories correspond to the main divisions in the tenth revision of the International Classification of Diseases. The codes for 'depression' and 'anxiety' (in the neurosis category) account for around 90 per cent of all psychiatric diagnoses.

Comorbidity by age group and drug misuse diagnosis

Figure 13.2 shows that both drug abuse and dependence peak at about 16–24 years old: thereafter the rate for drug abuse declines more rapidly. This supports the view that dependence reflects more chronic use while abuse may be transitory. For licit drug dependence, incidence gradually increases to a peak at 55–64 years. The incidence of licit drug dependence is higher than illicit abuse/dependence for those aged 55+ years. From age 55 years onwards, licit dependence is the most prevalent diagnosis.

Comorbidity by age group and psychiatric diagnosis

Figure 13.3 shows that all comorbid psychiatric diagnoses peak at ages 16–24 years or 25–34 years. There is an upsurge in psychoses at age 65+ years because of the presence of dementia and confusion diagnoses in this category.

Comorbidity and gender

In contrast to some findings of psychiatric morbidity in primary care, the comorbidity rate is higher among males than females [61 vs. 49 per 100,000 patient years of exposure (PYE)]. This is because illicit drug misuse is much more prevalent among males compared to females. Thus, up to age 44 years,

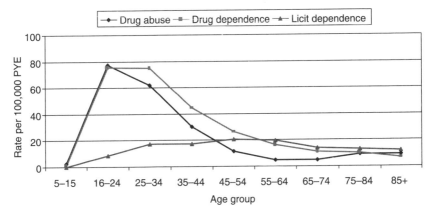

Figure 13.2 Comorbidity incidence rates stratified by age-band and type of drug misuse.

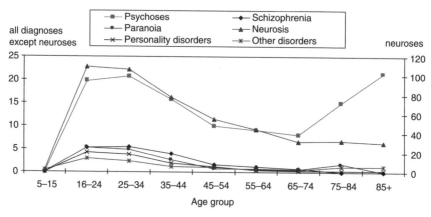

Figure 13.3 Comorbidity incidence rates stratified by age-band and type of psychiatric diagnosis (annual comorbid cases).

females have lower rates of comorbidity than males, while from 45 years onwards females have higher rates than males when licit dependence becomes more prevalent.

Comorbidity stratified by gender, age group and drug misuse

Figure 13.4 shows that male rates for abuse and dependence are similar throughout the age range. From the age of 55 years, rates of licit dependence are similar to those for illicit abuse and dependence. Figure 13.4 illustrates the much more prominent role of licit drug dependence in female comorbidity. There is also a wider gap between dependence and abuse compared to males. Among females, the prevalence of illicit dependence does not fall as sharply in older age groups. This perhaps indicates that chronicity of comorbid drug dependence is greater for females than for males.

Comorbidity and deprivation

In 2007, the UK government introduced what was claimed to be 'the most comprehensive programme ever seen in this country to address health inequalities'. This programme is underpinned by the Health Inequalities National Target, which is the aim to reduce health inequalities (as measured by infant mortality and life expectancy at birth) by 10 per cent by 2010. Drug misuse alone has been found to be strongly associated with socioeconomic deprivation, with higher concentrations of problematic drug use in areas of high unemployment, poverty and general social deprivation (see Butler 1996). Similarly, more people are admitted to psychiatric institutions from socially deprived areas compared with more affluent quarters (e.g. J. Harrison *et al.* 1995; Boardman *et al.* 1997; Croudace *et al.* 2000) – possibly due, at least in

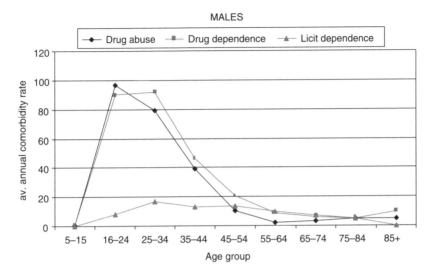

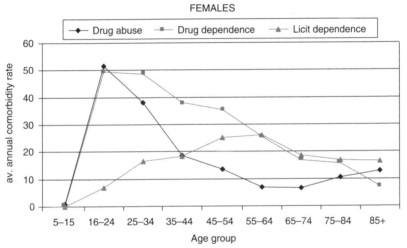

Figure 13.4 Annual comorbidity rates per 100,000 PYE by age-band for males and females.

part, to the greater social stress thought to result from deprivation (Peen and Dekker 2001).

It is thus not surprising that comorbidity is strongly associated with socioeconomic deprivation, as measured by the Practice Townsend Material Deprivation Score. This is a composite score calculated using information on unemployment, overcrowding, car availability and home ownership derived from census data: the percentage of (i) economically active residents aged 16–59/64 years who are unemployed; (ii) private households with more than one person per room; (iii) private households with no car; and (iv) private households not owner-occupied (Townsend *et al.* 1988). Each general practice was allocated to a quintile on the basis of the Townsend Score of the ward in which it is located.

There was a linear increase by Townsend Score. The rate was 20/100,000 in the most affluent quintile compared to 85/100,000 in the most deprived quintile. What is more surprising, however, is that between 1993 and 1998 comorbidity increased most rapidly among affluent practices. The rate increased by 120 per cent in the most affluent practices but by only 50 per cent in the least affluent practices. Thus there has been a reduction in inequality due to the more rapid increase in affluent areas rather than because of a reduction in poorer areas. A variation of this trend continued to 2005, with the most rapid increase being not in deprived areas but in the practices of average affluence. It appears that there has been a 'diffusion' of comorbidity from deprived to affluent areas: this is similar to previous findings that drug misuse has diffused from urban to rural areas (Frisher *et al.* 2002). (The diffusion hypothesis postulates that non-contagious diseases can nevertheless spread by social and cultural contact.)

Benzodiazepine dependence

Our study found benzodiazepine dependence to be the major form of licit drug misuse, particularly among patients aged 55 years and over. In a wide-ranging review of benzodiazepine dependence, Lennane (1986) notes that there is 'little therapeutic justification for the long-term administration of benzodiazepine drugs'. Dependence can occur in less than three months, and occasional patients, particularly those who have been dependent on other drugs, give anecdotal reports of almost instantaneous dependence on benzodiazepine drugs.

The government's Mental Health Czar has acknowledged that prescription data do not reveal the true extent of the problem of benzodiazepine overprescription. Whilst GPs consider the benefits of benzodiazepines alongside the risks (see Rogers *et al.* 2007), our study indicates that benzodiazepine dependence is still a considerable problem in primary care.

The present study also found licit drug dependence to be more prevalent among females. Women, particularly in later years, are more likely to be prescribed benzodiazepines (e.g. van der Waals *et al.* 1993). On the one hand, this may be a function of older women being more likely to visit their GP (e.g. Bertakis *et al.* 2000), supporting the view of iatrogenic dependence. However, women are also more likely to develop anxiety disorders (Kessler *et al.* 1994). This and other female-specific phenomena could explain such patterns of increased GP visits, as well as the higher benzodiazepine prescription rate itself, which would contradict the iatrogenic dependence hypothesis. Alternatively, there may be a degree of co-existence between these two perspectives.

Another point to consider is the more recent introduction of non-benzodiazepine hypnotics (Z-drugs) for the treatment of insomnia. These were developed partly to avoid the risk of tolerance, dependence and abuse associated with benzodiazepines (Dündar *et al.* 2004). However, there is no reliable evidence that Z-drugs pose any less risk for dependency than benzodiazepines (NICE 2004). A recent survey of general practice patients who had received at least one prescription for a Z-drug or benzodiazepine in the previous six months found that reported prescribing practices were often at variance with the licence for short-term use (Siriwardena *et al.* 2008).

What proportion of comorbidity have we captured?

Comorbidity between drug misuse and psychiatric disorder occurs whenever the two conditions are diagnosed for the same individual. It is known that much drug misuse occurring in the community is not brought to the attention of general practitioners. There is also evidence that much mental illness goes undetected by the health care services. From these observations it follows that the data reported here, which depend on recorded diagnosis by general practitioners, are likely to have underestimated the occurrence of comorbidity in the community as a whole.

A second concern is that, even when drug misuse has been brought to the attention of the health services, it may not be the sort of problem that gets recorded in the general practice records. This may occur if the route to the health services is via Accident & Emergency or specialist services. This may also apply to some forms of acute mental illness. However, we specifically addressed this issue in a validation study and have shown that over 90 per cent of a random sample of patients known to the specialist services as having a drug misuse or psychiatric problem were also found to have such problems recorded in their general practice records. We can conclude therefore that a study such as ours, based on general practice records, is unlikely to miss individuals, with either drug misuse or psychiatric illness or both, who have brought their problems to the attention of the health service by whatever route.

A third concern might be that there is under-recording of these problems in those patients who consult primary care. Computerized systems of coding morbidity are becoming more widely accepted and used in British general practice but there is widespread evidence of under-recording of problems. However, the GPRD is unique in this respect since it has specifically recruited and retained practices over the years which pass through a rigorous cycle of checks and audits to ensure the continuing completeness of their records.

Transition from mono- to comorbidity

Having described the nature and extent of comorbidity, we now consider the transition from mono-morbidity (where the diagnosis is either drug misuse or psychiatric) to comorbidity (the presence of both drug misuse and psychiatric illness). The key issue is how quickly do patients become comorbid?

Although it is well known that psychiatric patients have high rates of drug misuse and vice versa (N. Miller *et al.* 1990; Regier *et al.* 1990; Kessler *et al.* 1994), there is little information on the temporal ordering of diagnosis. This is of importance because the medical model of psychiatric services contrasts sharply with the psychosocial orientation of drug misuse services (Weaver *et al.* 1999). The patient's initial presentation to primary care could have considerable impact on his or her treatment.

In our study, the majority of comorbid cases had a psychiatric diagnosis prior to a drug misuse diagnosis (54 per cent); 41 per cent of cases had a drug misuse diagnosis first and 5 per cent of cases had a first diagnosis of both psychiatric illness and drug misuse on the same day. In terms of duration to comorbidity, 17 per cent of cases became comorbid within the first month of the first diagnosis, 50 per cent within six months and 75 per cent within two years. Where the first presentation was for drug misuse, the average interval before the comorbid psychiatric condition was 7.1 months. Where the first presentation was psychiatric, the average interval before the comorbid drug misuse condition was 11.4 months.

In the light of the current debate regarding the role of drug misuse in mental illness, the vast majority of schizophrenic patients are diagnosed with the psychiatric diagnosis prior to drug misuse (of course this does not mean that they have not been using drugs before, only that the GP has not recorded drug abuse as a diagnosis). In contrast, the majority of personality disorder diagnoses follow on from a drug misuse diagnosis (see Figure 13.5). This is perhaps surprising given previous research suggesting that, in most cases, personality disorder precedes substance use. However, it is important to consider that drug misuse may produce a syndrome diagnostically compatible with personality disorders. This interrelationship is an important factor when assessing health service provision and utilization. Indeed, a recent study found that high use of health care services among patients with personality disorders was confounded by comorbid substance misuse (Coid *et al.* 2006). In addition, personality disorders are the most prevalent form of comorbidity in drug dependence, accounting for 50–90 per cent of cases.

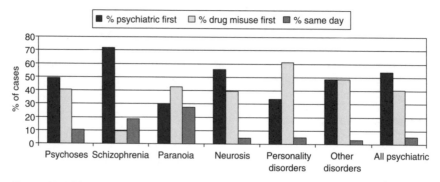

Figure 13.5 Time ordering of comorbidity.

So far we have looked at the development of comorbidity in terms of the average interval. Another approach is survival analysis, which is concerned with the distribution of times to an event – in this case comorbidity. The method was developed by Kaplan and Meier (1958). The key point about survival analysis is that it provides an estimate of survival for cases that have survived up until that point. In other words, it takes account not only of cases that have become comorbid but of all those cases which are censored. (A censored case is one that has left the database before the end of the follow-up period.) The survival analysis considers all cases which begin with a drug misuse diagnosis, some of which go on to develop comorbidity. In the study, 7,411 cases were eligible for analysis. Of these, 2,150 became comorbid (29 per cent) while 5,261 (71 per cent) did not have any psychiatric morbidity in the study period. Follow-up starts from date of drug misuse diagnosis and ends with (a) date of comorbid diagnosis or (b) end of follow-up period without comorbid diagnosis.

Figure 13.6 shows the survival curves for the categories of drug misuse (cases where psychiatric diagnosis precedes drug misuse have been excluded). The survival curves show a number of things about the development of comorbidity. First, for all three types of drug misuse, there is a gradual and continually increasing risk of becoming comorbid. There is no particular time at which there is a greater risk of becoming comorbid (i.e. the slope of the curve is fairly constant over the study period). Patients diagnosed with licit dependence have the highest risk of becoming comorbid (65 per cent of cases), compared to 60 per cent of dependence cases and 50 per cent of abuse cases.

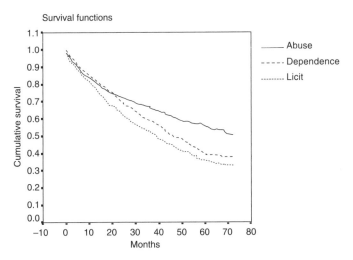

Figure 13.6 Survival analysis of 7,411 cases with a diagnosis of drug misuse.

Health service utilization

A key issue is whether comorbid patients make greater use of primary care than do other patients. In terms of their GP practice, they attend on average seventeen times per year. This is far more often than similar patients (matched by age/gender) who attend six times per year. Both mono drug misuse and mono psychiatric cases attend about twelve times per year. If extrapolated to the UK, comorbid cases would have 2 million more consultations than people of similar age and gender who do not have psychiatric or drugs problems.

Comorbid patients attend Accident & Emergency (A&E) more frequently than other patients: 25 per cent attended A&E per year compared to 15 per cent of mono patients and 6 per cent of matched controls. Interestingly, comorbid patients with secondary care psychiatric contact had lower rates of A&E attendance.

The impact of comorbidity in primary care

The GPRD analysis indicates a significant problem in terms of primary care workload. The numbers of individuals with newly developing comorbidity in primary care is increasing year-on-year. It is difficult for primary care as a whole to avoid the implication that comorbidity is placing high demands on the profession. Our data cannot show that the active early recognition of comorbidity would lead to better outcomes but there are indications that those who have contact with secondary care psychiatric services, for example, have fewer A&E visits. This suggests the potential of active engagement to reduce the need for crisis care.

Policy relevance

The research outlined here provides data on the prevalence of dual diagnosis in all areas of the UK. It enables service providers to assess what proportion of cases commencing with a diagnosis of drug abuse will progress to psychiatric illness. This chapter has looked at GP consultation rates but, in addition, we have analyzed hospital referral data and use of prescribed medications. This will enable an assessment of whether dually diagnosed patients make more intensive use of resources than singly diagnosed patients. The results of this research have the potential to directly influence policy aimed at the care of psychiatric patients, drug misusers and the dually diagnosed.

The Task Force to Review Services for Drug Misusers recommended that all drug misusers have access to primary care through normal registration with a GP. It also said that GPs are well placed to identify and offer advice to drug misusers who may not be in touch with specialist agencies (DH 1996). The role of the general practitioner in providing shared care for substance misusers is increasingly being recognized (Gerada and Tighe 1999) and family doctors are increasingly becoming the first point of contact for young drug misusers (DH 1999a; RCPsych/RCGP 2005). This has been paralleled by training initiatives for general practitioners, specific guidance for general practitioners with a special interest in substance misuse, and the new General Medical Services Contract (2004) [which includes provision of locally (LES) and nationally enhanced services (NES) for drug misusers and which offers remuneration, sets out the roles and responsibilities of doctors in the provision of treatment for drug and alcohol misusers and has established a clinical governance framework for the first time].

In addition, in 2007, NICE guidelines – on psychosocial interventions, and opioid detoxification for drug misuse, and technology appraisals on methadone, buprenorphine and naltrexone for the management of opioid dependence – were produced. Department of Health guidance (2007) has re-iterated that 'drug misusers have the same entitlements as other patients to the services provided by the National Health Service' and 'it is the responsibility of general practitioners to provide general medical services for drug misusers'.

A recent audit to assess the impact of the new General Medical Services Contract on drug misusers demonstrated that while capacity in specialist drug misuse services increased by 55 per cent from 2003 to 2005, this was not the case in shared care. Although quality of treatment had improved, capacity had not increased and it was mainly stable clients who were being treated. This suggests that there is still greater scope for primary care in the management of some of the more complex cases, particularly as the latest Drug Strategy has as its focus support and intervention for families and communities in re-establishing their lives (HM Government 2008). This philosophy is underpinned by the NTA's updated *Models of Care* (2006) which emphasizes that 'substitute prescribing alone does not constitute drug treatment'. It identifies the need for a care plan, which should include provision of, or access to, interventions for mental health needs. The GPRD study reported here provides timely information on drug users who are also experiencing mental illness and psychiatric patients with substance misuse disorders. Our study provides data on treatment patterns in primary care and enables trends and gaps in current treatment provision to be identified. As knowledge of and treatment for comorbidity improve, it is important that patients be offered the best interventions for their health and social needs in the most appropriate setting (Tiet and Mausbach 2007).

14 Offering a service to BME family members affected by close relatives' drug problems

Jim Orford, Alex Copello, Amanda Simon, Hameera Waheed, Qulsom Fazil, Hermine Graham, Majid Mahmood, Sheryllin McNeil and Gary Roberts

A model and methods to support work with affected family members

The present authors, and collaborators, have been carrying out a programme of research which is designed to lead to ways of involving family members that would be suitable for widespread incorporation into routine service provision in the UK. This is in line with the recently published guidelines on *Supporting and Involving Carers* produced by the National Treatment Agency for Substance Misuse (NTA 2008). We have carried out a series of studies which have (i) provided a detailed understanding of the experiences of family members and on that basis developed a stress–strain–coping–support (SSCS) model (Orford 1998; Orford *et al.* 2005), and (ii) developed and evaluated interventions that involve family members. These interventions have included the 5-Step approach, for use by GPs, health visitors and practice nurses in responding to family members (Copello *et al.* 2000a, 2000b, 2009; Orford *et al.* 2007a, 2007b; Templeton *et al.* 2007), and Social Behaviour and Network Therapy (SBNT), developed for the UK Alcohol Treatment Trial (UKATT) in which our group has been a partner (Copello *et al.* 2002, 2006; Williamson *et al.* 2007).

We have most recently taken our work into a dissemination phase. We have attempted to disseminate the SSCS model, and a flexible way of engaging and working with family members, based on the 5-Step and SBNT methods, via demonstration sites in primary and specialist health care and an internet site (Orford *et al.* 2008). The SSCS model underlies the approach: understanding it is the first necessary stage in all our dissemination activities. Unlike some other models of drugs and the family (e.g. codependency, systemic) it views family members as people who are seriously stressed by and concerned about a close relative's drug use, who are faced with difficult dilemmas about how to cope, about which they have little advice or support, and who, as a result, are at risk of showing signs of strain in the form of physical or mental ill health. It rejects the idea that families or individual family members are pathological or dysfunctional.

Box 14.1: The 5-Step method for family members affected by a close relative's drug problem

The 5-Step approach was designed to be used whenever a health or social care provider is trying to help someone who is affected by and concerned about the addictive behaviour of a close relative or friend. It might involve more than one such person – for example, the wife and daughter of a man with a drinking problem, or the mother and father of a young person with a drug problem. It might involve someone else in the social network such as a close friend or work colleague of someone with an addiction problem. But whoever it is, the key thing here is that this intervention is *delivered to people who are affected by someone else's addiction problem*. It is for concerned and affected others, not for the drug-misusing relative. It may be the appropriate intervention because the drug-misusing relative is not currently engaged in treatment at all; or because it is judged appropriate to provide a concerned and affected other person with an intervention on her/his own without the drug-misusing relative being present; or simply because it is the concerned and affected person who has asked for help. The five steps are as follows:

1 Listen non-judgementally – allowing the family or network member to talk about his or her experiences of the addiction, listening carefully and supportively to what is said.
2 Provide information – for example, information about types of drugs and their misuse or about the nature of dependence or addiction.
3 Discuss ways of coping – for example, discussing ways of supporting the user's efforts to change or ways of minimising the harm to oneself and the family from continued addiction.
4 Explore sources of support – encouraging family and network members to think of ways of improving their own social support.
5 Arrange further help if needed.

The full version of the method consists of working through the steps one by one. But, like all aspects of the integrated approach, it is intended to be used flexibly, adapted to the particular circumstances of family and network members. Only one or two of the steps may be thought appropriate: in nearly all cases, step 1 should come first, and sometimes that is all that time and circumstances will allow. Or the use of part of the 5-Step method may be just one component of the intervention that is being used.

Box 14.2: The Social Behaviour and Network Therapy (SBNT) method for engaging the support of family members in the treatment of drug problems

Elements of the SBNT method can be drawn upon whenever a service provider is working with a person with a drug or other addiction problem. The aim of

SBNT is to mobilise and/or develop positive social network support for that person's change. The main elements of the method are as follows:

- Always 'think network'.
- Draw a network diagram.
- Invite members of the network.
- Strengthen the network.
- Discuss themes of: communication, coping, information, joint activities.
- Work with any part of the network.
- Plan for the future.

Probably the most important elements of SBNT are the first two – identifying potentially supportive members of the drug-misusing client's social network. This is done by drawing a network diagram with the drug-misusing client's help. The diagram should ideally show all the most important people in the person's life, including those from whom s/he is currently estranged. Discussion of the relationship with each person in the diagram can lead to identifying a small number of people – who may be family or friends, and normally no more than one or two people – who are/may be the most supportive. If possible, they are invited to one or more subsequent sessions.

When the drug-misusing person and a family or network member(s) are jointly present in sessions, it is then possible to explore some of the same core issues that are highlighted in the 5-Step method – providing information, considering options for coping, and enhancing social support. But the particular strength of SBNT lies in the fact that those topics can be jointly discussed and, if all goes well, differences of view can be resolved or acknowledged, and joint action plans agreed upon. At the same time, improvements may be made to the way in which the drug-misusing client and network members communicate about issues related to the addiction.

The Birmingham BME family project

Project aims and objectives

The overall aim was to add to the dissemination phase of our work by disseminating this way of working with affected family members in the following two Birmingham black and minority ethnic (BME) communities:

1   The Pakistani/Kashmiri community in Birmingham. The Pakistani community is the largest ethnic minority group in the city, with 104,000 individuals representing 11 per cent of the city population. The written South Asian language for this group is Urdu but the spoken form for a large proportion of the Pakistani/Kashmiri population is Mirpuri. A survey of presentations to Birmingham drug services (Sangster *et al.* 2001) found that 9 per cent were by Pakistani or Bangladeshi drug users, supporting national, regional and other local studies providing evidence of problematic drug use in British South Asian communities. One of the

conclusions regarding the under-use of services by South Asian people was the inability of services to work appropriately with family members (Sangster *et al.* 2001).

2   The African Caribbean community in Birmingham. This is also a large ethnic minority group in the city, with 52,000 individuals representing over 5 per cent of the city population. The national evidence is that both drug and alcohol use and problematic use are as common amongst the young adult African Caribbean population as amongst the majority White population (Sangster *et al.* 2001; Orford *et al.* 2004).

The specific objectives were: (i) to identify and train a small group of practitioners, in each of the two communities, who would then go on to engage family members and to apply the intervention; and (ii) to provide a preliminary assessment of whether the service thus provided to family members was of benefit to them.

Project implementation

Networking/recruitment of organisations and practitioners – coming up against lack of service capacity

A variety of methods were used to try to locate interested practitioners and organisations that might nominate any of their practitioners for project training. Information was sent to all GP practices across those parts of the city where a high proportion of Birmingham's African Caribbean and Pakistani/ Kashmiri populations live. NHS addiction treatment services were contacted. We also contacted a wide variety of non-statutory organisations, having first made a thorough inventory of such organisations using internet search engines and website directories. Some of these were organisations specifically working with drug/alcohol problems, whilst others were not. Some organisations were community-specific, i.e. providing services for either African Caribbean or Muslim (or more generally South Asian) clients or for the BME population more generally. Others were not community-specific.

Figure 14.1 shows the total of nearly 200 organisations that were approached. The largest proportion of those in the statutory group were GP practices which were approached by mail in the first instance. In most other cases, the approach was made in person, by telephone or face-to-face. The figure also shows that a very high proportion of the non-statutory organisations expressed an interest (plus four individual practitioners who expressed an interest in being involved in the project independently of any organisation for which they currently worked or had worked in the past), whereas only a small proportion of the general practices and other statutory organisations did so. At the next stage, nearly half of the non-statutory organisations were represented on the project training courses but only a handful of statutory organisations.

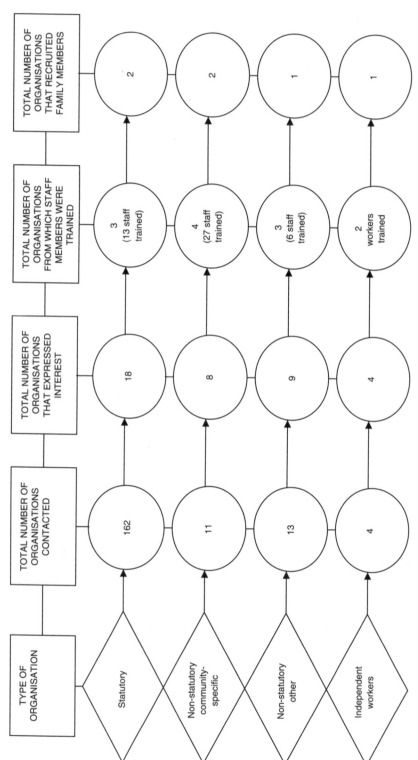

Figure 14.1 Organisation and practitioner networking flowchart.

The main difficulty identified by the general practices and other statutory organisations that showed interest but were unable to commit to the project was the lack of staff, resources and time they had to devote to training in particular and the project in general. The majority of organisations that were contacted initially envisaged that they would experience difficulties in recruiting clients who would fulfil the criteria for the project. Whilst some of these organisations stated that they did not have many African Caribbean or Pakistani/Kashmiri clients, others stated that they did not have much contact with family members or would find it difficult to make contact with them. Several stated that they already signposted family members to other organisations.

Training and support for practitioners

Five two-day training workshops were carried out. The aim was to equip practitioners to deliver the intervention with a flexible approach using elements of the 5-Step and SBNT methods as seemed appropriate to meet the requirements of individual family members. The response could vary from, at one extreme, providing a copy of a self-help manual with minimal orientation given face-to-face or by telephone, to several sessions held jointly with the family member(s) and the drug-misusing relative, at the other extreme. Options between those extremes include single- or multiple-session 5-Step counselling for the family member(s). The training incorporated mini-lectures, role-play exercises and discussion, supported by video and DVD material. The self-help manual, based on the five steps of the 5-Step method, developed in the course of our earlier work, played a large part in the intervention (Templeton *et al.* 2001). Three adaptations/translations were prepared for the project: a version adapted for the African Caribbean group (the adaptations were mainly to the case studies included in the manual); an English language version for the Pakistani/Kashmiri group; and an Urdu translation of the manual. Forty-eight practitioners were trained in total (20 in the Pakistani/Kashmiri arm and 28 in the African Caribbean arm).

Throughout the project, the researcher for each arm of the study kept in regular contact with trained practitioners in order to check up on progress, gauge any resource needs and give relevant advice where necessary. This communication was maintained through face-to-face meetings with practitioners as well as telephone and e-mail communication. In addition, researchers liaised closely with the principal investigators in relation to practitioner progress. With one particular organisation within the Pakistani/Kashmiri arm, regular meetings, attended by the principal investigators and researcher, were held to discuss cases, given the high volume of cases that this service was working with (twenty-nine in total over the duration of the project). Halfway through the project, a recap and evaluation session was also held by the project team with a number of practitioners in the African Caribbean arm of the project.

Working with BME family members affected by drug problems – what can be achieved

Following training, practitioners were asked to recruit clients through the various organisations with which they worked or had established connections. Various means of recruitment were employed, including sending letters out to potential clients, distributing leaflets and word of mouth. Practitioners were also given posters and leaflets which were displayed in their various organisations.

Practitioners were asked to keep records of all the project-related client work which they carried out. In total, work with forty family members was recorded. This was exactly half of the total number we had hoped for at the outset: we had planned for forty Pakistani/Kashmiri family members and forty African Caribbean. In practice, virtually all of the trained practitioners experienced difficulty in identifying suitable family member clients and applying the intervention. The most notable exception was that of a drug problems-specific, Muslim clients-specific organisation which, as the project started, was about to launch a new service specifically for women affected by drug problems in their families. The organisation and their practitioners, particularly the one woman practitioner who was to lead the new service, were enthusiastic about the project methods and from the outset used them as a core part of what they were offering. They worked with twenty-nine family member clients during the course of the project. Three other Pakistani/Kashmiri family members were recruited within statutory organisations, two by one GP and one by an assistant psychologist working with the statutory community drug services. In the African Caribbean arm of the project, eight family member clients were engaged, four by two practitioners at a single non-statutory organisation, one by a practitioner at a second non-statutory organisation, two via independent practitioners, and one who contacted the researcher about the project after seeing a poster advertisement.

All but two of the family members were women. The largest number were concerned about their son's drug problem (23, including 2 fathers), with a smaller number concerned about their husband (12), and a small number concerned about their brother (3), boyfriend (1) or friend (1). In twenty-five cases, family members were living with the relative they were concerned about, and in the remaining cases they were not living together, although they were closely and regularly involved with their drug-misusing relative. All were affected by their relative's illicit drug misuse, mostly involving class A drugs but in some cases focused exclusively on cannabis use. In several cases, alcohol misuse was a further cause of concern.

Practitioners were asked to describe the work they had carried out and what they believed to be the outcome. In as many cases as possible, the family member's consent was sought for a semi-structured follow-up interview with the researcher in order to obtain more detailed information about the family member's experience of the family drug problem and of the intervention and its outcome (ten such follow-up interviews were carried out).

A number of observations can be made on the basis of follow-up family member interviews and practitioner reports. The first concerns the nature of the problems facing the family members who were identified in the course of the project. Many were in a state of considerable distress over their relative's drug problems. Many had been facing these problems for a good many years. In several cases, there had been very worrying recent events, sometimes related to the illegal nature of the relative's drug-taking and/or associated activities. Financial stress was a big factor for a number of family members, particularly those concerned about a husband's drug misuse. The abusive behaviour of the drug user towards the family member and others was mentioned by many. Mothers were especially concerned about what they saw as the harmful effects of a husband's drug misuse on their children or, in the case of a son's drug misuse, effects on the drug misuser's siblings. Distress and worry were in a number of cases complicated by lack of support from other family members.

There was much variation in the nature of the work that was possible with family members. In some instances, including several of the African Caribbean family members, it was possible to do little more than make it known to the family member that the project intervention was available and give a copy of the self-help manual. At the other extreme, and particularly for a number of the Pakistani/Kashmiri family members being seen at the one non-statutory service, it proved possible to carry out a series of sessions (in several cases, ten or more) using the 5-Step principles, and, in addition, to hold joint sessions, using SBNT methods, attended by more than one family member and/or family member plus the drug-using relative (and occasionally a friend or another practitioner from the same or another agency). The self-help manual, either in English or Urdu, was given to the family member in most cases.

The outcome, as described to the researcher by the family member (and/or by the practitioner), also varied. At one extreme were a small number of family members who reported finding the intervention unhelpful, because the relative's behaviour remained unchanged or because the family member felt s/he was already receiving sufficient help or was unable to focus on the intervention due to current circumstances. In a few cases, the practitioner thought that the family member was not yet ready to reflect on the content of the intervention. However, the majority reported some benefit and a number – mostly seen at the one non-statutory service in the Pakistani/ Kashmiri arm – were able to describe considerable benefit. The benefits described were principally the following:

- Being able to speak about worries and concerns, to reflect on them, and as a result to clarify the nature of the problem.
- Experiencing a reduction in self-blame, for having been a cause of the

drug problem, for not having dealt with it, or for having taken action such as asking the drug-using relative to leave home.

- Achieving a better understanding of drugs the relative had been using and the effects of those drugs and in the process achieving greater understanding of the relative's behaviour.
- Finding a different way of dealing with the anger and frustration caused by the drug misuse, acting more calmly, and seeing the positive effects of this change on the drug user's behaviour.
- Deciding on new courses of action such as taking more control of family finances, helping the relative reduce his drug consumption, engaging in enjoyable joint leisure activities with the relative, putting limits on time spent with the drug user, moving home, or deciding to ask the relative to leave.
- Becoming more confident and engaging in rewarding activities for oneself such as enrolling in classes or taking a part-time job.
- Sometimes seeing consequent changes as the drug-misusing relative became more amenable, reduced drug use and/or engaged in treatment.

Boxes 14.3 to 14.7 provide a number of illustrations of the problems family members were facing and the ways in which the intervention was thought to have been helpful.

Box 14.3: Through a flexible combination of family member and network sessions, two parents find that following the intervention their stress is reduced and hope is sustained

A man in his sixties, separated from his wife who lives nearby, living with his now middle-aged drug-misusing son. He said he had to do everything for his son including cooking and laundry. He and his wife separated because of arguments about who was to blame for their son's drug-taking and how best to help him. He had four 5-Step sessions for himself and a number of SBNT sessions jointly with his wife and son. He reported that his 'upset was halved' by having someone to talk to. He had also found the self-help manual (in Urdu) helpful in giving him extra knowledge and the realisation that his stress 'was natural'. The joint sessions had given them a new opportunity to talk to each other about the problem. Both parents had felt benefit in terms of reduced stress and maintenance of hope, although they remained worried about their son's drug use and lack of change.

Box 14.4: A mother is comforted by talking about her own situation and knowing her son is receiving help

A woman living with her husband and several children including her drug-misusing youngest son. The son's drug use had led to him stealing money and jewellery at home and the rest of the family now locked all their doors carefully. She described herself as constantly 'upset, crying and depressed . . . [sitting in her] dark, prison-like house . . . [not wanting to] clean it or do anything'. She had four 5-Step sessions for herself and two SBNT sessions with her son. The intervention had helped her get her 'mood, energy, health and mind back up'. She had found the focus on her, as opposed to everything revolving around her son, 'refreshing'. She had been encouraged to pursue her own activities and was now attending exercise classes, and instead of eating unhealthy convenience food was now choosing healthy food and cooking it herself and feeling more energetic. Talking about her problems in confidence with a person outside the situation had been important. The joint sessions with her son had stood out as helpful because this was an opportunity to 'talk it out' which they otherwise did not do. Her other children had received the English version of the self-help manual.

Box 14.5: The intervention gives a wife somewhere to turn and plays a role in provoking her husband into changing

A woman living with her husband and their several young children. Her husband had been mixing use of a variety of illicit drugs and alcoholic drinks. Things came to a head when he was arrested for drunk driving. He was often missing from home for whole nights and she was worried that his drug use would move on to injecting heroin. The practitioner carried out four or five sessions with her at home, going through the steps in the self-help manual. Her husband was present for each of the sessions. She did not think that the manual itself had been helpful but described having a good relationship with the practitioner. She felt that it was good to have someone she could turn to when things were bad, and that the practitioner coming to talk to her had 'scared' her husband because he knew that 'finally people are taking notice of me', which made him think that he needed to sort himself out. She said that, as a result of the intervention, her husband had stopped hitting her. She had started to make friends again and had got herself a driving licence: 'I am a more open person, I like talking and laughing . . . [before] I was a very different person because when you're involved with someone who takes drugs then everything disappears around you, you lose your friends, family, social life.'

Box 14.6: A mother gains in confidence and becomes more independent

A single mother with several children, more than one of whom uses cannabis. She often found herself giving her sons money through fear that otherwise they would commit crimes. She felt trapped, on the one hand feeling that she was funding their drug habit and on the other not knowing what else to do. This also put her under great financial strain and she often had to go without things that she needed. Her concerns particularly focused on her youngest son who had become involved with the police. She felt stressed out by the problems surrounding her sons' drug use and felt the situation was 'hopeless . . . [I am] dragged in all directions'. At a low point, she had thought of suicide. She would have liked the children to get on with their own lives so she could get on with hers but felt she could not just 'abandon' them. She had seven 5-Step sessions. She and the practitioner met regularly for 'a coffee and a chat' about whatever was going on at the time and would then work through the manual exercises. These sessions took place outside the home, which gave her the chance to get out of the house. The practitioner also regularly called her to check up on her and she thought they had built up a good relationship in which she felt comfortable sharing her worries. As a result she now felt she had the option to 'go out there', i.e. to get out of the house and be more independent. For example, she had recently been away for a week by herself, something she would never have thought of doing without the children previously. She also thought she had gained a greater understanding of the problem, how it affected the user and how it would affect her in the future. She regretted not having the information beforehand and felt that if she had, 'things probably would not have got this bad'.

Box 14.7: A wife helps her husband gain control of his drug use

A wife living with her husband and three children. Her husband's drug use, of over ten years' standing, meant that they were struggling financially much of the time. Her relationship with her husband, although basically satisfactory, at times left her feeling very low. She thought it had affected the children. She said she had no support from her in-laws. She had a dozen 5-Step sessions for herself and eight SBNT sessions jointly with her husband (his keyworker had also joined these sessions). She was given the Urdu self-help manual. As a result, she put in a lot of hard work in trying to help her husband reduce his drug use and successfully implemented some changes. She started to manage his heroin intake, helping him reduce his spending on drugs from around £100 a day to about £20. Her husband started to take methadone. She also rebuilt connections with her in-laws. The home environment gradually improved and this had a positive effect on the children, reflected in their improved school work.

Discussion

The project findings are discussed along with the results of semi-structured interviews which were carried out towards the end of the project with fifteen of the participating practitioners. The discussion is also aided by the results of a systematic literature search that was carried out in conjunction with the project.

Neglect of BME family members affected by relatives' drug problems

The literature search revealed very little information with a specific focus on BME family members of substance-misusing relatives. One of the very few directly relevant British studies, which involved interviews with twenty-two 'carers' (Gooden 1999), concluded that family members were experiencing stress and strain associated with the substance misuse, were often marginalised because of the illicit nature of their relative's activities and, although some progress had been made, were still accorded a low priority in service provision. This corresponds with our experience of alcohol and drug problems and the family more generally and with our experience in the present project. We found that organisational support for practitioners' involvement in the kind of family work we were trying to promote was variable and rarely ideal. This was something that practitioners commented on during end-of-project interviews. In some instances the practitioner's organisation was said to have been little involved and two of the practitioners were working independently of any organisation. Some organisations sent a practitioner, or in some cases several practitioners, for project training but the way the organisation worked or the nature of its clientele made subsequent work with family members difficult. In some service organisations, there had been little opportunity to work with family members; in others there were relatively few BME clients. In only a small number of organisations did we find the circumstances very favourable, i.e. a very supportive organisation, wishing to develop family work in the context of drug services for BME clients. This had been particularly the case for the one service in the Pakistani/Kashmiri arm which had the greatest success recruiting family members.

Relevance of the project training and family intervention methods

We experienced considerable demand for the kind of training we were offering and comments on the training events organised as part of the project were generally very positive. The use of role-play methods received positive mention as did the opportunity to network with practitioners from other organisations. There was general agreement that involvement in the project had given practitioners new ideas about family work and about ways of working that could potentially be put into practice now or in the future. Several recognised, however, that putting the methods into practice remained an aspiration. Others could see the possibility of using elements of the methods.

A commonly expressed view was that the family methods being promoted by the project were as relevant to the African Caribbean and Pakistani/Kashmiri communities as they were to any others. The view was widely held that issues to do with shame and secrecy around drug use were important in the African Caribbean community, as they were around alcohol use in the Pakistani/Kashmiri community, but that these were not peculiar to BME groups and there was nothing in the methods that was not suitable whatever the cultural background. This is an important conclusion for the project since a main question for the research was whether our model and methods, developed in studies in which members of BME communities were in a small minority, were relevant for British BME communities. Nevertheless three of the African Caribbean practitioners were critical of the project because it was 'white, university based', and would have been better if it had come from African Caribbean community organisations, with greater consultation with community leaders. They were sceptical about the value of the project because in their view it ignored what were the core issues for African Caribbean people, failing to look at their core identity, issues of social justice, spiritual beliefs and the whole person.

How should services for BME family members be delivered in the future?

The difficulty that services have in attracting and working with BME clients was a main talking point in our interviews with practitioners. The failure of existing agencies to understand the needs of BME clients was seen as a main barrier to service access for affected BME family members. Agencies were thought not to be working hard enough to attract black clients: they needed to 'come out of their comfort zones', get beyond the stereotypes and embrace equal opportunities. As one practitioner put it, Black people often see services as 'White' and not culturally sensitive. The location and accessibility of the service were thought to be important, as were opening hours, style of language used, and who was on the frontline making the initial contact. The issue of trust was said to be central. There were sensitivities about agencies appearing to be judgemental, and more generally about the possibility of racism. It was important for practitioners to have awareness of the community, to have relevant knowledge – including knowledge of recent events and history, including the history of racism – to be able to assure clients that confidentiality would be safeguarded, to acknowledge the importance of spirituality for many clients, and in general to 'speak their language'.

This corresponds well with what appears in the literature regarding the under-use of drug services by BME drug users and carers. Various explanations have been given for this low uptake of services. They include: preference for seeking help within family and friendship networks; pride and the fear of stigma attached to the use of drug support services; fears about information leaking back into the community and concerns about letting down family members and peers (Gooden 1999); under-estimation of the drug problem within communities because of the taboo allied to drug use or drinking disclosure (Heim *et al.* 2004; Banton *et al.* 2005); lack of confidence in services, particularly regarding confidentiality, including fear that details may be passed on to the authorities, in some cases introducing the risk of deportation (Wanigaratne *et al.* 2003); perception of drug services as being

'White'-orientated or Euro-centric in nature which leads members of BME communities to believe that these services are unable to cater for their particular needs (Wanigaratne *et al.* 2003; Ruggiero and Khan 2006); a general lack of knowledge about available services (Gooden 1999; Heim *et al.* 2004); the narrow focus of services on opiate, injection-related drug problems as opposed to stimulant and cannabis use (Wanigaratne *et al.* 2003; Rassool 2006); and finally institutional racism or discrimination in services (Wanigaratne *et al.* 2003; Rassool 2006). In addition, we found very similar points being made by those who have studied the appropriateness of mental health services for BME clients (e.g. Tabassum *et al.* 2000; Fernando 2005).

Although the literature shows no clear-cut consensus on a good practice model for working with BME users and family members in the UK, there are some strong suggestions as to how current service delivery problems can be solved. A key debate within this area concerns the nature of service delivery organisations and in particular the relative merits of statutory and non-statutory bodies. There is a view, to which most of our practitioners subscribed, that non-statutory bodies, able to cater for specific groups, constituting less formal settings, characterised by more flexible practical arrangements, and often displaying greater cultural awareness, are more adequately equipped to deliver services to BME communities and may be more likely to assume that families will be involved (Gooden 1999; Banton *et al.* 2005; Fernando 2005). At the end of the present project, practitioners were generally in favour of using our family methods in their own organisations, and in a range of other locations, provided the service was in a position to work with family members and in a culturally appropriate way, as described above. It was voluntary/community organisations that were consistently mentioned as being best placed to do this work. Certainly the project's greater success was with non-statutory services, particularly one such service. Churches and mosques were also mentioned by most practitioners as being places to which family members naturally turned.

According to some of our practitioners, however, it is also important to note that some service users prefer mainstream delivery because they are concerned that members of their community should not be treated any differently (Heim *et al.* 2004). There are also confidentiality concerns with services that are run by BME community groups for members of BME communities. Service users from small communities in particular may be concerned about coming into contact with someone who knows them. For that reason, such services may still present access difficulties for BME community group members (Gooden 1999). As one of our practitioners put it, mainstream services should not be 'let off the hook' in providing services for affected BME family members. Several practitioners expressed the hope that the methods could also be used in the general practice primary care setting, although pressures in primary care were recognised: one practitioner recommended joint work between a GP surgery and a linking voluntary organisation.

Conclusions

1   Amongst these two BME communities, as in others, there is a need for services to provide for family members affected by close relatives' drug problems. Most of the family members who were recruited were under great stress and showing evidence of considerable distress.
2   The flexible family intervention promoted in the study was considered to be appropriate for the two communities and was reported by practitioners to be effective when opportunities were found to employ it. The training courses, designed to introduce the family intervention to practitioners, were popular and well received. The self-help manual for family members was successfully translated into Urdu for the Pakistani/Kashmiri arm of the study and is relevant for Urdu-literate family members throughout Britain.
3   The capacity for service organisations to take on this work is mostly very limited. Many organisations, including most general practices, are unlikely to be able to make it a priority to provide for BME family members affected by drug problems. Non-statutory organisations with experience of delivering services to a BME community (or communities) may be in a better position to provide such a service but most non-statutory organisations will also have difficulties because of lack of a drug focus or a family focus or for organisational reasons such as lack of secure funding. The project's greatest success was with a non-statutory organisation, specifically for Muslim clients, with a specific drug focus, which had just started a new service specifically for women affected by relatives' drug problems.

Acknowledgement

We wish to thank Professor Ray Hodgson and Mrs Pat Evans for their contributions to the work reported in this chapter.

A review of services for children
and young people with
drug-misusing carers

Daniel Clay and Judy Corlyon

Policy

In 2003, the Advisory Council on the Misuse of Drugs (ACMD) published *Hidden Harm*, a report which drew on a range of research to highlight the damage caused to children whose parents misuse drugs. This can start before a child is born, when maternal drug use during pregnancy can cause foetal harm, and can continue throughout childhood and beyond through the general ill effects of poverty, poor housing and/or frequent changes of residence, physical and emotional abuse or neglect, inadequate supervision, inappropriate parenting or parental behaviour, inconsistent school attendance, exposure to criminal activities and temporary or permanent separation from parents. Children of drug users often experience more than one of these and the result can be inadequate health care for children, delayed mental health development, emotional, cognitive and behavioural problems, poor educational attainment, substance misuse and offending behaviour. Children whose parents misuse alcohol can suffer the same ill effects (Turning Point 2006) but the illegality of drug use brings additional mental and emotional stress to families and leads to the added burden for children of having to deny its existence (Kroll 2004).

Hidden Harm contained six key messages for government, including recommendations that reducing the harm to children from parental problem drug use should become a priority for policy and practice and that services should work together to protect and improve the health and well-being of the children affected. The report also called for the evaluation of existing interventions aimed at supporting and improving outcomes for the children of drug misusers.

One year after the publication of *Hidden Harm*, a progress report on the government's ten-year Drug Strategy, *Tackling Drugs: Changing Lives* (Home Office 2004), promised rapid access to appropriate support where needed for children and young people in known risk groups, which included the children of those who misuse substances. In the following year, the government's response to *Hidden Harm* (DfES 2005) included a commitment to research to establish what types of interventions and services are successful in working with the children of problem drug users. This led to projects which have proved useful in raising the profile of children affected by parental substance misuse, sharing ideas on good practice and providing an opportunity for children and practitioners to meet and have input into national policy and practice-related developments. They have not, however, explored the nature and extent of service provision.

The research review

Phase II of the Department of Health's Drug Misuse Research Initiative – Research on Understanding Treatment Experiences and Services (ROUTES) – provided an ideal opportunity for a study to fill this gap in knowledge. The research attempted to identify which services were available throughout England to support the children of substance misusers, and to explore who provided the services and how they operated in terms of their aims and objectives, referral methods and criteria, client group and service delivery. It then looked in more detail at a small number of these services to establish what issues they were dealing with and whether and how they met the needs of their clients.

Information about services was obtained mainly, though not exclusively, from local Drug Action Teams (DATs) and this led to 141 services from a total of 127 DATs being identified. However, the information provided by the DATs was not always accurate and only eighty-two services, working across sixty-three areas, could be confirmed as undertaking direct work with children and young people whose parents misused drugs. Large areas of England, including major counties and large conurbations, had either limited or no provision. Services might well have existed in these areas but, if they did, they were not well known about.

Service characteristics

Just under three-quarters of the identified services were located in the voluntary sector but the vast majority received at least some of their funding from one or two statutory agencies, especially the local DATs and social services departments. (DATs have responsibility for commissioning, co-ordinating and communicating drug-related work taking place in their areas and were thus a main source of funding.) Large grant-giving bodies such as the Big Lottery Fund and Children in Need were also major sources of funding. Amounts tended to be relatively small (under £100,000 a year) and only a quarter of services, predominantly in the voluntary sector, had guaranteed funding for more than two years.

The majority of services, but especially voluntary ones, were engaged in a substantial amount of joint working, in particular with statutory sector social services, health and education. Although most had at least one service-level agreement in place, voluntary services had fewer than those in the statutory sector.

Referrals to the services came most frequently from social services, education and health professionals but self-referrals from children and families themselves were also quite common, indicating that services were both known about and seen as accessible by members of the public. Drug services for adults made few referrals to the services for children.

A diverse range of provision was offered, from play therapy through to leisure activities for children or the whole family. However, nearly all services provided some form of individual support or counselling, primarily to children and young people, though more than half also worked with parents in this capacity. Group work with children and young people was also offered by the majority of services and a small number also undertook group work with parents. Family support and/or family therapy were offered in two-fifths of services. The relatively large number of services working with parents as well as children suggested that providers were aware of the improved outcomes for children that came from using this approach (Smeaton 2004).

Meeting the needs of children and young people

The children and young people tended to present with a wide range of issues, the most commonly cited being a combination of child abuse, neglect and domestic violence. Anti-social behaviour, and problems at school, both outcomes highlighted in other research (ACMD 2003), were prominent issues for clients in around one-third of services. One-fifth of managers reported that their service dealt with issues around social isolation and a subsequent lack of social skills. Substance misuse amongst children of substance misusers was mentioned relatively infrequently, perhaps because clients were seen at an early stage and before they developed a problem with substances.

From the sixty-six services identified, ten were looked at in more detail to find out how they worked and whether this was effective for the children and young people who accessed the service. Interviews were conducted with managers of the ten services and with fourteen children/young people, aged between 9 and 17, who used the services.

At the time the interviews with providers and clients were conducted, government focus was primarily around the treatment and prevention of substance misuse. However, none of these projects specifically aimed to prevent substance misuse among their clients. Their main aims were, in fact, to increase the well-being of the child or young person through developing their resilience, providing them with the confidence and coping mechanisms with which to manage the situation they were in and to have a life of their own. They wanted to help children feel happier and more confident; communicate their thoughts and feelings to adults, including their parents; build better relationships with their family members and peers; understand their home situation; and improve their school attendance and educational attainment. In a number of services, the presenting needs of the clients dictated which of these outcomes had priority. Where services worked with parents as well as the children (which seven of the services did), there were additional aims related to achieving greater stability within the home, more consistent routines and better management of behaviour.

The magnitude of this task cannot be over-stated. Services not only had to cope with the expectations of funders – which, in some cases, focused on quantifiable outcomes such as reducing the number of children on the Child Protection Register and increasing school attendance – but also had to deal with a host of clients' presenting issues, often set against a backdrop of family disruption, chaos and dysfunctional relationships. Children were often acting as carers to their parents, truanting from school to remain at home, having limited social interaction and a substantial amount of unmet childhood need. Service providers found that where children had had to take control of what would otherwise have been a chaotic home environment, they often found it difficult to accept external boundaries. Others were left feeling out of control through the lack of predictable and consistent behaviour from their parents.

Only two of the fourteen children and young people interviewed lived with both parents (both drug users). All others were living with one parent or were cared for by other family members, including an elder sibling and grandparents. In some cases, grandparents were caring for children and the drug-using parent. For many, their living arrangements, in terms of both where and with whom they lived, had fluctuated over the years as they moved from one parent to the other, to grandparents and back to a parent. This not only caused practical and emotional disruption but it also impacted on children's and young people's family relationships, schooling and friendships and resulted in multiple experiences of loss:

> My dad was still living with me [at grandmother's] at that time [but] just about a year ago he moved [to live abroad] . . . because my step-mum broke up with him. And I don't get to see my [half-]sister . . . I haven't seen her in a year and . . . I mean my step-mum says she doesn't want anything to do with the past.
>
> (12-year-old male)

In some cases, a parent's continuing drug use prevented a child's contact with him/her, which younger children in particular struggled to understand. According to service providers, many clients blamed themselves for the situation they were in and clients themselves described how they did not know how to cope with it: 'I used to look at my mam and dad and when I used to try and talk to them I used to cry because I didn't know what to say to them' (13-year-old female).

Embarrassment and shame were compounded by fears for their parents' welfare: one 12-year-old who professed himself 'very disappointed' by his mother and her repeated drug use, also commented, 'I hope she goes into rehab soon and stops really, and I hope I have a very good life without it and hopefully she doesn't die early' (12-year-old male).

For younger children, school seemed to afford some degree of normality. Some of them received additional tuition and the personal attention this gave them proved to be a positive factor. This was not, however, the case with older children who typically preferred not to attend school and struggled with relationships with teaching staff. Teachers themselves did not always help the situation: one young person described receiving repeated detentions for wearing trainers to school because her mother, dealing with a new baby and impending homelessness, had not been able to buy regulation school shoes.

Mistrust of professionals was common among the children and young people. They had reached the conclusion that nothing said to people in positions of power remained confidential and that such people could not be relied upon. In such a situation, characterised by anxiety, shame, disaffection, isolation, lack of confidence, and mistrust, service providers faced a difficult task in achieving their aims. These children and young people were typically suspicious about engaging with services. With the exception of the few who had been properly briefed beforehand by their referrer, and – crucially – had remembered what they had been told, the majority experienced nervousness and apprehension on their first visit. Their perceptions of 'helping' and of 'support services' were dominated by unwelcome images of having to talk about feelings and experiences to a stranger, 'sitting in a room and talking all the time, and, like, just everything being low and depressed', as one 16-year-old young woman described it.

In all cases, the anxieties proved to be unfounded, partly because each project offered much more than talking therapy. Nine of the ten services did engage clients in one-to-one work but not in the form they had envisaged. Several services used creative therapeutic techniques such as art, drama and play, while others engaged with clients through leisure activities, such as playing pool. In addition, half of the services undertook group work with clients. These were typically run with specific age groups, for example, 7- to 11-year-olds or 12- to 15-year-olds. Where staffing permitted, several services ran two groups each week, one for younger children and one for older children. As well as providing children with an opportunity to socialise and have fun, sessions usually had a therapeutic or educational element.

Meetings tended to be held weekly after school, with the exception of one service where its activity-focused group work element (though not its one-to-one outreach work) was only provided during the holiday periods. Services providing individual support were more likely to be open-ended, though two did follow a time-limited programme of work which lasted between ten and twelve weeks. Three of the services offering group work also used a time-limited programme, varying between eight and fourteen weeks, with the longer interventions being more likely to have a therapeutic basis.

Unless it was activity-based, group work took place at the service. The one-to-one sessions took place at the service itself or at other locations hired by the service or on an outreach basis at locations where the clients felt comfortable. Outreach tended to be more common for work with older young people.

Overall, clients appreciated the service they were offered and this did not diminish with time: children and young people who had been attending a project for several years reported just as much enjoyment as those attending on a brief, time-limited basis. Some expressed a clear preference for working in groups, recognising the benefits of doing so in terms of personal enjoyment, but also seeing the potential to make friends and develop communication and team work skills: 'I think it's better in a group because, like, you learn, you meet new friends and stuff, to get along with them' (12-year-old male).

In addition, group work provided the fun aspect of involvement, whether a group functioned at the service or engaged in external activities, such as visits to leisure centres, and this was a rarity for many children and young people. A 12-year-old stated that since coming to the project he had had 'more fun . . . fun things came into my life'. For others, one-to-one support provided a rare opportunity to have time alone with an adult who listened to their problems – an aspect of their lives which was as important as being diverted from their concerns: 'Just going out for talking and like. . . . And like when I was living with my mum, I used to like getting time on my own if you know what I mean . . . used to go, like, [to] get things off my chest' (17-year-old female).

Notwithstanding individual preferences, in general it was a combination of having access to personal attention when it was needed, alongside group activities offering enjoyment, distraction and friendship, that most appealed:

> They should do more activities for like, like it kind of should be fun, yeah, but they should be like, like talking about more about how you feel and stuff about the fact that you found out that your mum's been doing this and that.
>
> (12-year-old male)

Projects were typically based in services which provided other support around substance misuse (both drugs and alcohol) to children, young people and, in a small number of cases, adults. All but two had a remit to work specifically with clients affected by parental substance misuse and employed dedicated staff for this task. For the majority of children and young people, it was the staff who defined the success of their involvement – in particular, project workers' ability to listen when needed, to engage in a respectful dialogue and to provide support were highlighted by respondents, for whom these aspects of social interaction were often missing. Many discussions about the benefits of their attendance focused on a named individual, highlighting the importance to participants of developing a strong, reliable and consistent relationship with one person: 'She said, just, "here, I'm gonna be working with you, so if you need anyone to talk to, I'm always here", gave us her number and that' (13-year-old female).

Consistency of support enhanced the degree to which children and young people felt able to share their feelings openly with workers but a vital component of this was the ability to trust and feel secure about the boundaries of confidentiality. This frequently contrasted with their previous experiences of what happened when they talked in personal terms to an adult in a position of authority. As one young woman remarked, 'She never t', told anyone what I'd said to her, like, but when everyone else I'd worked with, they always tell everybody' (13-year-old female).

Although able to take young people seriously, workers were not viewed as patronising or humourless. They were consistently described as 'fun' people who did not distance themselves from the young people by virtue of style or attitudes:

> They're down to earth. They're not snobby little people that walks round and thinks they're good. You know, like you get some social workers or workers thinks they're higher than you.
>
> (17-year-old female)

> They're really good actually. . . . I thought they would be like, like not trendy if you get what I mean but when K came . . . well she was just not like you think that they wore suits and things like that but she didn't, she just wore like normal teenager stuff.
>
> (16-year-old female)

Staff characteristics

So who were these people who were so uniformly well received and compared so favourably with other support workers? Of the ten services, six had one or two dedicated staff who worked primarily with children affected by parental substance misuse. In the others, staff and volunteers involved in other service work engaged with this client group. Three of the ten services were staffed with only part-time employees and volunteers, working between one and three days a week.

If the project was providing therapeutic work, staff with professional therapeutic and/or social work qualifications were recruited. Workers providing activity-based interventions or practical crisis support often had a youth work background. However, for other types of work, services were more relaxed about their requirements. The most important qualities were experience of working with young people and an ability to build a rapport with them. Knowledge about drugs and alcohol was not a prerequisite for employment: in some services it was desirable but, in others, the view was taken that it could be acquired fairly quickly in post. In fact, several service managers thought it unlikely that they could recruit someone with the primary skills and qualifications required as well as knowledge of substance misuse.

All services provided training for staff around substance misuse issues and most also provided a range of training, from formal, internal inductions, covering child protection and health and safety, for example, through to accredited external courses. Staff generally felt they had sufficient time to undertake training, and, likewise, felt well supported by their service, with regular line-management meetings and access to additional support if requested. This was seen as an important ingredient of staff satisfaction and competence. As one service manager stated, 'I think support for staff is really necessary, space for staff to gain access to support and feel contained in themselves to do a good enough job – that's a priority.'

The value of services

Finally, there is the question of whether those who used the services benefited from doing so, beyond enjoying the experience. Most children and young people cited a number of advantages from having been involved, all of which were in line with the stated aims of the projects. Projects, and in particular group activities, provided the opportunity to develop new relationships with others who had similar experiences to their own. In some cases, this appeared to remove the tension typically experienced by young people who were carrying around a guilty secret, and allowed them to engage in easier interaction with others: 'It's been easy meeting them. . . . 'Cos they're, they're like the same as me and then I don't feel awkward talking about stuff in front them' (13-year-old female). However, this was not always the case: for some young people, the covert and illicit nature of parental drug use remained a permanent barrier to disclosing personal information, even when friendships developed with others in the same situation as themselves.

Improvements in communication skills were noted by several young people as one of the key outcomes of their involvement in projects. From a starting point of being withdrawn, children and young people learned to talk openly to project workers and to engage with other members of their group. This, in turn, led to greater confidence, willingness to talk to others outside the project, and the ability to work in groups: 'Like I know how to communicate a bit more now. Because before I was a bit quiet, now I've come out me shell a bit more' (14-year-old female). For some young people, improved communication and coping skills had helped reduce the frustration which led to inappropriate patterns of behaviour and which had not served them well. Better communication skills also meant improvements in family interactions in the cases where the drug misuse was not so bad as to prevent this completely. Several examples were given where project workers helped children to work through specific issues with family members and supported them to practise and develop strategies for addressing difficult issues: 'I find it hard to talk to me Mam and when K's there she liked helped us talk to me Mam. Like tell her what was like problems I had and that . . . just like taught us how to say it in a nice way' (13-year-old female). In some cases project workers oiled the wheels of communication by initially acting as intermediaries and relaying information to family members which young people felt unable to communicate directly.

The majority of projects included some time devoted to explanations about substance misuse, its damaging effects on the individual and the difficulties it caused parents who were dependent users. This helped some children to make sense of their family circumstances and provided them with a degree of empathy, which not only improved the family relationship but made the child/ young person feel better about him/herself: 'It helped us understand what, why he was doing the things that he was doing, why, not why he had to do it but why he was doing it kind of thing' (16-year-old female). Moreover, and importantly in terms of government policy, having this information served as a deterrent to young people's own future use. Children of drug users are considered to be at increased risk of becoming users themselves but those interviewed here consistently and emphatically stated that they would not consider doing so. They were supported by service managers, who, notwithstanding the fact that they did not aim to prevent substance misuse, believed that their clients were less likely to become drug users because of their firsthand experience: 'I'd say mainly with the children that I work with, they are very anti-drug or alcohol use because of the effect that they have seen on their parents' (Service 6).

Thus, the majority of children and young people emerged from a service feeling more confident and aware and with the ability to form and maintain relationships. But this was not the case for all and, bearing in mind the point where services started, this is not surprising. Some young people who had enjoyed attending the project nevertheless were unable to identify a specific way in which it had helped them at home, or saw limits to the difference it could make. For some, the magnitude of their difficulties lay beyond the scope of the project to change. This was the case with one young man for whom the truth, and subsequent abandonment of hope, overwhelmed any positive benefit he might have felt from attending the project: 'It's understand me about mum and dad and that why I'm not allowed to live with them and that. That's it' (11-year-old male).

The future

Concerns have been raised that the government's focus is still on reducing drug-related crime rather than on promoting the wider welfare of children of substance misusers (ACMD 2007). The new ten-year plan, *Drugs: Protecting Families and Communities* (HM Government 2008) pays little attention to the provision of specific interventions for children and young people affected by parental substance misuse. However, it does adopt a more whole-family approach to addressing misuse than previous strategies have done. Early identification and treatment are still core to the strategy but there is an acknowledgement that this should be more holistic, 'family-friendly', and tailored to meet the individual needs of both parents and children.

The new strategy does acknowledge that greater levels of joint working and information sharing between adults' and children's services are needed to ensure that vulnerable children do not slip through the net. This is certainly an area where improvements can be made. The dearth of referrals from and lack of co-operative working with adult drugs services contributes to keeping hidden the harm experienced by children affected by their parents' misuse of drugs. It also does not fit with current policies either on drug misuse specifically or on family support generally both of which encourage a more co-operative approach between services helping families.

As we have seen, the children of drug users do derive benefit in a variety of ways from being able to access services designed to support them. However, it appears that such services are both sparse and randomly located across England. One, or possibly two, projects operated in some areas but in others there were none. As the vast majority of services worked only within their local authority and narrowed their focus further by targeting particularly deprived areas with notably high levels of substance misuse, this suggests that many children with drug-misusing parents are still left unsupported. Clearly greater provision, more uniformly spread across the country, would increase the chances of children and young people being able to access support designed to mitigate the negative effects of their parents' drug use. Alongside this should be better awareness on the part of DATs about which services are available in their local areas.

Secure funding for support services generally is not a new issue but it is particularly important for this client group whose lives are characterised by uncertainty and short-term solutions. As we saw in their relationship with project staff, reliability and consistency were central to their positive appraisal, and these aspects apply equally to the service itself. If funding disappeared and a service which they were accessing collapsed, any benefit they had gained might be quickly dispelled by yet another disappointment in their lives.

The central role that staff played in helping children and young people was evident here. Yet the practitioners' forum – the STARS National Initiative Practitioners' Forum which was funded by the then DfES and hosted by the Children's Society, and which came into effect in the wake of a recommendation in *Hidden Harm* that good practice should be shared – had only short-term funding and no longer exists, leaving workers with no central point for sharing emerging good practice. This is a substantial loss as services typically have a very small number of workers who, without a network, are left to plough a lonely furrow.

This and previous research shows that services for children of drug users do appear to bring positive personal, family and social benefits. Measuring such outcomes is not easy but it is important that the value of these, often personal, benefits is captured and recognised. A major unanswered question is how long these benefits might last, especially when the intervention is short. A brief period of pleasure and attention might be outweighed by the remorse-lessness of a chaotic and troubled life but, if this is the case, it would be better to know so that services can adapt to provide a more sustained intervention.

In 2003, the ACMD pointed out that the benefit of initiatives for the children of problem drug users was unknown for various reasons, which included the fact that few projects were specifically targeted at the children of drug-misusing parents and that several involved relatively small numbers of children or were confined to a few areas of the country. Some years later, the same concerns could be raised. The encouraging factor is the ability of service providers to bring about positive changes in and for these children and, given the appropriate resources, their potential to achieve more.

16 Dilemmas in intervening effectively in families where there is parental drug misuse

Brynna Kroll and Andy Taylor

They do love you but they *have* to put that [drugs] first. . . . However badly you want yourself to be number one to them, it'll never happen.

('Lizzie', 20, child of drug-misusing parents)

You're always constantly lying to yourself, fooling yourself . . . you do put yourself first. . . . Everything revolves around your hit – your next bit of gear.

('Harry', drug-misusing parent)

It is estimated that between 241,000 and 359,000 children in the UK are in the care of problem drug users, with between two and three per cent of children aged less than 16 years living with parents for whom this is an issue (ACMD 2003). Although not all such parents require intervention, research has highlighted the complex problems that many face, the emotional, social, educational and psychological implications for their children and the challenges that professionals encounter when attempting to intervene purposefully in their lives. We also know that parental drug misuse is frequently the reason that children are placed on child protection registers or enter the 'looked after' population (Forrester 2000), requiring substitute care either in foster placements or with relatives who are often unprepared for the challenges they present (Kroll 2006).

This chapter will explore some of the dilemmas encountered in intervening effectively in families where there is parental drug misuse (hereafter referred to as PDM). Drawing on data from a recently completed two-year research project, based on interviews with forty parents and forty-two children and young people, we will be highlighting some of the most critical issues for them, in relation to experiences of services, including some of the main barriers to intervention. We will also be conveying their suggestions for the way services need to change to meet the needs of all family members more effectively. This will be set alongside practice dilemmas identified from a sample of sixty professionals from health and social care in both child welfare and adult settings, and their perceptions of what needs to be done differently. Based on our findings, we will be arguing that, despite significant localized and individual endeavour and pockets of good practice, overall we are failing to meet the needs of these families, particularly children, and that, if the government's new drug strategy and the 'Care Matters' agenda for children are to move beyond rhetoric, significant changes in service configuration, policy and practice will need to take place.

We begin by providing the research backdrop against which this study took place, and examine its relevance to both drug and child care policy. We then outline the very specific social and demographic context in which our research was undertaken and describe how it was done. This will be followed by a summary of the key findings, illustrated by extracts from interviews. To ensure confidentiality, pseudonyms or professional titles have been used; where a quote is unattributed, this indicates it was said by several people. The implications for policy and practice will then be discussed.

In relation to both our study and what follows, 'drug misuse' is based on the definition provided by the Standing Conference on Drug Abuse (SCODA): 'the use of drugs which leads to harm (social, physical and psychological)' (SCODA 1997: 36).

Drug misuse, parenting and child wellbeing

The study took place against a backdrop of convincing research evidence which suggests that children living with a parent with a serious drug problem may encounter a range of barriers to satisfactory development, with obvious implications for their welfare (see, for example, Hogan 1998; Barnard and McKeganey 2004; Kroll and Taylor 2007b; Scaife 2008). We also know that drug misuse often has a complex aetiology, with its roots in troubled early histories of abuse and neglect (Etherington 2008), and that it rarely travels alone, frequently accompanied by domestic violence (Humphreys *et al.* 2005), mental health difficulties (Weir and Douglas 1999), criminal activities, social exclusion and poverty (Forrester and Harwin 2006). This 'collision of circumstances' (Kroll and Taylor 2003: 93) can mean, therefore, that family members are contending with a range of potentially problematic issues all at once.

The negative impact of PDM on parenting capacity, family dynamics and social and economic conditions is also well documented (Cleaver *et al.* 1999; Kroll and Taylor 2007a), as is the impact on parents' psychological availability (Hogan 1997; Barnard and McKeganey 2004; Kroll 2004). Because drug use is a chronic, relapsing condition, it brings with it a level of unpredictability and uncertainty for children, which undermines stability and security and leaves children feeling that they come a poor second to a substance (Barnard 2007). Although there are protective factors in the lives of children of drug-misusing parents which foster resilience, it is also clear that these are by no means reliable over time and rarely provide as much emotional ballast as is required (Bancroft *et al.* 2004). A clear distinction also needs to be made between 'resilience' and merely 'coping' (Templeton *et al.* 2006).

Because drug use is both illegal and characterized by secrecy and denial, there are various barriers to accessing services, with parents often falling through gaps in agency provision and children's needs not being met (Elliott and Watson 1998; Hogan and Higgins 2001; Kroll and Taylor 2003; Hart and Powell 2006; ACMD 2007; Cleaver *et al.* 2007). The conclusions reached suggest that interventions are not sufficiently targeted or not delivered effectively and that this has major implications for parents' motivation to enter drug treatment and the 'hidden harm' that many children experience.

The dilemmas and challenges for professionals

Working with parental drug misuse presents professionals with a range of dilemmas, including engagement, sustaining contact, assessment, intervention and decision-making, ensuring the 'visibility' of children, working with denial, effective inter-agency working, appropriate knowledge, training, support and supervision, and protocols regarding information sharing and confidentiality (Bates *et al.* 1999; Kearney *et al.* 2000; Hayden 2004; Taylor and Kroll 2004).

In response to an increasing sense of urgency about addressing the needs of families where there is PDM, models of assessment have been developed (Forrester 2004; Hart and Powell 2006) and inter-agency protocols and practice guidance produced in various areas of the UK (see for example Scottish Executive 2003). Examples of innovative services and specific projects have been identified (Harbin and Murphy 2000, 2006; ACMD 2006; Darby 2006) and a specialist Drug and Alcohol Court established in central London (DCSF 2008). However, many commentators conclude that there remains a need for more consistent, coordinated responses to this vulnerable group who remain a low priority. The emphasis on more effective, family-focused approaches, although frequently highlighted as of central importance to support families and protect children, often remains on the list of priorities for further research (Barnard 2007; Forrester and Harwin 2008). It was with a view to identifying the critical components for these that this study evolved, within a specific rural context.

Parental problems, drug misuse and child welfare: 'thinking family'

A range of government policies and initiatives focus on crucial crossover issues relating to adult drug problems and their impact on child welfare and family functioning. Most notably, the UK government's ten-year strategy for tackling drug misuse (HM Government 1998), the National Treatment Agency (NTA 2002b) and *Drug Misuse and Dependence: UK Guidelines on Clinical Management* (DH 2007) highlight the needs of both users and family members, emphasizing the importance of accessing and sustaining appropriate treatment. The government's *Drugs: Protecting Families and Communities:*

The 2008 Drug Strategy (HM Government 2008) further underlines the importance of acknowledging the individual needs of parents and children as well as the importance of a family focus and includes thirteen specific action points designed to prevent harm to children, young people and families affected by drug misuse. These include improving prompt access to treatment, supported by better child care provision, involving families in the development of better service delivery, more family-focused interventions, better support for kinship carers, and a recognition of the specific needs of child 'carers' in this context. In addition, shared inter-agency protocols to improve early identification and intervention and working-together practices across adult and child-care-focused services are emphasized.

Meanwhile, the agenda set by *Hidden Harm* (ACMD 2003) and *Hidden Harm Three Years On* (ACMD 2007) continues to influence child care policy and the government's 'Safeguarding' agenda. *Every Child Matters: Change for Children* (DfES 2004) focuses on more effective inter-agency training, identification, assessment and intervention where parental drug misuse is an issue. It also aims to support integrated working via the introduction of the 'Common Assessment Framework' (hereafter CAF), designed to help practitioners assess and respond to needs at an early stage and to place children at the centre of agencies' responses (DfES 2006). Alongside this, the Social Exclusion Task Force's review *Families at Risk* (Cabinet Office 2006) and *The Children's Plan: Building Brighter Futures* (DCSF 2007) raise broader considerations about the difficulties caused for children when families experience multiple social problems with their associated disadvantages – very much characteristic of the research population featured in this study. By the same token, the *Care Matters* implementation plan for children in care (DCSF 2008) emphasizes the vulnerability of children of drug-misusing parents and highlights the responsibility of corporate parents to listen to the wishes and feelings of children as well as to provide consistent support. Significantly, it underlines the needs of children 'on the edge of care' specifically as a consequence of parental substance misuse, which has prompted the establishment of the new Family Drug and Alcohol Court in London, referred to earlier.

About the study

The main aim of the study was to explore interventions for families where there was parental drug misuse in order to inform policy and develop good practice that would meet the needs of this vulnerable group more effectively. It was undertaken from March 2006 to March 2008, in collaboration with the local children and young people's service (formerly social services and hereafter referred to as CYPS), in a large, mainly rural area in the south-west of England, with an ethnic minority population of under 10 per cent. This chapter focuses on data from in-depth interviews with three groups of people: forty-two children and young people with drug-misusing parents, aged between 4 and 20 years (average age: 12.6 years); forty drug-misusing parents (and seven grandparents); and sixty health and social care professionals from voluntary and statutory sector drug services, statutory child care and primary health care. We also conducted a series of multi-professional focus groups.

Our research population was largely composed of white, working-class, socially disadvantaged single parents with longstanding, entrenched patterns of class A drug use (heroin, crack cocaine, cocaine). Use of benzodiazepines, amphetamines, cannabis and alcohol was also common. Most had also experienced or were currently struggling with a range of other problems (mental health, alcohol misuse, domestic violence, separation, loss). This was also an almost exclusively 'clinical' sample where the majority were in contact with either drug services, statutory child protection services or both. By the same token, the sample of children and young people was largely drawn from the families themselves or from agencies and many had experiences of the 'looked after' system. Findings cannot, therefore, be generalized to the wider population but may be representative of this specific group and of the population identified in the Drug Strategy as of most concern. Our group of professionals also reflected the ethnic population of the research area.

All interviews and focus groups were digitally audio-taped, transcribed verbatim and analyzed thematically using 'Framework', a well established method developed by the National Centre for Social Research (Ritchie and Lewis 2005). We then compared findings from the various sources in order to develop a sense of the way in which services were responding – or not – to the expressed needs of young people and parents, as well as the way that professionals were working in this very complex area of social welfare practice.

Key findings

Here we bring together young people's and parents' accounts of interventions and services alongside professionals' views about practice dilemmas. We also identify what respondents felt needed to change in order to meet the needs of families where there is PDM. We have chosen to focus on family members' general experiences of professionals, although there is a significant emphasis on the CYPS personnel, for obvious reasons. It is also important to stress, once again, that, by the time intervention took place, a crisis had generally been reached. The atmosphere of secrecy and denial that permeates families where there is PDM engendered high levels of fear and anxiety in all family members when a professional came into view.

Equally significant was the emotional landscape against which intervention took place, with young people's data reflecting the long shadow cast by the emotional and physical impact of parental drug misuse and its consequences. They were in no doubt that using drugs and caring for children did not mix and that drugs came first and were more important than they were. Although many of these young people were 'getting by', this often came at a price. Some, however, were not really getting by at all.

By the same token, parents' reflections on their own troubled histories and the aetiology of their substance problems highlighted the impact of adverse family experiences on them and on their children, with significant implications for parenting capacity and high levels of unmet need. It is significant that the vast majority of those interviewed had themselves grown up with parents with drug and/or alcohol problems and had experienced traumatic childhoods.

Exploring interventions: assessing and responding to need

Young people's experiences of statutory child care intervention, in the majority of cases, suggested that too little was offered too late, not enough was done to help families stay together – 'We wanted them to help our mums, not take them away from us' ('Tia', 16) – and, equally problematically, some children were not rescued early enough. They felt that developing any kind of trusting, fruitful relationship with professionals was hampered by frequent changes of personnel, who were often unreliable and inconsistent or appeared powerless to help. 'They just left . . . kept moving on . . . they think it doesn't affect children but it does . . . if you are going to be a social worker make sure you are committed' ('April', 17).

When children were removed, they thought that contact was rarely managed well and their attachment to parents was not appreciated. They also felt that some foster carers appeared ill equipped to deal with young people who were unused to rules and boundaries or actually being children. What they appreciated were workers who listened, tried to understand, helped the whole family and were reliable, kind and made them feel cared about.

For parents, it was apparent that both CYPS and drug service interventions often failed to address the complex roots of drug misuse, seeing only a 'drug problem', generally interpreted as the cause of current difficulties rather than a symptom of those in the past: 'Solve the problems in the life and the drugs will drop off – follows naturally!' ('Annabel', parent). This suggests a trend in which people are identified by 'problem' rather than seen in the round, despite evidence that makes a clear link between troubled histories, parenting capacity and child welfare, increasingly reflected in policy (DH 2000; DCSF 2007, 2008). Intervention seemed to be most successful and effective during pregnancy and the postnatal period, where motivation was also likely to be high, and tended to be multi-professional and led by a specialist PDM midwife. For some, the threat of children's removal was also effective. However, for many, interventions had a 'feast or famine' quality, with abrupt termination of support once recovery or drug management had been achieved. Ironically, however, for most parents, this was the beginning rather than the end of what they saw as a longer process, involving forging a new identity, major lifestyle changes and dealing with 'what's in here [points to heart]' ('Rosie', parent).

This research confirmed that reaching and responding to this group of families and children was extremely problematic. Professionals highlighted a variety of dilemmas including the often longstanding nature of the problem, the chaotic nature of both the use and the accompanying lifestyle, and the tendency of drug-misusing communities in rural locations to 'close ranks', contributing to the invisibility of children. Engaging parents sufficiently to obtain a clear picture of what they were using and how, together with high levels of denial, was also a major obstacle to effective working. Although many adult services were using more holistic approaches and recognized the need for better working relationships with child care agencies, visibility of children remained an issue. Despite the provision of a small number of dedicated and well regarded children's services, there was an urgent need for more therapeutic intervention in both rural and urban areas; provision was rarely forthcoming unless or until the child developed significant problems or was seen to be at risk.

Inter-agency working

From the professionals' point of view, the main difficulties were caused by varying thresholds for intervention between services, confusion about confidentiality, the interpretation of both protocols and the definition of 'significant harm', and insufficient assessments of the impact on children: 'There has to be a better balance between client confidentiality and the ability to make a decision on the child's behalf' (social worker). Multi-agency forums to discuss specific families were seen as particularly valuable, as was multi-agency training which assisted networking across disciplines. Multi-agency and joint working initiatives were also seen to be effective and the model of intervention with pregnant drug misusers was acknowledged as a template for good practice, transferable to other age groups of children.

A central finding, reflecting other recent research (Cleaver *et al.* 2007), was the need to free professionals to share information before the 'significant harm' threshold had been reached in a way that would lead to a more realistic assessment of children's circumstances: 'The big challenge is when it's *not* child protection' (GP); 'Sharing information if it's not section 47 [significant harm] or child protection . . . I don't think CYPS have resolved it. They don't know what constitutes child protection and what doesn't' (social work manager).

Despite the development of a variety of protocols, professionals were consistently inhibited from identifying children earlier by the complexity surrounding decisions about when information could be shared. Professionals almost universally acknowledged that far more had to be done for children at the 'child in need' stage. The extent to which the *Framework for the Assessment of Children in Need and their Families* (DH 2000) addressed the needs of children of drug-misusing parents (DMPs) was questioned and, whilst the introduction of the CAF was seen by some to encourage earlier intervention, others queried the extent to which it would provide a more robust system of identification and reach this particular group of vulnerable children. 'There is a clear lack of a model . . . or interaction that would improve outcomes for children. We need a definite model to target this population' (doctor).

A number of key principles for good practice emerged from professionals' focus group discussions, based on the central importance of identifying 'hidden harm' in all its complexity. These included viewing children of DMPs as 'children in need' as a presumption, consistent with Scottish protocols (Scottish Executive 2003), alongside ensuring that children remain 'visible' and are placed at the centre of decision-making. Establishing local, inter-agency, family-focused discussion forums, more open information sharing and inter-professional communication at the pre-child protection stage and greater clarity about confidentiality and information sharing were also highlighted as critical areas to address. Professionals across disciplines also advocated developing supportive but more assertive and direct methods in order to reach isolated and 'hidden' children, together with particular approaches for 'hard to reach families' within a rural dimension. Using successful, multi-professional pregnancy pathways as templates for children across the developmental spectrum was also seen as an important principle, as were joint visits by child care and drugs workers and a family focus as standard practice.

In relation to 'working together' practices, parents also felt that this was most effective when there was a lead professional with specialist knowledge of drug misuse, such as a health visitor, midwife or family support worker who was 'twin trained' and who orchestrated the network, reducing the need for repeating information – 'I don't have to keep repeating myself!' The main difficulties seen by parents seemed to be caused by professionals' failure to communicate either with one another or with the parent concerned.

Barriers to intervention

These findings highlighted the fact that, ironically, some of the greatest barriers to intervention were presented by the parents and young people themselves, who often made it very difficult for professionals to gain access to them. This tended to be linked to fears about the consequences of disclosure, particularly where social workers were concerned. The negative image of social workers as 'child snatchers', shared by all but a minority, was a major obstacle and was recognized as such by social workers themselves and by the professionals' network: 'They hate us' (social worker).

Although many young people were desperate for someone to notice what was happening at home, most said they could not or would not tell anyone about the impact of their parents' drug use: 'I tended to push people away who tried to help – dunno why' ('Lea', 14). Their main piece of advice to other young people, however, was 'tell someone!' On the one hand they wanted someone to know about what they were going through, without

198 Brynna Kroll and Andy Taylor

actually having to tell anyone explicitly. On the other, they often made it clear that disclosure and its consequences were too risky and, in any event, it was pointless asking professionals for help. As a result, attempts by workers to engage them often met with resistance. This emphasizes the considerable challenges posed by troubled, hard-to-reach young people whose anger with their circumstances becomes focused on the agencies designed to support them. It may also reflect the considerable pressure created by the culture of denial and secrecy so often characteristic of families where there is parental drug misuse (Kroll 2004).

Most parents were also ambivalent about getting help and it was clear that giving up drugs presented enormous challenges, where chasms threatened to open up beneath their feet. There was a sense that what they said they wanted and what they really wanted were at odds and that whatever they received would never be enough to deal with the issues they faced. This could perhaps account for the high level of criticism levelled at most of the professionals they encountered. Anxiety about the consequences of disclosure, including removal of children, was often compounded by professionals' perceived attitudes – 'It was a very derogatory help – a very looking down their noses at me help. That's how it felt' ('Bernard', parent); 'we are not lepers!' ('Janie', parent) – and what were perceived as threatening and punitive approaches. This was often coupled with what appeared to parents to be a lack of understanding about what drug use was about and the timescale for its management. Motivation to access help was also easily undermined by lengthy waits for rehab, detox and statutory and voluntary agency appointments.

Professionals also identified critical barriers to intervention – 'The agenda being presented is very different from the real agenda' (doctor); 'Assessment is affected by the difficulty of seeing beneath the surface' (health visitor); 'You think people are being honest but . . . I don't think you ever get a clear picture' (social worker). This had obvious implications for information sharing. In addition to the difficulties of penetrating rural communities, this was seen as an elusive group with complex problems and needs. Identifying what parents actually wanted, particularly from drug services, was an issue, as was working with the cycle of relapse and recovery. Lack of timely access to rehab and detox services, often hampered by complex funding arrangements, undermined motivation and progress. Social workers, in particular, felt that intervention was adversely affected by their crisis-oriented brief and the difficulties of overcoming their negative image.

Meeting the needs of children, young people and parents: what needs to change?

> Something I'd really like is someone to see me about this . . . I want someone to stop my mum and dad smoking [heroin] then I might be able to live with them.
>
> ('Rhondin', 7)

> [What's needed is] . . . some sort of team of special social workers or even existing social workers [who] change the way they do things so they *actually* come around and they just spend an hour or so with kids . . .
>
> ('Alexander', 16)

What all family members sought was a more concerted engagement with one key professional where trust could be established, albeit within some clear parameters where statutory powers were acknowledged. This was clearly crucial in facilitating disclosure about both drug use and the impact of history and complex personal circumstances.

Parents and young people also indicated that many of the social workers they encountered appeared to lack empathy, understanding or the capacity to listen or to hear, and thus seriously undermined the potential for establishing trust and rapport, so crucial for effective intervention – a finding reflected in other research (Forrester *et al.* 2008): 'When people aren't listening to you, you suddenly fall apart . . .' ('Haddie', parent). This seemed linked to both the tensions inherent in the statutory role as well as the increasingly bureaucratic approach to service delivery in statutory child welfare services.

What the data challenged was the assumption that, once the drug problem is solved, support is no longer required. What parents told us, however, as suggested earlier, was that, rather than being the end of the matter, this signalled the beginning of another more complex process – 'That's when the real work begins . . . it's no use . . . leaving them in their lives as they know it' ('Mary', parent). Most critically, from the child's point of view and underlined forcefully by the parents' data, this does not mean that the capacity to re-connect with children on an emotional level is restored. Post-recovery support, then, was a critical area to address.

Young people, parents and professionals were broadly agreed about the issues that needed to be addressed in relation to interventions for families where there was drug misuse. First, there were a number of barriers to overcome. These related to entering drug treatment (fears of child protection proceedings, stigma, and lack of child care either at home or at agencies), with faster and easier access to services required, especially for people in rural areas with limited transport (with implications for rural clinics and joint agency outreach). Tackling negative perceptions of social workers was identified by all as critical, if obstacles to disclosure and engagement for both young people and parents were to be overcome, together with avoiding frequent changes of worker. It was also crucial to reducing stigma and labelling for families in rural locations where 'visibility' is high.

In terms of service provision, better communication was required between agencies and professionals who needed to be trained more effectively in the area of PDM and its impact. 'Twin trained' workers were much appreciated and most agreed that numbers should be increased. Intervention should come sooner rather than later, with help for the whole family not just the 'user' and an awareness of the importance of post-recovery support. Much more help was needed for children of drug-using parents, including the development of specialist child-centred services. If children were removed, better training for foster carers to manage contact, appreciate parent/child bonds and increase placement stability was essential, and resources for kinship carers were also required.

Discussion: from rhetoric to reality

Although the government's ten-year Drug Strategy focuses on the need to respond more effectively where there is problematic parental drug misuse, particularly in relation to children, findings from this study suggest that a number of challenges will need to be overcome to achieve this. To what extent are the strategy's initiatives likely to succeed in the light of this research?

The families involved in our study fitted the profile of the strategy's target group, in relation to parental histories and patterns and type of drug misuse. They also highlighted the problems of achieving significant change in long-term users, providing appropriate treatment where there is co-morbidity, or support for multiple problems, and the need for both preventative and long-term and intensive interventions in order to prevent 'inter-generational harm' and support recovery (HM Government 2008: 24).

The strategy's aim 'that the needs of the children and families of drug users are given a greater priority' is to be achieved by 'a new package for families' supported by DCSF initiatives (HM Government 2008: 6). Whilst such aspirations seem admirable, our findings suggest that they may not sufficiently address the particular challenges to achieving such change, given the problems presented by this group of families and the way that services both are currently configured and work together.

First, adopting a family focus and identifying and engaging children is far more problematic than is acknowledged. The intense parental suspicion, resistance and ambivalence – often shared by children – that we encountered in our study were typical rather than exceptional responses, as a result of the contingencies of longstanding misuse, the accompanying family dynamics and negative experiences of services. Getting parents and their children to acknowledge what is happening and accept help, then, requires particular skills and strategies to foster trust and engagement that go beyond rhetoric and simply providing 'a new package'. Our findings also suggest that it seems particularly difficult to keep the child at the centre of the work, as numerous inquiries have made clear (Laming 2003).

These points have a number of implications. First, all professionals, including those in contact with children in non-specialist roles, need to have greater knowledge of the likely processes and barriers they will encounter and the appropriate training and skills to respond to them. This includes communicating with children. Second, the findings suggest the importance of *models* of intervention developed at agency level (as opposed to separate or distinct individual 'initiatives') which engage hard-to-reach families and combine assertiveness with support. The development and mainstreaming of more holistic approaches evolving from the synergy created by shared working and expertise amongst child- and adult-focused practitioners needs to be fostered and supported if this is to become a reality.

The findings also suggested that the current operation of the CYPS significantly undermined the potential for earlier identification and engagement. This was due to the way the service was perceived by parents and children (often unfairly) and a system of intervention too predicated on children being 'at risk' rather than 'in need'. Children were only likely to receive a service if there were child protection concerns, affecting both the focus and the style of the intervention offered. This in turn reinforced parents' and children's fears and fantasies, resulting in a vicious circle characterized by confrontation, avoidance and increased confrontation, and leaving the main statutory child protection agency with massive barriers to overcome. Tackling the adverse perception of child protection social workers is critical if key aspects of the strategy are to succeed.

By the same token, whilst the Drug Strategy comments on the need for better information-sharing arrangements as a way of reaching children sooner, these findings suggest that significant progress is unlikely unless the obstacles to this are faced more squarely. These include the cultural history and climate of inter-professional collaboration together with unresolved differences and dilemmas within the professional system in relation to confidentiality and the potential conflicts between children's needs and parents' rights. In our view, the combination of these factors significantly restricts the potential for earlier identification and assessment, leaving vulnerable children at increased risk. Certain types of inter-agency working were also seen to either increase or reduce parents' anxieties, children's fears and the potential to engage with family issues.

As other commentators have suggested (Cleaver *et al.* 2007; Scottish Executive 2007), whilst information sharing appeared more effective once the child protection stage had been reached, there was a lack of clarity about what should happen prior to that point. In our study it was face-to-face contact between professionals' groups, and well organized multi-agency meetings and forums (such as pregnancy pathways), that mitigated this problem, as information could be shared more openly at an earlier stage. This suggests the need not just for greater clarity between professional groups at a local level but for more guidance at national level about when information can be shared.

Although the development of shared inter-agency protocols where there are child welfare concerns provides good templates for this (Scottish Executive 2003, 2007), our study also suggests that these cannot work in isolation and need to be underpinned by a culture of good working relationships across services rather than being dependent on individual initiatives. Although the CAF was seen by some to encourage better identification and early multi-agency assessment, the extent to which it would be able to respond to children of DMPs was perceived as debatable, particularly as need was unlikely to be matched with resources – a concern shared by other commentators (Gilligan and Manby 2008).

The 'new package of support for families' referred to earlier will draw on what has been learnt so far from a range of pilot programmes and initiatives providing support for all the family. However our findings indicate that such initiatives tend to be very localized and vulnerable to cuts in funding and have yet to be translated into established approaches and embedded in mainstream services (in comparison with models in the adult treatment sector such as motivational interviewing).

It is also clear that there is an urgent need for an expansion of services for children at an earlier point of need, not just at the more acute 'child at risk' stage, nor only triggered as a result of children's extreme behaviour – surely a marker that early preventative services are either scarce or ineffective. Based on what children and young people say about living with parental drug misuse, and underlined by professionals' concerns, it is clear that they are almost inevitably 'children in need' and should be seen as such, as a matter of course. This has obvious implications for adequate support and intervention and for service configuration across child welfare and drug treatment agencies, if we are serious about responding purposefully to the needs of this vulnerable group of families.

These findings suggest that, whilst the Drug Strategy robustly identifies the issues that need to be tackled, it underestimates the challenges involved if the aspirations of the *Hidden Harm* agenda are to be achieved within the next generation.

Acknowledgements

We would like to thank the children, young people and parents who found the courage to talk to us about their often difficult and painful experiences. We would also like to thank the small but dedicated group of professionals who brokered access to the families concerned, and to all those from across the health and social care spectrum who gave their time to be interviewed and participated in focus groups.

17 Evidence and new policy questions

Susanne MacGregor

Overview of findings on drug treatment and care

Around 200,000 people are now receiving some treatment and care from the drug treatment system and the treatment workforce numbers about 9,000. Treatment usually provided today in a range of services is complex. Interventions available include care-planned prescribing, community detoxification, low threshold prescribing and Tier 2 interventions, and treatment for both drugs and alcohol misuse. Services range widely in size, and similarly there is a wide range in the size of caseloads. The overwhelming majority of services seem to have embraced case management principles and this approach is becoming more embedded and refined over time. In terms of performance, there is a significant 'agency effect' and the most important influence on engagement with treatment seems similarly to be the character of the treatment agency itself. Different kinds of agencies see people with different needs and, broadly speaking, these needs match the declared role of the agency. About half of these service users are reported to have children and a high proportion are in receipt of state benefits.

The conclusion seems also to be that 'treatment works' in that clear improvements in outcome measures six months after treatment have been described. Improvement does not however necessarily mean abstinence – the majority were still taking some drugs, illicit or prescribed. Patients who remain in treatment benefit from it but only a minority succeed in attaining complete abstinence quickly. Evidence supports arguments about drug use being a chronic relapsing condition and that motivation to change develops slowly over time (Gossop 2007). Services have to keep trying and have to be willing to take people back. Drug treatment is however cost-effective since, although health and social costs increase by virtue of providing care, there can be reductions in the use of the criminal justice system whose costs far outweigh those of health and social services. There is a case for improving the quality of therapy and improving training. Involving the patient or service user in decisions about their treatment seems also to be of benefit. It is important to establish a good relationship between practitioner and service user, ensuring consistency of care and helping to develop trust.

Key factors affecting take-up of treatment are age, referral source, previous experience of treatment and the agency attended. Those who drop out are most likely to be younger, homeless and not injecting. The needs of certain sub-groups remain inadequately met, including some IDUs (injecting drug users), some users of other drugs such as cannabis, some people who do not fit the 'junkie' image, people with complex needs, particularly with co-morbid mental illnesses, the children and families of substance misusers and members of BME (black and minority ethnic) communities. The implication is that a wider range of services is required, more adaptable to client needs and expectations. This set of conclusions presents quite a challenge to services and to practitioners. A change in the culture of drug treatment services might make a difference. A more active approach to drug treatment might be an answer, raising expectations about what can be achieved and making more demands on service users. Still, it is worth noting that service users have generally expressed some satisfaction with the services they have received, but stigma continues to impact on the way services are delivered and on attitudes and behaviours at different agencies.

Severe poly-drug use is the norm in the drug treatment service population and misuse of alcohol a common complication. Complex needs require sophisticated interventions. While there has been an expansion of care and treatment in dedicated drug treatment services since 2003, this is not the case with shared care. There is a need to pay more attention to treatment and care in the wider community, including general practice. Care plans need to pay attention not just to substitute prescribing but also to offering interventions which take into account mental health needs and the needs of the children and families of drug misusers. One of the major gaps in service provision highlighted in this collection is the lack of services for the children of drug-misusing parents. A striking and consistent fact emerging from a number of studies of users of drug treatment services is that about half are parents. This challenges the out-of-date image of the single, migrant, homeless, heroin user which grew from earlier experience and studies. As drug-taking has become more widespread, the characteristics of drug misusers have changed – although to some extent this reflects also belated recognition of an important set of needs. It would require a change in service configuration, policy and practice to deal with this major issue.

The chapters in this volume suggest a need to mainstream the issue of substance misuse more widely as it is a complicating factor affecting a range of services – recognition of and response to it cannot be confined to dedicated drug treatment services, given the increased numbers and wide range of needs exposed. Other hospital services, such as those for mentally ill patients, Accident & Emergency and general surgery and medicine, all have to take into account the substance use of their patients (including excessive use of alcohol and tobacco). Services in the community, especially general practice and children and young people's services, are all affected and the burden of care is increasing. This draws attention to the need for an expansion of training both in basic courses and through continuing professional development and more support for community-based and non-statutory services.

The need is thus for a wider range of services than those which have been developed so far, including those support services which help to prevent relapse, maintain stability and overcome the barriers to social integration so prevalent in the employment and housing fields.

Continuity and change in drugs strategies

The chapters in this collection demonstrate that the New Labour government which came to power in 1997 adopted and built upon much of the previous Conservative policy with regard to drugs (MacGregor 2006a, 2006b). But the new administration added its own distinctive aspects and, importantly, stressed the role of coercion into treatment and increased expenditure on services and on related research. Core features of the underlying philosophy were optimism about the benefits of improved management and about the possibility of personal change and reintegration. No one would be written off even if this meant some coercion and offering tough choices. The 'new paternalism' which underlies New Labour social policy extended into drugs policy also (MacGregor 1998: 255).

Overall assessments of the impact of the Ten Year Strategy have concluded, 'much done much still to do' – the motto used by Labour to describe its policies in general – 'while we have made a great deal of progress more remains to be done', announced the new drugs strategy (HM Government 2008: 10). The government's own assessment of its achievements was that there had been reductions in drug-related harm and drug-related crime and increased treatment provision, with increasing numbers of offenders referred into treatment from the criminal justice system (HM Government 2008: 8). The Public Service Agreement (PSA) target to direct 1,000 drug-misusing offenders into treatment each week had been largely achieved (HM Government 2008: 9). More people were now receiving treatment, with the number in contact with treatment services increasing from 85,000 in 1998 to 195,000 by 2006/7. Three-quarters of new entrants to treatment were now retained in treatment for twelve weeks or more, the government claimed (HM Government 2008: 28). Waiting times had been reduced. There was in addition a new qualifications framework and suite of occupational standards for drugs treatment workers.

The Drug Interventions Programme (DIP) in particular was seen as playing an important part. Local multi-agency drug teams (Criminal Justice Integrated Teams – CJITs) aim to provide a seamless service and adopt a case management approach. Over £600 million was invested in DIP between 2003 and 2008. A reduction in offending is one of the key aims of DIP and it was claimed that around half of drug misusers who came into contact with the programme showed a 79 per cent decline in offending. DIP's target had been to get 1,000 drug-misusing offenders into treatment each week via the criminal justice system by March 2008: this target was achieved two months early. Since January 2008 more than 4,000 people a month were now entering treatment (DIP newsletter, July 2008, Central Office of Information).

A 2007 review conducted for UKDPC concluded that where UK drug policy has made its most valuable contribution has been in reducing the damage and harms to individuals and communities caused by problem drug use. This overview pointed out that the number of dependent heroin users increased from around 5,000 in 1975 to about 281,000 in England in 2007, with over 50,000 in Scotland. The authors agreed with the government that the bulk of drug-related harm (death, illness, crime and other social problems) occurs among the relatively small number of people who become dependent on class A drugs, notably heroin and cocaine. The review noted the large and unparalleled increase in expenditure on treatment services. It agreed that the number of dependent drug users entering treatment had increased and observed that the majority of this treatment involved the prescription of heroin substitute drugs, mostly methadone. It noted the continuing problem of Hepatitis C among injecting drug users and concluded that future policy should focus on expansion and innovation in treatment and harm reduction services (Reuter and Stevens 2007).

In November 2007, however, the drugs treatment lobby was challenged when the BBC Home Affairs Editor, Mark Easton, publicised the fact that only 3 per cent of patients 'recover' from addiction. This was largely true in the sense that only this proportion emerged from treatment 'drug-free' in 2006 (Ashton 2008). This excluded of course the numbers who continued to 'use drugs' in that they were being prescribed substitutes like methadone as part of a package aimed at stabilising them and occasionally or often would top these up with other illegally acquired drugs. If these were included as 'successes' of treatment then the system would appear to be doing better. Reflecting these concerns, the 2008 strategy admitted that 'too many drug users relapse, do not complete treatment programmes, or stay in treatment too long before re-establishing their lives . . . while we have been successful at fast tracking people into treatment, we need to focus more upon treatment outcomes'. There are no instant solutions, the strategy said, but the aim would be 'that those who do use drugs not only enter treatment but complete it and re-establish their lives'.

The 2008 strategy also set out in some distinctively new directions to 'focus more on families, addressing the needs of parents and children as individuals as well as working with whole families to prevent drug use, reduce risk and get people into treatment' (HM Government 2008: 5). It would aim to ensure 'that children's social services know about drug using parents where children are at risk'. It was admitted that the impact of parental drug use had previously been underestimated – it would now become a priority to identify children and families at risk from substance misuse and provide appropriate interventions.

Significantly, it needed to be made clear that 'drug users have a responsibility to engage in treatment in return for the help and support available'. The priority for treatment would continue to be those causing most harm to communities and families, and policy continued to be to get offenders, and parents whose drug use may put their children at risk, into effective treatment quickly (HM Government 2008). A variety of interventions are appropriate, it was acknowledged, from abstinence-based treatment for some to drug replacement over time for others, and innovative treatments, including injectable heroin and methadone, could be used where they have been proven to work and reduce crime. The impact of the resources spent on treatment would be maximised by better targeting and tailoring of interventions and supporting users to move on from treatment and reintegrate into communities (HM Government 2008: 11). In future, new treatment approaches would be piloted, including use of contingency management and prescription of injectable heroin or methadone.

Another important innovation was that policy would ensure that the benefits system supports the new focus on reintegration and personalisation. At a minimum, drug misusers on out-of-work benefits would have to attend a discussion with an appropriate specialist treatment provider. Links would be encouraged between agencies so that benefit-claiming drug users could be referred to specialist services. [There was a possible implication that these changes might reduce the sums available for treatment services conventionally defined, since the strategy proposed allowing the Pooled Treatment Budget to be used alongside other funding streams to provide advice on reintegration support and case management (HM Government 2008: 31).]

New PSA targets for 2008–11 would be measured by indicators. PSA25 was to reduce the harm caused by alcohol and drugs: with regard to drugs, success would be measured by the number of drug users recorded as being in effective treatment; the rate of drug-related offending; and the percentage of the public who perceive drug use or dealing to be a problem in their area. PSA14 – to increase the number of children and young people on the path to success – would be measured by the proportion of young people frequently using illicit drugs, alcohol or volatile substances (HM Government 2008: 12). There would be a cross-government programme of research and pilot programmes in support of the new strategy.

Drugs strategies and related social policies

The new drugs strategy, as in other areas of current social policy, continues to expand on the principles of the new paternalism and the new public health – choice and market solutions for the majority, coercion for the outsider minorities (Peterson and Lupton 1996; Mead 1997; MacGregor 1998). The 2008 drugs strategy emphasises that 'drug users have a responsibility to engage in treatment in return for the help and support available' and that 'in return for benefit payments, claimants will have a responsibility to move successfully through treatment and into employment' (HM Government 2008: 6). Of the 330,000 people currently defined as Problematic Drug Users (PDUs) in

England, two-thirds are said to be on benefits and half are in drug treatment. The aim now is to use the benefit system to identify PDUs and get them into treatment. The Department of Health will be funding a network of drug coordinators in JobCentre Plus offices to link drug treatment with employment support (NTA website, accessed 21 August 2008). This work is being led by the Department for Work and Pensions (DWP) which has a national UK remit and the Department of Health which has responsibility for the treatment element of the new approach in England only. This means that in Scotland, which has devolved powers in health, agreement will have to be secured between the DWP and Scottish Health Ministers. Sanctions which might apply could involve a two-week benefit cut for failure to turn up for treatment, and after a third offence loss of benefit for twenty-six weeks. This element in the new Drug Strategy has been criticised as a blot on what is otherwise an encouraging document.

Rights and responsibility are central to the new thinking in drugs policy, as they have been in social policy since the Third Way was articulated in the mid-1990s and expanded on further by advisers at the Prime Minister's Strategy Unit (Halpern *et al.* 2004). The Green Paper on the future of welfare (DWP 2008), published on 21 July 2008, and the ensuing White Paper aim to create a system that rewards responsibility, and both emphasise that no one will be 'written off'. A new benefit has replaced the former income support and incapacity benefit. This is called Employment and Support Allowance (ESA) and was introduced in October 2008. All new 'customers' receiving ESA will be required to undertake general work-related activity. (This benefit will be available only to those who have worked for around six months and paid contributions.) The severely disabled will not be expected to take part in work-related activity and the medical certification system will be overhauled to help implement this with a Work Capability Assessment at the core. Important to our discussion here, drug users receiving benefit will be required to undergo treatment to overcome their addiction and get back to work. Those identified as having problems with crack cocaine and opiates (specifically) would be required to take action to stabilise their drug habit and to take steps towards employment in return for receiving benefits. Failure to undertake general 'work-related activity' would lead to benefit being reduced. Writing in the *Health Services Journal*, on 14 August 2008, Paul Hayes, Chief Executive at the NTA, denied that the government intends to force drug users into treatment. He said that the NTA had been closely involved in advising the DWP on the Green Paper and that the aim was to get more drug users into treatment and get drug users in treatment into jobs. The aim was to remove barriers to work. However, since this was written, the onset of economic recession must raise doubts about how likely this will be.

The value of these policies is seen to be in making people more self-sufficient, removing them from out-of-work benefits and thus reducing the cost to the Exchequer. Support from the state is only available to those who accept responsibility to work because paid employment is seen as of short- and long-term benefit to the individual and to the overall economy. Work programmes run by private and voluntary providers will form part of the activities required of those who find it difficult to move quickly into a job. Private, public and voluntary sector providers delivering back-to-work support would be rewarded from the benefit expenditure they save.

The chapters in this collection provide a lot of evidence that many problem drug users are very unhealthy, often related partly to heavy tobacco smoking, and would not be fit for work. They also have well above average mental and physical health problems, as well as other social problems, with personality disorder, depression and anxiety figuring as important components in this complexity, something which can be difficult to treat and manage and whose implications seem insufficiently recognised in current policy proposals.

Raistrick and colleagues found that, in the majority of the drug treatment agencies in their study, less than half of these service users were in receipt of state benefit. So it is possible to combine drug-taking with other means of generating income. A study conducted for the DWP by Hay and Bauld (2008) estimated that in 2006 there were approximately 267,000 PDUs accessing the main DWP benefits in England. (This was drawn from DTORS data which counted 80 per cent of their sample as on main benefits.) Claimants were most commonly in receipt of Income Support (44 per cent) with smaller proportions receiving Incapacity Benefit (26 per cent) or Job Seekers Allowance (20 per cent). This represented about 6 or 7 per cent of all individuals accessing such benefits.

The most likely impact of the more challenging schemes being talked about in these welfare reform proposals is that some will indeed benefit while others will disappear and find other ways of surviving: how desirable this might be in the long term for them, their families and the wider society is debatable. As Neale and colleagues have pointed out (Chapter 8), keeping to the demands of employers is not a simple matter for IDUs. Remaining employable was hard for them when they had so many other appointments to keep. This emerged in other chapters too: being a PDU is a very time-consuming business. Once in the 'system', they found they had to try to keep appointments all over the place, across town and country, at the doctor, the clinic, the benefit office, with the social worker, the probation officer, the housing office, perhaps attending court, taking children to school, collecting them. Especially if you are poor and have to rely on infrequent bus services, this can take up a lot of time and employers are unlikely to be relaxed about such behaviour and time-keeping.

One concern of commentators is that in future treatment services will be tied not only as they have been in recent years to the criminal justice system but also to the welfare to work system. Decisions about treatment and care will be influenced not only by evidence and good practice guidelines emerging from the medical and other professions and from within the Department of Health, but also from managers and budget holders in the Home Office, DWP and Department for Children, Schools and Families. Of course the principles of joined-up working have encouraged this, from *Tackling Drugs Together* in 1995 to the new drugs strategy in 2008, so this is not new. But a clash of priorities may become more likely if the core principles and priorities of each department diverge. The formal role of the National Treatment Agency (NTA) is to promote and monitor the effective commissioning of high quality drug services and to progress against particular policy priorities set by and agreed with government, including achievement against the PSA. This surely requires considerable skill in negotiating to get the best budget and the best system for clients and staff. The role of the NTA and of local commissioners is likely to be even more important in future.

Breaking the consensus?

Since autumn 2007 there has been a renewed debate on drug treatment, focusing on the abstinence record of the English treatment services, while at the same time in Scotland a similar controversy raged. The debate was sparked by the BBC's Mark Easton, followed up by a substantial article by Mike Ashton, Editor of *Drug and Alcohol Findings*, in *Druglink* (Ashton 2008), numerous entries on Mark Easton's blog (http://www.bbc.co.uk/blogs/ thereporters/markeaston) and discussions at meetings organised by the NTA, Conference Consortium and DrugScope among others. The key issues identified in these exchanges focused on the question of what is meant by 'effective treatment' – how can the success and quality of treatment best be measured? What do service users themselves want? Many pointed out that this is not a new debate but one which explodes periodically. Why has this debate arisen again? The main explanation seems to be that with current constraints on public expenditure, there is more questioning of whether drug treatment costs are delivering the results claimed for them. Most thoughtful commentators involved in these discussions concluded that a range of approaches are needed on a continuum from harm reduction to abstinence: there are a variety of needs and different people have different needs at different times.

The Scottish drugs strategy is linked to the SNP Administration's first Budget, which was passed with Conservative support amid reports that a deal had been done to end 'over-reliance' on methadone and give more focus to abstinence. However, shortly afterwards the Community Safety Minister moved to defuse criticism from supporters of methadone programmes and underlined the need for a range of treatment options. The main aim of the Scottish strategy would be recovery, and abstinence would be one facet of that. While worrying about 'over reliance on methadone', he said, 'this is not, and cannot be, at the expense of measures to reduce harm' (quoted in *SDF Bulletin*, February 2008: 2).

The findings presented in Metrebian and colleagues' chapter (Chapter 9) help to illuminate some of these issues. They found that methadone accounts for the majority of prescriptions written currently in drug treatment services, and these are overwhelmingly not for injectables. Only a tiny proportion of prescriptions are currently for heroin. Their attempt to conduct a trial of injectable methadone treatment was difficult because it was hard to recruit sufficient numbers of opiate-dependent drug users given the strict eligibility criteria they used. This indicates that the proportion of the current treatment population who might be suitable for treatment by prescription of injectables is only around one in ten. The majority of the people presenting for treatment at the sites in their study wanted to receive oral methadone detoxification. These authors observe that injectable opiate treatment is now being considered as an option but that we still do not know if it is more effective than oral maintenance treatment, nor how it should best be delivered. Findings from current and future research may help to answer these questions.

Beyond the specific questions of improvements to the drugs treatment system lie larger issues relating to the whole tenor of drugs policy. Some see harm reduction as equivalent to calls for legalisation and others see discussion of abstinence as tantamount to support for prohibition. These dichotomies over-simplify the issues. However, there are important questions around the criminalisation of drug use. Signs of a growing questioning of this premise in policy began to emerge and were encapsulated in a report to the UKDPC (McSweeney *et al.* 2008). Following up on this, a blog contribution from a former government adviser, Julian Critchley, exposed the issues. He wrote:

> Several years ago I was Director of the UK Anti-Drug Coordination Unit in the Cabinet Office . . . [this was when Keith Hellawell was Drugs Czar] . . . it became apparent to me that available evidence pointed very clearly to the fact that enforcement and supply side interventions were largely pointless. . . . In the Spending Review that we undertook we did successfully manage to reallocate resources towards treatment programmes but even then I had misgivings about the effectiveness of those programmes . . . what harms society is the illegality of drugs and all the costs associated with that . . . ultimately people will make choices which harm themselves, whether that involves their diet, smoking, drinking, lack of exercise, sexual activity or pursuit of extreme sports . . . what was truly depressing about my time in UKADCU was that the overwhelming majority of professionals I met, including those from the police, the health service, government and voluntary sectors held the same view: the illegality of drugs causes far more problems for society and the individual than it solves. Yet publicly, all those intelligent, knowledgeable people were forced to repeat the nonsensical mantra that the Government would be 'tough on drugs' . . . the tragedy of our drugs policy is that it is dictated by tabloid irrationality, and not by reference to evidence.
>
> (entry 73, 30 July 2008, *Mark Easton blogsite*)

While it is surely not true that all civil servants and professionals are in favour of restricting activities devoted to the reduction of supply and law enforcement, as long as the question of drugs misuse is approached in a sensational and hysterical manner, a reasoned and intelligent debate seems impossible. Yet if greater engagement and participation, and changes in their behaviour, are needed from citizens to achieve better health and social cohesion, then better understanding of science and evidence will be needed and more respect for the views of those professionals, practitioners and public servants active in the middle layers of society. What is required is a better informed civic society to counter the current simplification of social questions arising from the dominant politics–media axis.

The Drugs Misuse Research Initiative was set within the context of the Ten Year Strategy and expected to contribute to it. Its two phases reflect developments and changing priorities over these years. But such periodisation is somewhat unreal in the worlds of policy and practice. Many of the research questions and methods built on evidence accumulated before this time and the findings will contribute to developments over the next ten years. Policy development is a complex process and research evidence is just one of the influences on what happens. However, all the contributors to this volume adhere to the precepts of the evidence-based movement in health care and have written their chapters to contribute to ongoing discussions among policy communities and more widely in the hope that better evidence will lead to improvements in social provision and thus in the health and wellbeing of the population, especially those most closely affected by drug misuse. However, it is also acknowledged that there is a limit to what treatment services alone can deliver. Contributions from the wider society are also needed if substantial impact on this social problem is to be achieved. As well as arguing for a rebalancing from punishment to treatment, research evidence demonstrates the need for much greater attention to prevention, which would require addressing wider cultural values, which together with poverty, deprivation and inequality, underlie poor health and certain forms of criminality.

References

Aas, K.F. (2005) *Sentencing in the Age of Information: From Faust to MacIntosh*, London: Glasshouse Press.

Abou-Saleh, M.T. (2004) 'Psychopharmacology of substance misuse and comorbid psychiatric disorders', *Acta Neuropsychiatrica*, 16: 19–25.

ACMD (Advisory Council on the Misuse of Drugs) (1982) *Treatment and Rehabilitation*, London: Home Office.

—— (1988) *AIDS and Drug Misuse, Part One*, London: HMSO.

—— (1989) *AIDS and Drug Misuse, Part Two*, London: HMSO.

—— (1991) *Drug Misuse and the Criminal Justice System, Part One: Community Resources and the Probation Service*, London: HMSO.

—— (1993) *AIDS and Drug Misuse – Update*, London: HMSO.

—— (1994) *Drug Misusers and the Criminal Justice System, Part Two: Police, Drug Misusers and the Community*, London: HMSO.

—— (1996) *Drug Misusers and the Criminal Justice System, Part Three: Drug Misusers and the Prison System – an Integrated Approach*, London: HMSO.

—— (2003) *Hidden Harm: Responding to the Needs of Children of Problem Drug Users*, London: Home Office.

—— (2005) *Further Consideration of the Classification of Cannabis under the Misuse of Drugs Act 1971*, London: Home Office.

—— (2006) *Pathways to Problems*, London: Home Office.

—— (2007) *Hidden Harm Three Years On: Realities, Challenges and Opportunities*, London: Home Office.

—— (2008) *Cannabis: Classification and Public Health*, London: Home Office.

Addenbrooke, W.M. and Rathod, N.H. (1990) 'Relationship between waiting time and retention in treatment amongst substance misusers', *Drug and Alcohol Dependence*, 26(3): 255–264.

ADFAM (2001) *Engaging Experts*, London: ADFAM.

Amato, C., Minozzi, S., Davoli, M., Vecchi, S., Ferri, M. and Mayet, S. (2007) *Psychosocial and Pharmacological Treatments versus Pharmacological Treatments for Opioid Detoxification*, Cochrane Database of Systematic Reviews, 4.

Ames, B.N. and Gold, L.S. (1997) 'The causes and prevention of cancer: gaining perspective', *Environmental Health Perspectives*, 105 (supplement 4): 865–873.

Amos, A., Wiltshire, S., Bostock, Y., Haw, S. and McNeill, A. (2004) ' "You can't go without a fag . . . you need it for your hash" – a qualitative exploration of smoking, cannabis and young people', *Addiction*, 99: 77–81.

Andreasson, S., Allebeck, P., Engstrom, A. and Rydberg, U. (1987) 'Cannabis and schizophrenia. A longitudinal study of Swedish conscripts', *Lancet*, 2: 1483–1486.

Appleby, L., Shaw, J., Amos, T. *et al.* (1999a) 'Suicide within 12 months of contact with mental health services: national clinical survey', *British Medical Journal*, 318: 1235–1239.

Appleby, L., Shaw, J., Amos, T. *et al.* (1999b) *Safer Services – Report of the National Confidential Inquiry into Suicide and Homicide by People with Mental Illness*, London: Department of Health.

Arnull, E., Eagle, S., Patel, S.L. and Gammampila, A. (2007) *An Evaluation of the Crack Treatment Delivery Model*, London: NTA.

Arseneault, L., Cannon, M., Poulton, R., Murray, R., Caspi, A. and Moffit, T.E. (2002) 'Cannabis use in adolescence and risk for adult psychosis: longitudinal prospective study', *British Medical Journal*, 325: 1212–1213.

Arseneault, L., Cannon, M., Witton, J. and Murray, R.M. (2004) 'Causal association between cannabis and psychosis: examination of the evidence', *British Journal of Psychiatry*, 184: 110–117.

Åsberg, M., Montgomery, S., Perris, C. *et al.* (1978) 'A Comprehensive Psychopathological Rating Scale', *Acta Psychiatrica Scandinavica*, 271(suppl.): 5–27.

Ashton, M. (2008) 'The new abstentionists', *Druglink*, Special insert, December/January: 1–16.

Atkinson, R. and Flint, J. (2001) *Accessing Hidden and Hard-to-Reach Populations: Snowball Research Strategies. Social Research Update Issue 33*, Guildford: University of Surrey.

Audit Commission (2002) *Changing Habits: The Commissioning and Management of Community Drug Treatment Services for Adults*, London: Audit Commission.

Avants, S.K., Margolin, A., Sindelar, J.L., Rounsaville, B.J., Schottenfield, R., Stine, S., Cooney, N.L., Rosenheck, R.A., Shou-Hua, L. and Kosten, T.R. (1999) 'Day treatment versus enhanced standard methadone services for opioid dependent patients: a comparison of clinical efficacy and cost', *American Journal of Psychiatry*, 156: 27–33.

Baer, J.S., Ball, S., Campbell, B.K., Miele, G.M., Schoener, E.P. and Tracey, K. (2007) 'Training and fidelity monitoring of behavioral interventions in multi-site addiction research', *Drug and Alcohol Dependence*, 87: 107–118.

Ball, S., Martino, S., Corvino, J., Morgenstern, J. and Carroll, K. (2002) *Independent Tape Rater Guide: Manual for Rating Therapist Adherence and Competence for the NIDA Clinical Trials Network Protocols 4 and 5*, Washington: NIDA.

Bammer, G., Dobler-Mikola, A., Fleming, P.M., Strang, J. and Uchtenhagen, A. (1999) 'The heroin prescribing debate: integrating science and politics', *Science*, 284: 1277–1278.

Bancroft, A., Wilson, S., Cunningham-Burley, S., Backett-Milburn, K. and Masters, H. (2004) *Parental Drug and Alcohol Misuse: Resilience and Transition among Young People*, York: Joseph Rowntree Foundation.

Banerjee, S., Clancy, C. and Crome, I. (eds) (2002) *Co-existing Problems of Mental Disorder and Substance Misuse (Dual Diagnosis): An Information Manual*, London: The Royal College of Psychiatrists' Research Unit.

Banton, P.M., Dhillon, H., Johnson, M.R.D. and Subhra, G. (2005) *Alcohol Issues and the South Asian and African Caribbean Communities: Improving Education, Research and Service Development. A Report Commissioned by the Alcohol Education Research Council*, London: AERC.

Barnard, M. (2007) *Drug Addiction and Families*, London: Jessica Kingsley Publishers.

Barnard, M. and McKeganey, N. (2004) 'The impact of parental drug use on children: what is the problem and what can be done to help?', *Addiction*, 99: 552–559.

Barnes, M. and Wistow, G. (1994) 'Achieving a strategy for user involvement in community care', *Health and Social Care in the Community*, 2: 347–356.

Barrowclough, C., Haddock, G., Tarrier, N. *et al.* (2001) 'Randomized controlled trial of motivational interviewing, cognitive behavior therapy, and family intervention for patients with comorbid schizophrenia and substance use disorders', *American Journal of Psychiatry*, 158: 1706–1713.

Barrowclough, C., Haddock, G., Tarrier, N. *et al.* (2003) 'Cognitive-behavioural therapy and motivational intervention for schizophrenia and substance misuse: 18-month outcomes of a randomized controlled trial', *British Journal of Psychiatry*, 183: 418–426.

Barrowclough, C., Haddock, G., Fitzimmons, M. *et al.* (2006) 'Treatment development for psychosis and co-occurring substance misuse: a descriptive review', *Journal of Mental Health*, 15: 619–632.

Barton, A. (1999) 'Sentenced to treatment: criminal justice orders and the health service', *Critical Social Policy*, 19(4): 463–483.

Barton, A. and Quinn, C. (2002) 'Risk management of groups or respect for the individual? Issues for information sharing and confidentiality in Drug Treatment and Testing Orders', *Drugs: Education, Prevention and Policy*, 9(1): 35–43.

Bates, E. (1983) *Health Systems and Public Scrutiny: Australia, Britain and the United States*, London: Croom Helm.

Bates, T., Buchanan, J., Corby, B. and Young, L. (1999) *Drug Use, Parenting and Child Protection: Towards an Effective Interagency Response*, Liverpool: University of Central Lancashire.

Battersby, M., Farrell, M., Gossop, M., Robson, P. and Strang, J. (1992) 'Horse trading – prescribing injectable opiates to opiate addicts. A descriptive study', *Drug and Alcohol Review*, 11: 35–42.

Bean, P. (2004) *Drugs and Crime*, Cullompton: Willan Publishing.

Beck, A.T., Wright, F.D., Newman, C.F. and Liese, B.S. (1993) *Cognitive Therapy of Substance Abuse*, New York: Guilford.

Becker, J. and Duffy, C. (2002) *Women Drug Users and Drugs Service Provision: Service Level Responses to Engagement and Retention*, London: Drugs Prevention Advisory Service, Home Office.

Belenko, S., Patapis, N. and French, M.T. (2005) *Economic Benefits of Drug Treatment: A Critical Review of the Evidence for Policy Makers*, Treatment Research Institute at the University of Pennsylvania.

Bell, J., Caplehorn, J.R.M. and McNeil, D.R. (1994) 'The effect of intake procedures on performance in methadone maintenance', *Addiction*, 89: 463–471.

Berridge, V. (1990) 'Drug research in Britain: the relation between research and policy', in V. Berridge (ed.), *Drug Research and Policy in Britain*, Aldershot: Avebury.

—— (1999) *Opium and the People: Opiate Use and Drug Control in Nineteenth and Early Twentieth Century England*, London: Free Association Books.

Bertakis, K.D., Azari, R., Callahan, E.J. and Robbins, J.A. (2000) 'Gender differences in the utilization of health care services', *Journal of Family Practice*, 49: 147–152.

Best, D. (2004) 'Delivering better treatment: what works and why?' *NTA National Conference*, London: NTA.

Best, D., Noble, A., Ridge, G., Gossop, M., Farrell, M. and Strang, J. (2002) 'The relative impact of waiting time and treatment entry on drug and alcohol use', *Addiction Biology*, 7(1): 67–74.

Beynon, C., Bellis, M. and McVeigh, J. (2006) *Trends in Drop Out, Drug Free Discharge and Rates of Re-presentation: A Retrospective Cohort Study of Drug Treatment Clients in the North West of England*, Liverpool: Liverpool John Moores University.

Bird, M. (2006) 'Presentation: services for stimulant users', *Conference of the Federation of Drug and Alcohol Professionals*, London, 8 November 2006.

Boardman, A.P., Hodgson, R.E., Lewis, M. *et al.* (1997) 'Social indicators and the prediction of psychiatric admission in different diagnostic groups', *British Journal of Psychiatry*, 171: 457–462.

Boreham, R., Cronberg, A., Dollin, L. and Pudney, S. (2007) *The Arrestee Survey 2003–2006*, Home Office Statistical Bulletin 12/07, London: Home Office.

Brooner, R.K., King, V.L., Kidorf, M. *et al.* (1997) 'Psychiatric and substance misuse co-morbidity among treatment-seeking opioid abusers', *Archives of General Psychiatry*, 54: 71–80.

Brown, B.S., Hickey, J.E., Chung, A.S., Craig, R.D. and Jaffe, J.H. (1989) 'The functioning of individuals on a drug abuse treatment waiting list', *American Journal of Drug and Alcohol Abuse*, 15(3): 261–274.

Budd, T., Collier, P., Mhlanga, B., Sharp, C. and Weir, G. (2005) *Levels of Self-report Offending and Drug Use Among Offenders: Findings from the Criminality Surveys*, Home Office Online Report 18/05, London: Home Office.

Burney, E. (2005) *Making People Behave: Anti-social Behaviour Politics and Policy*, Cullompton: Willan Publishing.

Burns, T., Creed, F., Fahy, T. *et al.* (1999) 'Intensive versus standard case management for severe psychotic illness: a randomized trial', *Lancet*, 353: 2185–2189.

Burrows, J., Clarke, A., Davison, T., Tarling, R. and Webb, S. (2000) *The Nature and Effectiveness of Drugs Throughcare for Released Prisoners*, Home Office Research Findings 109, London: Home Office.

Butler, S. (1996) 'Substance misuse and the social work ethos', *Journal of Substance Misuse*, 1(3): 149–154.

Cabinet Office (1999) *Modernising Government*, Cmnd 4310, London: Cabinet Office.

—— (2006) *Reaching Out: Think Family: Analysis and Themes from the 'Families at Risk' Review*, London: Social Exclusion Task Force. Available at http://www.cabinetoffice.gov.uk/social exclusion task force/families at risk

Campbell, R., Starkey, F., Holliday, J., Audrey, S., Bloor, M., Parry-Langdon, N., Hughes, R. and Moore, L. (2008) 'An informal school-based peer-led intervention for smoking prevention in adolescence (ASSIST): a cluster randomized trial', *Lancet*, 371: 1595–1602.

Carey, M.P., Carey, K. and Meisler, A.W. (1991) 'Psychiatric symptoms in mentally ill chemical abusers', *Journal of Nervous and Mental Disease*, 179: 136–138.

Carnwath, T. (2003) 'Viewpoint – Not such a bad treatment after all', *Journal of Substance Use*, 8: 7–8.

Carpenter, W. (2003) 'Foreword', in R.M. Murray, P.B. Jones, E. Susser, J. Van Os and M. Cannon (eds), *The Epidemiology of Schizophrenia*, Cambridge: Cambridge University Press, pp. xv–xvi.

Carr, C.J.A., Xu, J., Redko, C., Lane, D.T., Rapp, R.C., Goris, J. and Carlson, R.G.

(2008) 'Individual and system influences on waiting time for substance abuse treatment', *Journal of Substance Abuse Treatment*, 34: 192–201.

Carroll, K.M. (1997) 'Integrating psychotherapy and pharmacotherapy to improve drug abuse outcomes', *Addictive Behaviours*, 22(2): 233–245.

—— (1998a) *Therapy Manuals for Drug Addiction: A Cognitive Behavioural Approach – Treating Cocaine Addiction, Exhibit 14: CBT Rating Scale*, Rockville, MD: National Institute on Drug Abuse.

—— (1998b) *Therapy Manuals for Drug Addiction: A Cognitive Behavioural Approach – Treating Cocaine Addiction, Exhibit 13: CBT Therapist Checklist*, Rockville, MD: National Institute on Drug Abuse.

Carroll, K.M. and Rounsaville, B.J. (1992) 'Contrast of treatment-seeking and untreated cocaine abusers', *Archives of General Psychiatry*, 49: 464–471.

Carroll, K., Kadden, R.M., Donovan, D.M., Zweben, A. and Rounsaville, B.J. (1994) 'Implementing treatment and protecting the validity of the independent variable in treatment matching studies', *Journal of Studies on Alcohol*, 12: 149–155.

Carroll, K., Nich, C., Sirfry, R.L., Nuro, K.F., Frankforter, T.L., Ball, S., Fenton, L. and Rounsaville, B.J. (2000) 'A general system for evaluating therapist adherence and competence in psychotherapy research in the addictions', *Drug and Alcohol Dependence*, 57: 225–238.

Cartwright, A., Hyams, G. and Spratley, T. (1996) 'Is the interviewer's therapeutic commitment an important factor in determining whether alcoholic clients engage in treatment?' *Addiction Research and Theory*, 4(3): 215–230.

Chakrapani, V., Velayudham, J., Michael, S. and Shanmugam, M. (2008) *Barriers to Free Antiretroviral Treatment Access for Injecting Drug Users in Chennai, India*, Chennai: Indian Network for People Living with HIV and AIDS (INP+).

Chambers, R.A., Sajdyk, T.J., Conroy, S.K. *et al.* (2006) 'Neonatal amygdala lesions: co-occurring impact on social/fear-related behavior and cocaine sensitization in adult rats', *Behavioral Neuroscience*, 121(6).

Checkoway, B., Thomas, B., O'Rourke, T.W. and Bull, D. (1984) 'Correlates of consumer participation in health planning agencies: findings and implications from a national survey', *Policy Studies Review*, 3: 296–310.

Cleaver, H., Unell, I. and Aldgate, J. (1999) *Children's Needs, Parenting Capacity: The Impact of Parental Mental Illness, Problem Alcohol and Drug Use and Domestic Violence on Children's Development*, London: Stationery Office.

Cleaver, H., Nicholson, D., Tarr, S. and Cleaver, D. (2007) *Child Protection, Domestic Violence and Parental Substance Misuse*, London: Jessica Kingsley.

Coid, J., Yang, M., Tyrer, P., Roberts, A. and Ullrich, S. (2006) 'Prevalence and correlates of personality disorder in Great Britain', *British Journal of Psychiatry*, 188: 423–431.

Collison, M. (1993) 'Punishing drugs: criminal justice and drug use', *British Journal of Criminology*, 33(3): 382–399.

Commission for Healthcare Audit and Inspection (2006) *Improving Services for Substance Misuse: A Joint Review*, London: CHAI.

Connock, M., Juarez-Garcia, A., Jowett, S., Frew, E., Liu, Z., Taylor, R.J., Fry-Smith, A., Day, E., Lintzeris, N., Roberts, T., Burls, A. and Taylor, R.S. (2007) 'Methadone and buprenorphine for the management of opioid dependence: a systematic review and economic evaluation', *Health Technology Assessment*, 11(9).

Conservative Party (2007) *Ending the Costs of Social Breakdown*, Social Justice Policy

Group, Chairman Rt Hon Iain Duncan Smith MP, July, London: Conservative Party.

Copeland, J. (1997) 'A qualitative study of barriers to formal treatment among women who self manage change in addictive behaviours', *Journal of Substance Abuse Treatment*, 14: 183–190.

Copello, A., Orford, J., Velleman, R., Templeton, L. and Krishnan, M. (2000a) 'Methods for reducing alcohol and drug related family harm in non-specialist settings', *Journal of Mental Health*, 9: 319–333.

Copello, A., Templeton, L., Krishnan, M., Orford, J. and Velleman, R. (2000b) 'A treatment package to improve primary care services for relatives of people with alcohol and drug problems', *Addiction Research*, 8: 471–484.

Copello, A., Orford, J., Hodgson, R., Tober, G. and Barrett, C. on behalf of the UKATT Research Team (2002) 'Social Behaviour and Network Therapy: basic principles and early experiences', *Addictive Behaviours*, 27: 345–366.

Copello, A., Williamson, E., Orford, J. and Day, E. (2006) 'Implementing and evaluating Social Behaviour and Network Therapy in drug treatment practice in the UK: a feasibility study', *Addictive Behaviours*, 31: 802–810.

Copello, A., Templeton, L., Velleman, R., Orford, J., Patel, A., Moore, L., Macleod, J. and Godfrey, C. (2009) 'The relative efficacy of two primary care brief interventions for family members affected by the addictive problem of a close relative: a randomized trial', *Addiction*, 104: 49–58.

Coulter, A. (2002) 'Involving patients: representation or representativeness?' *Health Expectations*, 5: 1.

Coupland, H. and Maher, L. (2005) 'Clients or colleagues? Reflections on the process of participatory action research with young injecting drug users', *International Journal of Drug Policy*, 16: 191–198.

Coyle, D., Godfrey, C., Hardman, G. and Raistrick, D. (1997) 'Costing substance misuse services', *Addiction*, 92(8): 1007–1015.

Crawford, M., Rutter, D., Manley, C., Bhui, K., Weaver, T., Fulop, N. and Tyrer, P. (2002) 'Systematic review of involving patients in the planning and development of health care', *British Medical Journal*, 325: 1263–1265.

Crawford, M.J., Aldridge, T., Bhui, K., Rutter, D., Manley, C., Weaver, T. and Tyrer, P. (2003) 'User involvement in the planning and delivery of mental health services: a cross-sectional survey of service users and providers', *Acta Psychiatrica Scandinavica*, 107: 410–414.

Crawford, M.J., Rutter, D. and Thelwall, S. (2004) *User Involvement in Change Management: A Review of the Literature*, London: NHS Service Delivery and Organisation Research and Development.

Crawford, V. and Crome, I. (2001) *Co-existing Problems of Mental Health and Substance Misuse (Dual Diagnosis): A Review of Relevant Literature*, London: Royal College of Psychiatrists.

Crome, I.B. (1999) 'Substance misuse and psychiatric comorbidity: towards improved service provision', *Drugs: Education, Prevention and Policy*, 6: 151–174.

Croudace, T.J., Kayne, R., Jones, P.B. and Harrison, G.L. (2000) 'Non-linear relationship between an index of social deprivation, psychiatric admission prevalence and the incidence of psychosis', *Psychological Medicine*, 30: 177–185.

Dale-Perera, A. (2005) 'What is the treatment effectiveness strategy?' Launch of NTA Treatment Effectiveness Strategy, July.

Dalrymple, T. (2006) *Romancing Opiates: Pharmacological Lies and the Addiction Bureaucracy*, London: Encounter Books.

Darby, A. (2006) 'Under the same roof', *Community Care*, 17–23 August: 32–33.

Davey Smith, G. and Ebrahim, S. (2002) 'Data dredging, bias or confounding', *British Medical Journal*, 325: 1437–1438.

—— (2003) ' "Mendelian randomisation": can genetic epidemiology contribute to understanding environmental determinants of disease?' *International Journal of Epidemiology*, 32: 1–22.

Davey Smith, G. and Phillips, A. (1990) 'Declaring independence: why we should be cautious', *Journal of Epidemiology and Community Health*, 44: 257–258.

—— (1992) 'Confounding in epidemiological studies: why "independent" effects may not be all they seem', *British Medical Journal*, 305: 757–759.

Davies, P. (2004) 'Is evidence based government possible?' *Jerry Lee Lecture, 2004, 4th Annual Campbell Collaboration Colloquium*, Washington, DC.

Daykin, N., Evans, D., Petsoulas, C. and Sayers, A. (2007) 'Evaluating the impact of patient and public involvement initiatives on UK health services: a systematic review', *Evidence and Policy: A Journal of Research*, 3: 47–65.

Deck, D. and Carlson, M.J. (2004) 'Access to publicly funded methadone maintenance treatment in two western states', *Journal of Behavioral Health Services and Research*, 31: 164–177.

Degenhardt, L. and Hall, W. (2006) 'Is cannabis use a contributory cause of psychosis?' *Canadian Journal of Psychiatry*, 51: 556–565.

Degenhardt, L., Hall, W. and Lynskey, M. (2003) 'Testing hypotheses about the relationship between cannabis use and psychosis', *Drug and Alcohol Dependence*, 71: 37–48.

DeLeon, G. and Jainchill, N. (1986) 'Circumstances, motivation, readiness and suitability', *Journal of Psychoactive Drugs*, 18: 203–208.

Dennis, M.L., Ingram, P.W., Burks, M.E. and Rachal, J.V. (1994) 'Effectiveness of streamlined admission to methadone treatment: a simplified time-series analysis', *Journal of Psychoactive Drugs*, 26(2): 207–216.

DCSF (Department for Children, Schools and Families) (2007) *The Children's Plan: Building Brighter Futures*, London: Stationery Office.

—— (2008) *Care Matters: Time to Deliver for Children in Care: An Implementation Plan*, London. Available at http://www.teachernet.gov.uk/publications

Department of Health, Scottish Home and Health Department and Welsh Office (1991) *Drug Misuse and Dependence: Guidelines on Clinical Management*, London: HMSO.

DfES (Department for Education and Skills) (2004) *Every Child Matters: Change for Children. Young People and Drugs*. Available at www.everychildmatters.gov.uk

—— (2005) *Government Response to Hidden Harm: The Report of an Inquiry by the Advisory Council on the Misuse of Drugs*, London: HMSO.

—— (2006) *The Common Assessment Framework for Children and Young People: Practitioners' Guide*, London: DES. Available at http://www.everychildmatters. gov.uk

DH (Department of Health) (1995) *Building Bridges*, London: HMSO.

—— (1996) *Task Force to Review Services for Drug Misusers: Report of an Independent Review of Drug Treatment Services in England* (Chairman: the Reverend Dr John Polkinghorne), London: HMSO.

—— (1997) *Purchasing Effective Treatment and Care for Drug Misusers. Guidance for Health Authorities and Social Services Departments*, London: Department of Health.

—— (1998a) *Modernising Mental Health Services*, London: Department of Health.

—— (1998b) *Our Healthier Nation*, London: HMSO.

—— (1999a) *Drug Misuse and Dependence: Guidelines on Clinical Management*, London: Department of Health.

—— (1999b) *A National Service Framework for Mental Health: Modern Standards and Service Models*, London: Department of Health.

—— (2000) *Framework for the Assessment of Children in Need and Their Families*, London: Stationery Office.

—— (2001) *Mental Health Policy Implementation Guide*, London: Department of Health.

—— (2002) *Mental Health Policy Implementation Guide: Dual Diagnosis Good Practice Guide*, London: Department of Health.

—— (2007) *Drug Misuse and Dependence: UK Guidelines on Clinical Management*, London: Department of Health and the devolved administrations.

DHSS (Department of Health and Social Security) (1984) *Guidelines of Good Clinical Practice in the Treatment of Drug Misuse*, London: DHSS.

Digiusto, E. and Treloar, C. (2007) 'Equity of access to treatment, and barriers to treatment for illicit drug use in Australia', *Addiction*, 102: 958–969.

Donmall, M., Watson, A., Millar, T. and Dunn, G. (2005) *Outcome of Waiting Lists (OWL) Study. Waiting Times for Drug Treatment: Effects on Uptake and Immediate Outcomes*, London: NTA.

Donovan, D.M., Rosengren, D.B., Downey, L., Cox, G.B. and Sloan, K.L. (2001) 'Attrition prevention with individuals awaiting publicly funded drug treatment', *Addiction*, 96(8): 1149–1160.

Dorn, N. and South, N. (1994) 'The power behind practice: drug control and harm minimisation in inter-agency and criminal law contexts', in J. Strang and M. Gossop (eds), *Heroin Addiction and Drug Policy: The British System*, Oxford: Oxford University Press.

Downes, D. (1988) 'The sociology of crime and social control in Britain 1960–1987', in P. Rock (ed.), *A History of British Criminology*, Oxford: Clarendon Press.

Drake, R.E., Mercer-McFadden, C., Mueser, K.T. *et al.* (1998) 'Review of integrated mental health and substance abuse treatment for patients with dual disorders', *Schizophrenia Bulletin*, 24: 589–608.

Driessen, M., Veltrup, C., Weber, J. *et al.* (1998) 'Psychiatric co-morbidity, suicidal behaviour and suicidal ideation in alcoholics seeking treatment', *Addiction*, 93: 889–894.

DrugScope (2008) 'Drug strategy: can the government deliver?' Press release, 27 February, London: DrugScope.

Drumm, R.D., McBride, D.C., Metsch, L., Page, J.B., Dickerson, K. and Jones, B. (2003) ' "The rock always comes first": drug users' accounts about using formal health care', *Journal of Psychoactive Drugs*, 35: 461–469.

Drummond, D.C., Kouimtsidis, C., Reynolds, M., Russell, I., Godfrey, C., McCusker, M., Coulton, S., Parrott, S., Davis, P., Tarrier, N., Turkington, D., Sell, L., Williams, H., Abou-Saleh, M.T., Ghodse, A.H. and Porter, S. (2004) *The Effectiveness and Cost Effectiveness of Cognitive Behaviour Therapy for Opiate Misusers in Methadone Maintenance Treatment: A Multi-centre Randomized Controlled Trial*

(UKCBTMM). *Final Report to the Department of Health*, London: St George's Hospital Medical School.

Duke, K. (2003) *Drugs, Prisons and Policy-making*, London: Palgrave Macmillan.

—— (2006) 'Out of crime and into treatment? The criminalization of contemporary drug policy since Tackling Drugs Together', *Drugs: Education, Prevention and Policy*, 13(5): 409–415.

Duke, K., MacGregor, S. and Smith, L. (1996) *Activating Local Networks: A Comparison of Two Community Development Approaches to Drug Prevention*, Paper 10, London: Home Office Drugs Prevention Initiative.

Duke, P.J., Pantelis, C., McPhillips, M.A. and Barnes, T.R.E. (2001) 'Comorbid substance misuse among people with schizophrenia in the community: an epidemiological study in central London', *British Journal of Psychiatry*, 179: 501–513.

Duncan, S. (2005) 'Towards evidence inspired policy', *Social Sciences*, 61: 10–11.

Dündar, Y., Boland, A., Strobl, J., Dodd, S. *et al.* (2004) 'Newer hypnotic drugs for the short-term management of insomnia: a systematic review and economic evaluation', *Health Technology Assessment*, 8: 1–25.

DWP (Department of Work and Pensions) (2008) *No-one Written Off: Reforming Welfare to Reward Responsibility*, Green Paper consultation on future of welfare, London: DWP.

Eaton, G., Morleo, M., Lodwick, A., Bellis, M.A. and McVeigh, J. (2005) *United Kingdom Drug Situation: Annual Report to the European Monitoring Centre for Drugs and Drug Addiction 2005*, London: Department of Health.

Elliott, E. and Watson, A. (1998) *Fit to be a Parent: The Needs of Drug Using Parents in Salford and Trafford*, Manchester: Public Health Research and Resource Centre, University of Salford.

Etherington, K. (2008) *Trauma, Drug Misuse and Transforming Identities*, London: Jessica Kingsley.

EuroQol Group (1990) 'A new facility for the measurement of health-related quality of life', *Health Policy*, 16: 199–208.

Evans, C., Connell, J., Barkham, M., Margison, F., McGrath, G., Mellor-Clark, J. and Audin, K. (2002) 'Towards a standardized brief outcome measure: psychometric properties and utility of the CORE-OM', *British Journal of Psychiatry*, 180: 51–60.

Farabee, D., Prendergast, M. and Anglin, M. (1998) 'The effectiveness of coerced treatment for drug-abusing offenders', *Federal Probation*, 62(1): 3–10.

Farrell, M., Howes, S., Taylor, C., Lewis, G. *et al.* (1998) 'Substance misuse and psychiatric co-morbidity: an overview of the OPCS National Psychiatric Morbidity Survey', *Addictive Behaviours*, 23: 909–918.

Fergusson, D.M., Horwood, L.J. and Swain-Campbell, N.R. (2003) 'Cannabis dependence and psychotic symptoms in young people', *Psychological Medicine*, 33: 15–21.

Fernando, S. (2005) 'Multicultural mental health services: projects for minority ethnic communities in England', *Transcultural Psychiatry*, 42: 420–436.

Ferri, M., Davoli, M. and Perucci, C.A. (2006) 'Heroin maintenance treatment for chronic heroin dependent individuals. A Cochrane systematic review of effectiveness', *Journal of Substance Abuse Treatment*, 30(1): 63–72.

Festinger, D.S., Lamb, R.J., Kountz, M.R., Kirby, K.C. and Marlowe, D. (1995) 'Pretreatment drop-out as a function of treatment delay and client variables', *Addictive Behaviour*, 20(1): 111–115.

Fielding, N.G. and Fielding, J.L. (1986) *Linking Data*, London: Sage.

Fiorentine, R., Nakashima, J. and Anglin, M.D. (1999) 'Client engagement with drug treatment', *Journal of Substance Abuse Treatment*, 17(3): 199–206.

Fischer, B., Rehm, J., Kirst, M., Casas, M., Hall, W., Krausz, M., Metrebian, N. *et al.* (2002) 'Heroin assisted treatment as a response to the public health problem of opiate dependence in established market economics – an overview', *European Journal of Public Health*, 12: 228–234.

Fischer, B., Oviedo-Joekes, E., Blanken, P., Haasen, C., Rehm, J., Schechter, M.T., Strang, J. and van den Brink, W. (2007) 'Heroin-assisted Treatment (HAT) a decade later: a brief update on science and politics', *Journal of Urban Health*, 84(4).

Ford, C. and Ryrie, I. (1999) 'Prescribing injectable methadone in general practice', *International Journal of Drug Policy*, 10: 39–45.

Ford, P. (2003) 'Evaluation of the Dartmouth Assessment of Lifestyle Inventory and the Leeds Dependence Questionnaire for use among detained psychiatric inpatients', *Addiction*, 98: 111–118.

Forrester, D. (2000) 'Parental substance misuse and child protection in a British sample: a survey of children on the child protection register in an inner London district office', *Child Abuse Review*, 9: 235–246.

—— (2004) 'Social work assessments with parents who misuse drugs or alcohol', in R. Phillips (ed.), *Children Exposed to Parental Substance Misuse: Implications for Family Placement*, London: British Association for Adoption and Fostering.

Forrester, D. and Harwin, J. (2006) 'Parental substance misuse and child care social work: findings from the first stage of a study of 100 families', *Child and Family Social Work*, 11: 325–335.

—— (2008) 'Parental substance misuse and child welfare: outcomes for children two years after referral', *British Journal of Social Work*, 38: 1518–1535.

Forrester, D., McCambridge, J., Waissbein, C. and Rollnick, S. (2008) 'How do child and family social workers talk to parents about child welfare concerns?' *Child Abuse Review*, 17: 23–35.

Fountain, J., Strang, J., Griffiths, P., Powis, B. and Gossop, M. (2000) 'Measuring met and unmet need of drug misusers: integration of quantitative and qualitative data', *European Addiction Research*, 6: 97–103.

Fountain, J., Bashford, J. and Winters, M. (2003) *Black and Minority Ethnic Communities in England: A Review of the Literature on Drug Use and Related Service Provision*, London: National Treatment Agency.

Freund, P.D. and Hawkins, D.W. (2004) 'What street people reported about service access and drug treatment', *Journal of Health and Social Policy*, 18: 87–93.

Frisher, M., Norwood, J., Heatlie, H., Millson, D. *et al.* (2000) 'A comparison of trends in problematic drug misuse from two reporting systems', *Journal of Public Health Medicine*, 22: 362–367.

Frisher, M., Anderson, S., Hickman, M. and Heatlie, H. (2002) 'Diffusion of drug misuse in Scotland: findings from the 1993 and 1996 Scottish Crime Surveys', *Addiction Research*, 10: 83–95.

Frisher, M., Crome, I., Macleod, J., Millson, D. and Croft, P. (2005) 'Substance misuse and psychiatric illness: prospective observational study using the general practice research database', *Journal of Epidemiology and Community Health*, 58: 847–850.

Garrett, D. and Foster, J. (2005) 'Fumbling in the dark', *Druglink*, June: 12.

Gerada, C. (2005) 'The GP and the drug misuser in the new NHS: a new "British system" ', in J. Strang and M. Gossop (eds), *Heroin Addiction and the British System, Vol. 2: Treatment and Policy Responses*, London: Routledge.

Gerada, C. and Tighe, J. (1999) 'A review of shared care protocols for the treatment of problem drug use in England, Scotland and Wales', *British Journal of General Practice*, 439: 125–126.

Gilligan, P. and Manby, M. (2008) 'The Common Assessment Framework: does the reality match the rhetoric?' *Child and Family Social Work*, 1: 177–187.

GLADA (Greater London Alcohol and Drug Alliance) (2005) *Lessons Learned; Some Approaches, Tools and Good Practice for Improving Drug User Involvement*, London: GLADA.

Goddard, E. and Green, H. (2005) *Smoking and Drinking among Adults, 2004*, London: National Statistics.

Godfrey, C., Stewart, D. and Gossop, M. (2004) 'Economic analysis of costs and consequences of the treatment of drug misuse: 2-year outcome data from the National Treatment Outcome Research Study (NTORS)', *Addiction*, 99(6): 697–707.

Gooden, T. (1999) *Carers and Parents of African Caribbean and Asian Substance Users in Nottingham: A Needs Analysis, A Report Prepared for Nottingham Black Drugs Initiative, Organisational Change Innovation Development (ORCHID)*, Nottingham: ORCHID.

Gossop, M. (2006) *Treating Drug Misuse Problems: Evidence of Effectiveness*, London: National Treatment Agency for Substance Misuse.

—— (2007) *Living with Drugs*, 6th edn, Aldershot: Ashgate.

Gossop, M., Darke, S., Griffiths, P. *et al.* (1995) 'The Severity of Dependence Scale (SDS): psychometric properties of the SDS in English and Australian samples of heroin, cocaine and amphetamine users', *Addiction*, 90: 607–614.

Gossop, M., Marsden, J., Stewart, D., Lehmann, P., Edwards, C., Wilson, A. and Segar, G. (1998) 'Substance use, health and social problems of service users at 54 drug treatment agencies. Intake data from the National Treatment Outcome Research Study', *British Journal of Psychiatry*, 173: 166–171.

Gossop, M., Stewart, D., Browne, N. and Marsden, J. (2003) 'Methadone treatment for opiate dependent patients in general practice and specialist clinic settings: outcomes at 2-year follow-up', *Journal of Substance Abuse Treatment*, 24(4): 313–321.

Gostin, L. (1991) 'Compulsory treatment for drug-dependent persons: justifications for a public health approach to drug dependency', *The Milbank Quarterly*, 69(4): 561–593.

Gray, J.A.M. (2001) *Evidence-based Health Care*, 2nd edn, London: Churchill Livingstone.

Gregg, L., Barrowclough, C. and Haddock, G. (2007) 'Reasons for increased substance use in psychosis', *Clinical Psychology Review*, 27(4): 494–510.

Grund, J.P.C., Blanken, P., Adriaans, N.F.P., Kaplan, C.D., Barendregt, C. and Meeuwsen, M. (1992) 'Reaching the unreached: targeting hidden IDU populations with clean needles via known user groups', *Journal of Psychoactive Drugs*, 24(1): 41–47.

Haasen, C., Verthein, U., Degkwitz, A., Berger, J., Krausz, M. and Naber, N. (2007) 'Heroin-assisted treatment for opioid dependence', *British Journal of Psychiatry*, 191: 55–62.

Hall, W. (1996) 'What have population surveys revealed about substance use disorders and their co-morbidity with other mental disorders?', *Drug and Alcohol Review*, 15(2): 57–170.

—— (1997) 'The role of legal coercion in the treatment of offenders with alcohol and heroin problems', *Australian and New Zealand Journal of Criminology*, 30(2): 103–120.

Hall, W. and Farrell, M. (1997) 'Co-morbidity of mental disorders with substance misuse', *British Journal of Psychiatry*, 171: 4–5.

Hall, W. and Solowij, N. (1998) 'Adverse effects of cannabis', *Lancet*, 352: 1611–1616.

Halpern, D., Bates, C., Beales, G. and Heathfield, A. (2004) *Personal Responsibility and Changing Behaviour: The State of Knowledge and its Implications for Public Policy*, London: HMSO.

Ham, C. and Alberti, K. (2002) 'The medical profession, the public and the government', *British Medical Journal*, 324: 838–842.

Harbin, F. and Murphy, M. (eds) (2000) *Substance Misuse and Child Care: How to Understand, Assist and Intervene when Drugs Affect Parenting*, Lyme Regis: Russell House Publishing.

—— (eds) (2006) *Secret Lives: Growing with Substance: Working with Children and Young People Affected by Familial Substance Misuse*, Lyme Regis: Russell House Publishing.

Harrison, J., Barrow, S. and Creed, F. (1995) 'Social deprivation and psychiatric admission rates among different diagnostic groups', *British Journal of Psychiatry*, 167: 456–462.

Harrison, S. and Mort, M. (1998) 'Which champions, which people: public and user involvement in health care as a technology of legitimation', *Social Policy and Administration*, 32(1): 60–70.

Harrison, S., Dowswell, G. and Milewa, T. (2002) 'Guest editorial: public and user "involvement" in the UK National Health Service', *Health and Social Care in the Community*, 10(2): 63–66.

Hart, D. and Powell, J. (2006) *Adult Drug Problems, Children's Needs: Assessing the Impact of Parental Drug Use – a Toolkit for Practitioners*, London: National Children's Bureau.

Hartnoll, R., Mitcheson, M., Battersby, A. *et al.* (1980) 'Evaluation of heroin maintenance in controlled trials', *Archives of General Psychiatry*, 37: 877–883.

Hay, G. and Bauld, L. (2008) *Population Estimates of Problematic Drug Users Who Access DWP Benefits*, DWP working paper WP 46.

Hay, G., Gannon, M., MacDougall, J., Millar, T., Eastwood, C. and McKeganey, N. (2007) *National and Regional Estimates of the Prevalence of Opiate Use and/or Crack Cocaine Use 2005/6: A Summary of Key Findings*, Home Office Online Report 21/07, London: Home Office.

Hayden, C. (2004) 'Parental substance misuse and child care social work; research in a city social work department in England', *Child Abuse Review*, 13: 18–30.

Haywood, T.W., Kravitz, H.M., Grossman, L.S. *et al.* (1995) 'Predicting the "revolving door" phenomenon among patients with schizophrenic, schizoaffective and affective disorders', *American Journal of Psychiatry*, 152: 856–861.

Heginbotham, C., Carr, J., Hale, R., Walsh, T. and Warren, L. (1994) *Report of the Independent Panel of Inquiry Examining the Case of Michael Buchanan*, London: North West London Mental Health NHS Trust.

Heim, D., Hunter, S.C., Ross, A.J., Bakshi, N., Davies, J.B., Flatley, K.J. and Meer, N. (2004) 'Alcohol consumption, perceptions of community responses and attitudes to service provision: results from a survey of Indian, Chinese and Pakistani young people in Greater Glasgow, Scotland, UK', *Alcohol and Alcoholism*, 39: 220–226.

Henquet, C., Krabbendam, L., Spauwen, J., Kaplan, C., Lieb, R., Wittchen, H. *et al.*

(2005) 'Prospective cohort study of cannabis use, predisposition for psychosis, and psychotic symptoms in young people', *British Medical Journal*, 330: 11–14.

Hickman, M., Sutcliffe, H., Sondhi, A. and Stimson, G. (1997) 'Validation of a regional drug misuse database: implications for policy and surveillance of problem drug use in the UK', *British Medical Journal*, 315: 581.

Hickman, M., Vickerman, P., Macleod, J., Kirkbride, J. and Jones, P.B. (2007) 'Cannabis and schizophrenia: model projections of the impact of the rise in cannabis use on historical and future trends in schizophrenia in England and Wales', *Addiction*, 102: 597–606.

Hildebrandt, E. (1994) 'A model for community involvement in health program development', *Social Science and Medicine*, 39(2): 247–254.

Hill, A.B. (1965) 'The environment and disease: association or causation', *Proceedings of the Royal Society of Medicine*, 58: 295–300.

HM Government (1990) *The National Health Service and Community Care Act*, London: HMSO.

—— (1995) *Tackling Drugs Together: A Strategy for England 1995–1998. Cm 2846*, London: HMSO.

—— (1998) *Tackling Drugs to Build a Better Britain: The Government's Ten Year Strategy for Tackling Drugs Misuse. Cm 3945*, London: Stationery Office.

—— (2002) *Health and Social Care Act 2001*, London: Stationery Office.

—— (2008) *Drugs: Protecting Families and Communities. The 2008 Drug Strategy*, London: Stationery Office.

Hogan, D.M. (1997) *The Social and Psychological Needs of Children of Drug Users: Report on Exploratory Study*, Dublin: Children's Research Centre, University of Dublin (Trinity College).

—— (1998) 'Annotation: the psychological development and welfare of children of opiate and cocaine users: review and research needs', *Journal of Child Psychology and Psychiatry*, 39: 609–619.

Hogan, D. and Higgins, L. (2001) *When Parents Use Drugs: Key Findings from a Study of Children in the Care of Drug-Using Parents*, Dublin: Children's Research Centre, University of Dublin (Trinity College).

Hollowell, J. (1997) 'The general practice research database: quality of morbidity data', *Population Trends*, 87: 36–40.

Home Affairs Select Committee (2002) *The Government's Drug Policy: Is It Working?* Third Report Session 2001–2002 HC 318, London: Stationery Office.

Home Office (2002) *Updated Drug Strategy 2002*, London: Home Office.

—— (2004) *Tackling Drugs: Changing Lives*. Accessed at: http://drugs.homeoffice. gov.uk/communications-and-campaigns/tackling-drugs/

—— (2005) *Offender Management Caseload Statistics 2004. Home Office Statistical Bulletin 17/05*, London: Home Office.

Hough, M. (2002) 'Drug user treatment within a criminal justice context', *Substance Use and Misuse*, 37(8–10): 985–996.

Hough, M., Clancy, A., McSweeney, T. and Turnbull, P. (2003) *The Impact of Drug Treatment and Testing Orders on Offending: Two-year Reconviction Rates*, Research Findings 184, London: Home Office.

Howard, R., Beadle, P. and Maitland, J. (1994) *Across the Divide: Building Community Partnerships to Tackle Drug Misuse*, London: Department of Health.

Humphreys, C., Regan, L., River, D. and Thiara, R.K. (2005) 'Domestic violence and substance use: tackling complexity', *British Journal of Social Work*, 35: 1303–1320.

Hunt, N. and Stevens, A. (2004) 'Whose harm? Harm reduction and the shift to coercion in UK drug policy', *Social Policy and Society*, 3(4): 333–342.

ISDD (1989) *Study of Help-seeking and Service Utilization by Problem Drug Takers*, London: ISDD.

Jacobson, N.S., Roberts, L.J., Berns, S.B. and McClinchey, J.B. (1999) 'Methods for defining and determining the clinical significance of treatment effects: description, application and alternatives', *Journal of Consulting and Clinical Psychology*, 67: 300–307.

Jenkins, R., Bebbington, P., Brugha, T.S. *et al.* (1998) 'British Psychiatric Morbidity Survey', *British Journal of Psychiatry*, 173: 4–7.

Jick, H. (1997) 'A database worth saving', *Lancet*, 350: 1045.

Joe, G.W., Simpson, D.D. and Broome, K.M. (1998) 'Effects of readiness for drug abuse treatment on client retention and assessment of process', *Addiction*, 93(8): 1177–1190.

Johnson, S. (1997) 'Dual diagnosis of severe mental illness and substance misuse: a case for specialist services?' *British Journal of Psychiatry*, 171: 205–208.

Jones, A., Weston, S., Moody, A., Millar, T., Dollin, L., Anderson, T. and Donmall, M. (2007) *The Drug Treatment Outcome Study (DTORS): Baseline Report*, Home Office Research Report 3, London: Home Office.

Kaplan, E. and Meier, P. (1958) 'Non-parametric estimation from incomplete observations', *Journal of the American Statistical Association*, 53: 457–481.

Kearney, P., Levin, E. and Rosen, G. (2000) *Working with Families: Alcohol, Drug and Mental Health Problems*, London: National Institute of Social Work.

Kerr, T., Douglas, D., Peace, W., Pierre, A. and Wood, W. (2001) *Responding to an Emergency: Education Advocacy and Commissioning Care by a Peer Driven Organisation of Drug Users. A Case Study of Vancouver Area Network of Drug Users (VANDA)*, Ontario: Health Canada.

Kessler, R.C., McGonagle, K.A., Zhao, S.Y., Nelson, C.B. *et al.* (1994) 'Lifetime and 12 month prevalence of DSM-III R psychiatric disorders in the United States: results from the National Comorbidity Survey', *Archives of General Psychiatry*, 51: 8–19.

Kokkevi, A. and Hartgers, C. (1995) 'Europe ASI: European adaptation of a multi-dimensional assessment instrument for drug and alcohol dependence', *European Addiction Research*, 1(4): 208–210.

Kouimtsidis, C., Reynolds, M., Drummond, C., Davis, P. and Tarrier, N. (2007) *Cognitive Behavioural Therapy in the Treatment of Addiction: A Treatment Planner for Clinicians*, London: Wiley.

Kraft, M.K., Rothbard, A.B., Hadley, T.R., McLellan, A.T. and Asch, D.A. (1997) 'Are supplementary services provided during methadone maintenance really cost effective?' *American Journal of Psychiatry*, 154: 1214–1219.

Kroll, B. (2004) 'Living with an elephant: growing up with parental substance misuse', *Child and Family Social Work*, 9: 129–140.

—— (2006) 'A family affair? Kinship care and parental substance misuse', *Child and Family Social Work*, 12: 84–93.

Kroll, B. and Taylor, A. (2003) *Parental Substance Misuse and Child Welfare*, London: Jessica Kingsley.

—— (2007a) *Research Review: Parental Substance Misuse, Child Maltreatment and Parenting Capacity*, Community Care. Available at http://www.ccinform. co.uk

—— (2007b) *Research Review: The Impact of Parental Substance Misuse on Children*, Community Care. Available at http://www.ccinform.co.uk

Labour Party (1996) *Breaking the Vicious Circle: Labour's Proposals to Tackle Drug Related Crime*, London: Labour Party.

Laming, H. (2003) *The Victoria Climbie Inquiry: Report of an Inquiry by Lord Laming*, London: Stationery Office.

Lancet (1995) 'Care-management: a disastrous mistake', *Lancet*, 345: 399–401.

Lawlor, D.A., Davey Smith, G. and Ebrahim, S. (2004) 'Commentary: The hormone replacement–coronary heart disease conundrum: is this the death of observational epidemiology?' *International Journal of Epidemiology*, 33: 464–467.

Layder, D. (1998) *Sociological Practice: Linking Theory and Social Research*, London: Sage.

LDAN Senior Managers Group (2008) 'Guideline changes prompt scrutiny of NDTMS', *LDAN News*, August/September: 4.

Lee, M. (1994) 'The probation order: a suitable case for treatment', *Drugs: Education, Prevention and Policy*, 1(2): 121–133.

Leitner, M., Shapland, J. and Wiles, P. (1993) *Drug Usage and Drug Prevention: The Views and Habits of the General Public*, London: HMSO.

Lennane, K.J. (1986) 'Treatment of benzodiazepine dependence', *The Medical Journal of Australia*, 144, 26 May.

Lewis, D. and Bellis, M. (2001) 'General practice or drug clinic for methadone maintenance? A controlled comparison of treatment outcomes', *International Journal of Drug Policy*, 12(1): 81–89.

Ley, A., Jeffery, D.P., McLaren, S. and Siegfried, N. (1999) *Treatment Programmes for People with Both Severe Mental Illness and Substance Misuse (Cochrane Review)*, in *The Cochrane Library* Issue 2, Oxford: Update Software.

Lintzeris, N., Strang, J., Metrebian, N., Byford, S., Hallam, C., Lee, S. and RIOTT Group (2006) 'Methodology for the Randomized Injecting Opioid Treatment Trial (RIOTT): evaluating injectable methadone and heroin treatment versus optimized oral methadone treatment in the UK', *Harm Reduction Journal*, 3: 28.

MacGregor, S. (1998) 'A New Deal for Britain?', in H. Jones and S. MacGregor (eds), *Social Issues and Party Politics*, London: Routledge, pp. 248–272.

—— (2006a) 'Tackling drugs together: ten years on', *Drugs: Education, Prevention and Policy*, 13(5): 393–398.

—— (2006b) ' "Tackling Drugs Together" and the establishment of the principle that "treatment works" ', *Drugs: Education, Prevention and Policy*, 13(5): 399–408.

MacGregor, S., Ettorre, B., Coomber, R., Crosier, A. and Lodge, H. (1991) *Drugs Services in England and the Impact of the Central Funding Initiative*, ISDD Research Monograph Series No. 1, London: Institute for the Study of Drug Dependence.

Macleod, J. (2007) 'Cannabis use and symptom experience amongst people with mental illness: a commentary on Degenhardt *et al.*', *Psychological Medicine*, 22: 1–4.

—— (2008) 'The natural history of cannabis use by young people and the implications of this for health', *Addiction*, 103: 450–451.

Macleod, J., Davey Smith, G., Heslop, P., Metcalfe, C., Carroll, D. and Hart, C. (2002) 'Psychological stress and cardiovascular disease: empirical demonstration of bias in a prospective observational study of Scottish men', *British Medical Journal*, 324: 1247–1251.

Macleod, J., Oakes, R., Copello, A., Crome, I., Egger, M., Hickman, M., Oppenkowski, T., Stokes-Lampard, H. and Davey Smith, G. (2004a) 'The psychosocial sequelae of use of cannabis and other illicit drugs by young people: systematic review of longitudinal, general population studies', *Lancet*, 363: 1579–1588.

Macleod, J., Oakes, R., Oppenkowski, T., Stokes-Lampard, H., Copello, A., Crome, I., Davey Smith, G., Egger, M., Hickman, M. and Judd, A. (2004b) 'How strong is the evidence that illicit drug use by young people is an important cause of psychological or social harm? Methodological and policy implications of a systematic review of longitudinal, general population studies', *Drugs: Education, Policy and Practice*, 11: 281–297.

Macleod, J., Hickman, M., Bowen, E., Alati, R., Tilling, K. and Davey Smith, G. (2008) 'Parental drug use, early adversities, later childhood problems and children's use of tobacco and alcohol at age 10: birth cohort study', *Addiction*, 103: 1731–1743.

MacMaster, S.A. (2005) 'Experiences with, and perceptions of, barriers to substance abuse and HIV services among African American women who use crack cocaine', *Journal of Ethnicity in Substance Abuse*, 4: 53–75.

Magidson, J. and Brandyberry, G. (2001) 'Putting customers in the "wish mode" ', *Harvard Business Review*, 79(8): 26–28.

Maglione, M., Chao, B. and Anglin, M.D. (2000) 'Correlates of outpatient drug treatment drop-out among methamphetamine users', *Journal of Psychoactive Drugs*, 32(2): 221–228.

Maki, P., Veijola, J., Jones, P.B., Murray, G.K., Koponen, H., Tienari, P. *et al.* (2005) 'Predictors of schizophrenia – a review', *British Medical Bulletin*, 73 and 74: 1–15.

March, J.C., Oviedo-Joekes, E., Perea-Milla, E., Carrasco, F. and the PEPSA Team (2006) 'Controlled trial of prescribed heroin in the treatment of opioid addiction', *Journal of Substance Abuse Treatment*, 31: 203–211.

Marlatt, G.A. and Gordon, J. (1985) *Relapse Prevention: Maintenance Strategies for Addictive Behaviors*, New York: Guilford.

Marsch, L.A. (1998) 'The efficacy of methadone maintenance interventions in reducing illicit opiate use, HIV risk behaviour and criminality: a meta-analysis', *Addiction*, 93: 515–532.

Marsden, J., Gossop, G., Stewart, D., Best, D., Farrell, M., Lehmann, P., Edwards, C. and Strang, J. (1998) 'The Maudsley Addiction Profile (MAP): a brief instrument for assessing treatment outcome', *Addiction*, 93: 1857–1867.

Marsden, J., Stewart, D., Gossop, M., Rolfe, A., Bacchus, L., Griffiths, P., Clarke, K. and Strang, J. (2000) 'Assessing client satisfaction with treatment for substance use problems and the development of the Treatment Perceptions Questionnaire', *Addiction Research and Theory*, 8: 455–470.

Marsh, J.C., D'Anino, T.A. and Smith, B.D. (2000) 'Increasing access and providing social services to improve drug abuse treatment for women and children', *Addiction*, 95(8): 1237–1248.

Marshall, M. (1996) 'Case management: a dubious practice', *British Medical Journal*, 312: 523–524.

Marshall, M., Lockwood, A. and Gath, D. (1995) 'Social services case management for long term mental disorders: a randomized controlled trial', *Lancet*, 345: 409–412.

Marshall, M., Gray, A., Lockwood, A. and Green, R. (1998) *Case Management for People with Severe Mental Disorders (Cochrane Review)*, in *The Cochrane Library*, Issue 2, Oxford: Update Software.

Marshall, M., Gray, A., Lockwood, A. and Green, R. (2003) (first published 1996)

Case Management for People with Severe Mental Disorders (Cochrane Review), in *The Cochrane Library*, Issue 3, Oxford: Update Software.

Mattick, R.P., Oliphant, D., Ward, J. and Hall, W. (1998) 'The effectiveness of other opioid replacement therapies: LAAM, heroin, buprenorphine, naltrexone and injectable maintenance', in J. Ward, R.P. Mattick and W. Hall (eds) *Methadone Maintenance Treatment and Other Opioid Replacement Therapies*, Amsterdam: Harwood Academic Publishers.

Maughan, B. and McCarthy, G. (1997) 'Childhood adversities and psychosocial disorders', *British Medical Bulletin*, 53: 156–169.

May, T., Duffy, M., Warburton, H. and Hough, M. (2007) *Policing Cannabis as a Class C Drug: An Arresting Change?* York: Joseph Rowntree Foundation.

McCambridge, J. and Strang, J. (2004) 'The efficacy of single-session motivational interviewing in reducing drug consumption and perceptions of drug-related risk and harm among young people: results from a multi-site cluster randomized trial', *Addiction*, 99: 39–52.

McCollum, E.E. and Trepper, T.S. (1995) ' "Little by little, pulling me through": Women's perceptions of successful drug treatment: a qualitative inquiry', *Journal of Family Psychotherapy*, 6: 63–82.

McCusker, C. and Davies, M. (1996) 'Prescribing drug of choice to illicit heroin users: the experience of a UK community drug team', *Journal of Substance Abuse Treatment*, 13(6): 521–531.

McFarlane, M. and Thomson, A. (1998) 'Asking around: changing a service from the inside – on the inside', *Druglink*, March/April: 18–20.

McGrath, J.J. and Saha, S. (2007) 'Thought experiments on the incidence and prevalence of schizophrenia "under the influence" of cannabis', *Addiction*, 102: 514–551.

McGrath, M. and Grant, G. (1992) 'Supporting needs-led services – implications for planning and management systems', *Journal of Social Policy*, 21: 71–97.

McGuffin, P., Farmer, A.E. and Harvey, I. (1991) 'A polydiagnostic application of operational criteria in studies of psychotic illness: development and reliability of the OPCRIT system', *Archives of General Psychiatry*, 48: 764–770.

McLellan, A.T., Arndt, I.O., Metzger, D.S., Woody, G.E. and O'Brien, C.P. (1993) 'The effects of psychosocial services in substance abuse treatment', *Journal of the American Medical Association*, 269: 1953–1959.

McSweeney, T., Stevens, A. and Hunt, N. (2006) *The Quasi-compulsory Treatment of Drug Dependent Offenders in Europe: The Final National Report – England*, London: Institute for Criminal Policy Research.

McSweeney, T., Stevens, A. Hunt, N. and Turnbull, P. (2007) 'Twisting arms or a helping hand? Assessing the impact of "coerced" treatment and comparable "voluntary" drug treatment options', *British Journal of Criminology*, 47(3): 470–490.

McSweeney, T., Turnbull, P. and Hough, M. (2008) *The Treatment and Supervision of Drug-dependent Offenders: A Review of the Literature Prepared for the UK Drug Policy Commission*, London: UKDPC.

Mead, L. (ed.) (1997) *The New Paternalism: Supervisory Approaches to Poverty*, Washington, DC: Brookings Institution Press.

Menezes, P.R., Johnson, S., Thornicroft, G. *et al.* (1996) 'Drug and alcohol problems among individuals with severe mental illness in South London', *British Journal of Psychiatry*, 168: 612–619.

Metrebian, N., Shanahan, W., Wells, B. and Stimson, G.V. (1998) 'Feasibility of prescribing injectable heroin and methadone to opiate-dependent drug users: associated health gains and harm reductions', *Medical Journal of Australia*, 168: 596–600.

Metrebian, N., Shanahan, W., Stimson, G.V., Small, C., Lee, M., Mtutu, V. and Wells, B. (2001) 'Prescribing drug of choice to opiate dependent drug users: a comparison of clients receiving heroin with those receiving injectable methadone at a West London drug clinic', *Drug and Alcohol Review*, 20: 267–276.

Metrebian, N., Carnwath, T., Stimson, G.V. and Soltz, T. (2002) 'Survey of doctors prescribing diamorphine (heroin) to opiate dependent drug users in the United Kingdom', *Addiction*, 97: 1155–1161.

Metrebian, N., Stimson, G.V., Shanahan, W., Alcorn, R., Sell, L., Nunn, A., Gabe, R. et al. (2003) *Pilot UK Injectable Methadone Trial: Final Report*, Report to the Department of Health.

Metrebian, N., Carnwath, Z., Mott, J., Carnwath, T. and Stimson, G.V. (2006) 'Patients receiving a prescription for diamorphine (heroin) in the United Kingdom', *Drug and Alcohol Review*, 25: 115–121.

Metrebian, N., Mott, J., Carnwath, Z., Carnwath, T. and Stimson, G.V. (2007) 'Pathways into receiving a prescription for diamorphine (heroin) for the treatment of opiate dependence in the United Kingdom', *European Addiction Research*, 13: 144–147.

Metsch, L.R. and McCoy, C.B. (1999) 'Drug treatment experiences: rural and urban comparisons', *Substance Use and Misuse*, 34: 763–784.

Meylan, G.L. (1910) 'The effects of smoking on college students', *The Popular Science Monthly*, 77: 170–177.

Milewa, T. (1997) 'Community participation and health care priorities: reflections on policy, theatre and reality in Britain', *Health Promotions International*, 12: 161–167.

Millar, T., Beatty, S., Jones, A., Donmall, M. and Gemmell, I. (2003) *Arrest Referral – Treatment Uptake, Retention and Behaviour Change*, London: Home Office.

Millar, T., Donmall, M. and Jones, A. (2004) *Treatment Effectiveness: Demonstration Analysis of Treatment Surveillance Data about Treatment Completion and Retention*, London: National Treatment Agency for Substance Misuse.

Miller, N., Millman, R. and Keskinen, B. (1990) 'Outcome at six and twelve months post inpatient treatment for cocaine and alcohol dependence', *Advances in Alcohol and Substance Abuse*, 9: 101–119.

Miller, W.R., Rollnick, S. and Conforti, K. (2002) *Motivational Interviewing: Preparing People for Change*, 2nd edn, New York: Guilford Press.

Miller, W.R., Yahne, C.E., Moyers, T.B., Martinez, J. and Pirritano, M. (2004) 'A randomised trial of methods to help clinicians learn motivational interviewing', *Journal of Consulting and Clinical Psychology*, 72: 1050–1062.

Ministry of Health (1926) *Report of the Departmental Committee on Morphine and Heroin Addiction* (The Rolleston Report), London: HMSO.

Ministry of Health and Scottish Home and Health Department (1965) *Drug Addiction: The Second Report of the Interdepartmental Committee* (The Second Brain Report), London: HMSO.

Mitcheson, M. (1994) 'Drug clinics in the 1970s', in J. Strang and M. Gossop (eds), *Heroin Addiction and Drug Policy: The British System*, London: Oxford Medical Publications, pp. 331–340.

Mold, A. (2008) *Heroin: The Treatment of Addiction in Twentieth Century Britain*, Dekalb, IL: Northern Illinois University Press.

Montgomery, S.A. and Åsberg, M. (1979) 'A new depression scale designed to be sensitive to change', *British Journal of Psychiatry*, 134: 382–389.

Moore, T.H.N., Zammit, S., Lingford Hughes, A., Barnes, T.R.E., Jones, P.B., Burke, M. and Lewis, G. (2007) 'Cannabis use and risk of psychotic or affective mental health outcomes: a systematic review', *Lancet*, 370: 319–328.

Morton, N.E. (2008) 'Into the post-HapMap era', *Advances in Genetics*, 60: 727–742.

Mueser, K.T. and Drake, R.E. (2003) 'Integrated dual diagnosis treatment in New Hampshire (USA)', in H.L. Graham (ed.), *Substance Misuse in Psychosis: Approaches to Treatment and Service Delivery*, Chichester: Wiley.

Mueser, K.T., Bellack, A.S. and Blanchard, J.J. (1997) 'Comorbidity of schizophrenia and substance abuse: implications for treatment', in G.A. Marlatt and G.G. VandenBos (eds), *Addictive Behaviors: Readings on Etiology, Prevention and Treatment*, New York: Pergamon Press.

National Audit Office (2004) *The Drug Treatment and Testing Order: Early Lessons*, Report by the Comptroller and Auditor General HC 366 Session 2003–2004, 26 March, London: National Audit Office.

National Statistics (2006) *Unemployment Highlights*, London: National Statistics.

Nazareth, I., King, M., Haines, A., Rangel, I. and Myer, S. (1993) 'Accuracy of diagnosis of psychosis on general practice computer system', *British Medical Journal*, 307: 32–34.

Neale, J., Godfrey, C., Parrott, S., Sheard, L. and Tompkins, L. (2006) *Barriers to the Effective Treatment of Injecting Drug Users*, Final Report submitted to the Department of Health.

Neale, J., Sheard, L. and Tompkins, C. (2007) 'Factors that help injecting drug users to access and benefit from services: a qualitative study', *Substance Abuse Treatment, Prevention and Policy*, 2: 31.

Neale, J., Tompkins, C. and Sheard, L. (2008) 'Barriers to accessing generic health and social care services: a qualitative study of injecting drug users', *Health and Social Care in the Community*, 16: 147–154.

Negrete, J.C. (1988) 'What's happened to the cannabis debate?' *British Journal of Addiction*, 83: 359–372.

Nestler, E.J. and Landsman, D. (2001) 'Learning about addiction from the genome', *Nature*, 409: 834–835.

Newcombe, R. (2007) 'Trends in the prevalence of illicit drug use in Britain', in M. Simpson, T. Shildrick and R. MacDonald (eds), *Drugs in Britain: Supply, Consumption and Control*, Basingstoke: Palgrave Macmillan, pp. 13–38.

—— (2008) 'A model for harm reduction?', video presentation. Accessed 5 August 2008: http://www.lifeline.org.uk

NHS Executive (1999) *Patient and Public Involvement in the New NHS*, Leeds: Department of Health.

NHSME (National Health Service Management Executive) (1994a) *HSG (94)5 Introduction of Supervision Registers for Mentally Ill People from 1st April 1994*, London: Department of Health.

—— (1994b) *HSG (94)27 Guidance on the Discharge of Mentally Disordered People and their Continuing Care in the Community*, London: Department of Health.

NICE (National Institute for Clinical Excellence) (2004) *Guidance on the Use of*

Zaleplon, Zolpidem and Zopiclone for the Short-term Management of Insomnia: Technology Appraisal 77, London: NICE.

—— (2007a) *Drug Misuse: Opioid Detoxification (Clinical Guideline 52)*, London: NICE.

—— (2007b) *Drug Misuse: Psychosocial Interventions (Clinical Guideline 51)*, London: NICE.

—— (2007c) *Methadone and Buprenorphine for the Management of Opioid Dependence (NICE Technology Appraisal Guidance 114)*, London: NICE.

Nolan, J.L. (1998) *The Therapeutic State: Justifying Government at Century's End*, New York: New York University Press.

NTA (National Treatment Agency for Substance Misuse) (2002a) *Making the System Work: Guidance on Managing and Reducing Waiting Times for Specialist Drug Treatment Services in England*, London: NTA.

—— (2002b) *Models of Care for the Treatment of Adult Drug Misusers*, London: NTA.

—— (2003) *Injectable Heroin (and Injectable Methadone): Potential Roles in Drug Treatment*, London: NTA.

—— (2005) *More Treatment, Better Treatment, Fairer Treatment* (Effectiveness Strategy), London: NTA.

—— (2006a) *Models of Care for the Treatment of Adult Drug Misusers: Update 2006*, London: NTA.

—— (2006b) *Performance Information*, London: NTA.

—— (2006c) *NTA Guidance for Local Partnerships on User and Carer Involvement*, London: NTA.

—— (2006d) *Care Planning Practice Guide*, London: NTA.

—— (2007a) *Annual Report 2006/7*, London: NTA.

—— (2007b) *Good Practice in Care Planning*, London: NTA.

—— (2008) *Supporting and Involving Carers*, London: NTA.

Nutley, S.M., Walter, I. and Davies, H.T.O. (2007) *Using Evidence: How Research Can Improve Public Services*, Bristol: Policy Press.

Nutt, D., King, L.A., Saulsbury, W. and Blakemore, C. (2007) 'Development of a rational scale to assess the harm of drugs of potential misuse', *Lancet*, 369(9566): 1047–1053.

Onyett, S. (1992) *Case Management in Mental Health*, London: Chapman and Hall.

Orford, J. (1998) 'The coping perspective', in R. Velleman, A. Copello and J. Maslin (eds), *Living with Drink: Women Who Live with Problem Drinkers*, London: Longman.

Orford, J., Johnson, M. and Purser, R. (2004) 'Drinking in second generation Black and Asian communities in the English West Midlands', *Addiction Research and Theory*, 12: 11–30.

Orford, J., Natera, G., Copello, A., Atkinson, C., Mora, J., Velleman, R., Crundall, I., Tiburcio, M., Templeton, L. and Walley, G. (2005) *Coping with Alcohol and Drug Problems: The Experiences of Family Members in Three Contrasting Cultures*, London: Brunner-Routledge.

Orford, J., Templeton, L., Patel, A., Copello, A. and Velleman, R. (2007a) 'The 5-Step family intervention in primary care: I. Strengths and limitations according to family members', *Drugs: Education, Prevention and Policy*, 14: 29–47.

Orford, J., Templeton, L., Patel, A., Velleman, R. and Copello, A. (2007b) 'The 5-Step family intervention in primary care: II. The views of primary health care professionals', *Drugs: Education, Prevention and Policy*, 14: 117–135.

Orford, J., Templeton, L., Copello, A., Velleman, R., Ibanga, A. and Binnie, C. (2008) 'Increasing the involvement of family members in alcohol and drug treatment services: the results of an action research project in two specialist agencies', *Drugs: Education, Prevention and Policy* (in press).

Ovretveit, J. and Davies, K. (1988) 'Client participation in mental handicap services', *Health Services Management*, 84: 112–116.

Parascandola, M. and Weed, D.L. (2001) 'Causation in epidemiology', *Journal of Epidemiology and Community Health*, 55: 905–912.

Parker, H. (2004) 'The new drugs intervention industry: what outcomes can drugs/criminal justice treatment programmes realistically deliver?', *Journal of Community and Criminal Justice*, 51(4): 379–386.

Patterson, S., Weaver, T., Agath, K., Albert, E., Rhodes, T., Rutter, D. and Crawford, M. (2009a) ' "They can't solve the problem without us": a qualitative study of stakeholder perspectives on user involvement in drug treatment services in England', *Health and Social Care in the Community*, 17: 54–62.

Patterson, S., Weaver, T., Agath, K., Rutter, D., Albert, E. and Crawford, M.J. (2009b) 'User involvement in efforts to improve the quality of drug misuse services in England: a national survey', *Drugs: Education, Prevention and Policy*, in press.

Patterson, S., Weaver, T. and Crawford, M. (2009c) 'Drug Service User Groups: only a partial solution to the problem of developing user involvement', *Drugs: Education, Prevention and Policy*, in press.

Patton, G.C., Coffey, C., Carlin, J.B., Sawyer, S.M. and Lynskey, M. (2005) 'Reverse gateways? Frequent cannabis use as a predictor of tobacco initiation and nicotine dependence', *Addiction*, 100: 1518–1525.

Pearson, G. (1990) 'Drugs, law and criminology', in V. Berridge (ed.), *Drugs Research and Policy in Britain*, Aldershot: Avebury.

Peen, J. and Dekker, D. (2001) 'Social deprivation and psychiatric service use for different diagnostic groups', *Social Science and Medicine*, 53: 1–8.

Perneger, T.V., Giner, F., Del Rio, M. and Mino, A. (1998) 'Randomized trial of heroin maintenance programme for addicts who fail in conventional drug treatments', *British Medical Journal*, 317: 13–18.

Peters, R.H., Haas, A.L. and Murrin, M.R. (1999) 'Predictors of retention and arrest in drug courts', *National Drug Court Review*, 2(1): 33–60.

Peterson, A. and Lupton, D. (1996) *The New Public Health: Health and Self in the Age of Risk*, London: Sage.

Petitti, D. (2004) 'Commentary: hormone replacement therapy and coronary heart disease: four lessons', *International Journal of Epidemiology*, 33: 461–463.

Phelan, M., Slade, M., Thornicroft, G. *et al.* (1995) 'The Camberwell Assessment of Need: the validity and reliability of an instrument to assess the needs of people with severe mental illness', *British Journal of Psychiatry*, 167: 589–595.

Phillips, A.N. and Davey Smith, G. (1991) 'How independent are "independent" effects? Relative risk estimation when correlated exposures are measured imprecisely', *Journal of Clinical Epidemiology*, 44: 1223–1231.

Potvin, S., Sepehry, A.A. and Stip, E. (2006) 'A meta-analysis of negative symptoms in dual diagnosis schizophrenia', *Psychological Medicine*, 36(4): 431–440.

Poulton, R., Caspi, A., Milne, B.J., Thomson, W.M., Taylor, A., Sears, M.R. and Moffitt, T.E. (2002) 'Association between children's experience of socioeconomic disadvantage and adult health: a life-course study', *Lancet*, 360: 1640–1645.

Project MATCH Research Group (1998) 'Matching patients with alcohol disorders to treatments: clinical implications from Project MATCH', *Journal of Mental Health*, 7(6): 589–602.

Quinn, C. and Barton, A. (2000) 'The implications of the drug treatment and testing orders', *The Nursing Standard*, 14(27): 38–41.

Radcliffe, P. and Stevens, A. (2008) 'Are drug treatment services only for "thieving junkie scumbags"? Drug users and the management of stigmatised identities', *Social Science and Medicine*, 67(3): 1065–1073.

Raistrick, D., Bradshaw, J., Tober, G., Weiner, J., Allison, J. and Healey, C. (1994) 'Development of the Leeds Dependence Questionnaire', *Addiction*, 89: 563–572.

Raistrick, D., Heather, N. and Godfrey, C. (2006) *Review of the Effectiveness of Treatment for Alcohol Problems*, London: NTA.

Raistrick, D., Tober, G., Heather, N. and Clark, J. (2007) 'Validation of the Social Satisfaction Questionnaire for outcome evaluation in substance use disorders', *Psychiatric Bulletin*, 31: 333–336.

Ramsay, M. (2003) *Prisoners' Drug Use and Treatment: Seven Research Studies*, Home Office Research Study 267, London: Home Office.

Ramsay, M. and Partridge, S. (1999) *Drug Misuse Declared in 1998: Results from the British Crime Survey*, London: Home Office, Research and Statistics Directorate.

Randall, G. and DrugScope (2002) *Drug Services for Homeless People – a Good Practice Handbook*, London: Home Office.

Rassool, H. (2006) 'Substance abuse in black and minority ethnic communities in the United Kingdom: a neglected problem?', *Journal of Addictions Nursing*, 17: 127–132.

RCPsych/RCGP (Royal College of Psychiatrists and Royal College of General Practitioners) Joint Substance Misuse Working Group (2005) *Roles and Responsibilities of Doctors in the Provision of Treatment for Drug and Alcohol Misusers*, London: Royal College of Psychiatrists.

Regier, D., Farmer, M., Rae, D., Locke, B. *et al.* (1990) 'Co-morbidity of mental disorders with alcohol and other drug abuse: results from the Epidemiologic Catchment Area (ECA) study', *Journal of the American Medical Association*, 264: 2511–2518.

Reuter, P. and Stevens, A. (2007) *An Analysis of UK Drug Policy: A Monograph Prepared for the UK Drug Policy Commission*, London: UKDPC.

Richardson, A. and Bray, C. (1987) *Promoting Health Through Participation: Experience of Groups for Patient Participation in General Practice*, London: Policy Studies Institute.

Ritchie, J., Dick, D. and Lingham R. (1994) *The Report of the Inquiry into the Care and Treatment of Christopher Clunis*, London: Stationery Office.

Ritchie, R. and Lewis, L. (eds) (2005) *Qualitative Research Practice*, London: Sage.

Robertson, J.R., Macleod, J., Hickman, M., Copeland, L. and McKenzie, J. (2007) 'Lifecourse antecedents and possible consequences of injection drug use: follow-up of a cohort of injection opiate users recruited in primary care' (Abstract from a presentation at the annual scientific meeting of the Society for Social Medicine), *Journal of Epidemiology and Community Health*, 61(Suppl. 1): A1–A44.

Rogers, A., Pilgrim, D., Brennan, S., Ilyas, S. *et al.* (2007) 'Prescribing benzodiazepines in general practice: a new view of an old problem', *Health*, 11: 181–198.

Rose, D. (1998) *In Our Experience: User-Focused Monitoring of Mental Health Services*, London: Sainsbury Centre for Mental Health.

Rothman, K.J. (1976) 'Causes', *American Journal of Epidemiology*, 104: 587–592.

Rowlingson, K. (2001) 'Child poverty and the policy response', in M. May, R. Page and E. Brunsdon (eds), *Understanding Social Problems: Issues in Social Policy*, Oxford: Blackwell, pp. 107–117.

RSA (2007) *Drugs – Facing Facts. The Report of the RSA Commission on Illegal Drugs, Communities and Public Policy*, London: RSA.

Ruggiero, V. and Khan, K. (2006) 'British South Asian communities and drug supply networks in the UK: a qualitative study', *International Journal of Drug Policy*, 6: 473–483.

Rutter, D., Manley, C., Weaver, T., Crawford, M.J. and Fulop, N. (2004) 'Partners or patients? Case studies of user involvement from two mental health trusts', *Social Science and Medicine*, 58: 1973–1984.

Rutter, M. and Smith, D.J. (1995) *Psychosocial Disorders in Young People: Time Trends and Their Causes*, Chichester: Wiley.

Sandwick, R. (1912) 'The use of tobacco as a cause of failures and withdrawals in one high school', *The School Review*, 20: 623–625.

Sangster, D., Shiner, M., Patel, K. and Sheikh, N. (2001) *Delivering Drug Services to Black and Minority Ethnic Communities*, London: Home Office.

Sarfraz, A. and Alcorn, R. (1999) 'Injectable methadone prescribing in the United Kingdom – current practice and future policy guidelines', *Substance Use and Misuse*, 34(12): 1709–1721.

Saunders, J.B., Aasland, O.G., Babor, T.F. *et al.* (1993) 'Development of the Alcohol Use Disorders Identification Test (AUDIT): WHO collaborative project on early detection of persons with harmful alcohol consumption II', *Addiction*, 88: 791–804.

Scaife, V.H. (2008) 'Maternal and paternal drug misuse and outcomes for children: identifying risk and protective factors', *Children and Society*, 22: 53–62.

Schneider, J., Brandon, T., Wooff, D., Carpenter, J. and Paxton, R. (2006) 'Assertive outreach: policy and reality', *Psychiatric Bulletin*, 30(3): 89–94.

Schulte, S., Moring, J., Meier, P.S. and Barrowclough, C. (2007) 'User involvement and desired service developments in drug treatment: service user and provider views', *Drugs: Education, Prevention and Policy*, 14: 277–287.

SCODA (Standing Conference on Drug Abuse) (1997) *Drug Using Parents: Policy Guidelines for Inter-agency Working*, London: Local Government Association Publications.

Scott, H., Johnson, P., Menezes, P. *et al.* (1998) 'Substance misuse and risk of aggression and offending among the severely mentally ill', *British Journal of Psychiatry*, 172: 345–350.

Scottish Executive (2003) *Getting Our Priorities Right: Policy and Practice Guidelines for Working with Children and Families Affected by Problem Drug Use*, Edinburgh: Scottish Executive. Available at http://www.scotland.gov.uk

—— (2007) *Letters of Assurance 2: Children Affected by Drug Misusing Parents*. Available at http://www.scotland.gov.uk/publications/2007/08/09/1163225

Seddon, T. (2000) 'Explaining the drug–crime link: theoretical, policy and research issues', *Journal of Social Policy*, 29(1): 95–107.

—— (2006) 'Drugs, crime and social exclusion', *British Journal of Criminology*, 46(4): 680–703.

—— (2007) 'Coerced drug treatment in the criminal justice system: conceptual, ethical and criminological issues', *Criminology and Criminal Justice*, 7(3): 1–16.

Sell, L. and Zador, D. (2004) 'Patients prescribed injectable heroin or methadone – their opinions and experiences of treatment', *Addiction*, 99: 442–449.

Sell, L., Segar, G. and Merrill, J. (2001) 'Patients prescribed injectable opiates in the North West of England', *Drug and Alcohol Review*, 20: 57–66.

Semple, D.M., McIntosh, A.M. and Lawrie, S.M. (2005) 'Cannabis as a risk factor for psychosis: systematic review', *Journal of Psychopharmacology*, 19: 187–194.

Shaw, G.B. (1911) *The Doctor's Dilemma*, London: Constable.

Shaw, J., Appleby, L., Amos, T. *et al.* (1999) 'Mental disorder and clinical care in people convicted of homicide: national clinical survey', *British Medical Journal*, 318: 1240–1244.

Shiner, M., Thom, B. and MacGregor, S. (2004) *Exploring Community Responses to Drugs*, York: Joseph Rowntree Foundation Drug and Alcohol Research Programme.

Simpson, D.D., Joe, G.W., Rowan-Szal, G.A. and Greener, J.M. (1997) 'Drug abuse treatment process components that improve retention', *Journal of Substance Abuse Treatment*, 14(6): 565–572.

Simpson, E.L. and House, A.O. (2002) 'Involving users in the delivery and evaluation of mental health services: systematic review', *British Medical Journal*, 325(7375): 1265–1270.

Single, E. (1989) 'The impact of marijuana decriminalization', *Journal of Public Health Epidemiology*, 10: 456–466.

Siriwardena, A.N., Qureshi, M.Z., Dyas, J.V., Middleton, H. and Orner, R. (2008) 'Magic bullets for insomnia? Patients' use and experiences of newer (Z drugs) versus older (benzodiazepine) hypnotics for sleep problems in primary care', *British Journal of General Practice*, 58(551): 417–422.

Skodbo, S., Brown, G., Deacon, S., Cooper, A., Hall, A., Millar, T., Smith, J. and Whitham, K. (2007) *The Drug Interventions Programme (DIP): Addressing Drug Use and Offending through 'Tough Choices'*, Home Office Research Report 2, London: Home Office.

Smart, C. (1984) 'Social policy and drug addiction: a critical study of policy development', *British Journal of Addiction*, 79: 31–39.

Smeaton, E. (2004) *Evaluation of the STARS Project, Nottingham – April 2003 to March 2004*, London: The Children's Society.

Smit, F., Bolier, L. and Cuijpers, P. (2004) 'Cannabis use and the risk of later schizophrenia: a review', *Addiction*, 99: 425–430.

Smith, M.K. (1998) 'Empowerment evaluation: theoretical and methodological considerations', *Evaluation and Program Planning*, 21(3): 255–261.

South, N. (1994) 'Drugs: control, crime and criminological studies', in M. Maguire, R. Morgan and R. Reiner (eds), *The Oxford Handbook of Criminology*, Oxford: Clarendon Press.

Southwell, M. (2002) *A Guide to Involving and Empowering Drug Users*, London: National Treatment Agency in partnership with National Drug Users Development Agency.

Staton, M., Leukefeld, C. and Logan, T.K. (2001) 'Health service utilization and victimization among incarcerated female substance users', *Substance Use and Misuse*, 36: 701–716.

Sterk, C.E., Elifson, K.W. and Theall, K. (2000) 'Women and drug treatment experiences: a generational comparison of mothers and daughters', *Journal of Drug Issues*, 30: 839–862.

Stevens, A. (2004) 'The treatment/punishment hybrid: selection and experimentation', Paper presented at the 4th Annual Conference of the European Society of Criminology, Amsterdam, August.

—— (2007) 'When two dark figures collide: evidence and discourse on drug-related crime', *Critical Social Policy*, 27(1): 1–38.

Stevens, A., Berto, D., Kerschl, V., Oeuvray, K., van Ooyen, M., Steffan, E., Heckmann, W. and Uchtenhagen, A. (2003) *Summary Literature Review: The International Literature on Drugs, Crime and Treatment*, QCT Europe Project, EISS, University of Kent.

Stevens, A., Berto, D., Heckmann,W., Kerschl, V., Oeuvray, K., vanOoyen, M., Steffan, E. and Uchtenhagen, A. (2005) 'Quasi-compulsory treatment of drug dependent offenders: an international literature review', *Substance Use and Misuse*, 40: 269–283.

Stevens, A., Berto, D., Frick, U., Hunt, N., Kerschl, V., McSweeney, T., Oeuvray, K., Puppo, I., Santa Maria, A., Schaaf, S., Trinkl, B., Uchtenhagen, A. and Werdenich, W. (2006) 'The relationship between legal status, perceived pressure and motivation in treatment for drug dependence: results from a European study of quasi-compulsory treatment', *European Addiction Research*, 12: 197–209.

Stevens, A., Radcliffe, P., Hunt, N. and Sanders, M. (2008) 'Early exit: estimating and explaining early exit from drug treatment', *Harm Reduction Journal*, 5(13).

Stewart, D., Gossop, M., Marsden, J. and Strang, J. (2000) 'Variation between and within drug treatment modalities: data from the National Treatment Outcome Research Study (UK)', *European Addiction Research*, 6(3): 106–114.

Stimson, G. (1990) 'Reviewing policy and practice: new ideas about the drugs problem', in J. Strang and G. Stimson (eds), *AIDS and Drugs Misuse: The Challenge for Policy and Practice in the 1990s*, London: Routledge.

Stimson, G.V. and Oppenheimer, E. (1982) *Heroin Addiction: Treatment and Control in Britain*, London: Tavistock.

Strang, J. and Gossop, M. (eds) (1994) *Heroin Addiction and Drug Policy*, Oxford: Oxford University Press.

Strang, J. and Sheridan, J. (1997) 'Heroin prescribing in the "British System" of the mid 1990s: data from the 1995 national survey of community pharmacies in England and Wales', *Drug and Alcohol Review*, 16: 7–16.

Strang, J., Sheridan, J. and Barber, N. (1996) 'Prescribing injectable and oral methadone to opiate addicts: results from the 1995 national postal survey of community pharmacists in England and Wales', *British Medical Journal*, 313: 270–272.

Strang, J., Witton, J. and Hall, W. (2000a) 'Improving the quality of the cannabis debate: defining the different domains', *British Medical Journal*, 320: 108–110.

Strang, J., Marsden, J., Cummins, M., Farre, M., Finch, E., Gossop, M., Stewart, D. and Welch, S. (2000b) 'Randomised trial of supervised injectable versus oral methadone maintenance: a report of feasibility and six month outcome', *Addiction*, 95(11): 1631–1645.

Strang, J., Best, D., Ridge, G. and Gossop, M. (2004). *Randomized Clinical Trial of the Effects of Time on a Waiting List on Clinical Outcomes in Opiate Users Awaiting Out-patient Treatment*, London: NTA.

Strang, J., Manning, V., Mayet, S., Ridge, G., Best, D. and Sheridan, J. (2007) 'Does prescribing for opiate addiction change after national guidelines? Methadone and buprenorphine prescribing to opiate addicts by general practitioners and hospital doctors in England, 1995–2005', *Addiction*, 102: 761–770.

Susser, M. (1991) 'What is a cause and how do we know one?A grammar for prag-matic epidemiology', *American Journal of Epidemiology*, 133: 635–648.

Swartz, M.S., Swanson, J.W., Hiday, V.A. *et al.* (1998) 'Violence and severe mental illness: the effects of substance abuse and non-adherence to medication', *American Journal of Psychiatry*, 155: 226–231.

Swift, W. and Copeland, J. (1996) 'Treatment needs and experiences of Australian women with alcohol and other drug problems', *Drug and Alcohol Dependence*, 40: 211–219.

Szasz, T. (1976) *Ceremonial Chemistry: The Ritual Persecution of Drugs, Addicts, and Pushers*, Holmes Beach, FL: Learning Publications.

Tabassum, R., MaCaskill, A. and Ahmad, I. (2000) 'Attitudes towards mental health in an urban Pakistani community in the United Kingdom', *International Journal of Social Psychiatry*, 46: 170–181.

Taylor, A. and Kroll, B. (2004) 'Working with parental substance misuse: dilemmas for practice', *British Journal of Social Work*, 34: 1115–1132.

Taylor, J., Lloyd, D.A. and Warheit, G.J. (2006) 'Self-derogation, peer factors, and drug dependence among a multiethnic sample of young adults', *Journal of Child and Adolescent Substance Abuse*, 15(2): 39–51.

Taylor, P.J. and Gunn, J. (1999) 'Homicides by people with mental illness: myth and reality', *British Journal of Psychiatry*, 174: 9–14.

Templeton, L., Patel, A., Copello, A., Velleman, R. and Orford, J. (2001) *'A self-help manual for family members of relatives with drink or drug problems'* (unpublished – obtainable from first author).

Templeton, L., Zohadi, S., Galvani, S. and Velleman, R. (2006) *Looking Beyond Risk: Parental Substance Misuse Scoping Study*, Edinburgh: Scottish Executive.

Templeton, L., Zohhadi, S. and Velleman, R. (2007) 'Working with family members in specialist drug and alcohol services: findings from a feasibility study', *Drugs: Education, Prevention and Policy*, 14: 137–150.

Tien, A.Y. and Anthony, J.C. (1990) 'Epidemiological analysis of alcohol and drug use as risk factors for psychotic experiences', *Journal of Nervous and Mental Disease*, 178: 473–480.

Tiet, Q.Q. and Mausbach, B. (2007) 'Treatments for patients with dual diagnosis: a review', *Alcoholism: Clinical and Experimental Research*, 31: 513–536.

Tober, G. (2000) *'The nature and measurement of change in substance dependence'*, University of Leeds PhD thesis.

Tober, G., Brearley, R., Kenyon, R., Raistrick, D. and Morley, S. (2000) 'Measuring outcomes in a health service addiction clinic', *Addiction Research*, 8: 169–182.

Tober, G., Godfrey, C., Parrott, S., Copello, A., Farrin, A., Hodgson, R., Kenyon, R., Morton, V., Orford, J., Russell, I. and Slegg, G. (2005) 'Setting standards for train-ing and competence: the UK Alcohol Treatment Trial', *Alcohol and Alcoholism*, 40: 413–418.

Tober, G., Kline, W., Finnigan, O., Farrin, A. and Russell, I., in collaboration with the UKATT Research Team (in press) 'Validation of a scale for rating the delivery of psychosocial treatments for alcohol dependence and misuse: the UKATT Process Rating Scale (PRS)', *Alcohol and Alcoholism*.

Todd, S., Felce, D., Beyer, S., Shearn, J., Perry, J. and Kilsby, M. (2000) 'Strategic planning and progress under the All Wales Strategy: reflecting the perceptions of stakeholders', *Journal of Intellectual Disability Research*, 44: 31–44.

Tompkins, C.N.E., Neale, J., Sheard, L. and Wright, N. (2007) 'Experiences of prison among injecting drug users in England: a qualitative study', *International Journal of Prisoner Health*, 3: 189–203.

Townsend, P., Phillimore, P. and Beattie, A. (1988). *Health and Deprivation: Inequalities and the North*, London: Croom Helm.

Turnbull, P., McSweeney, T., Hough, M., Webster, R. and Edmunds, M. (2000) *Drug Treatment and Testing Orders: Final Evaluation Report. Research Study 212*, London: Home Office.

Turning Point (2004) *Routes into Treatment: Drugs and Crime*, London: Turning Point.

—— (2006) *Bottling It Up: The Effects of Alcohol Misuse on Children, Parents and Families*, London: Turning Point.

Tyrer, P. (2000) 'Quick Personality Assessment Schedule: PAS-Q', in P. Tyrer (ed.), *Personality Disorders: Diagnosis, Management and Course*, 2nd edn, London: Arnold, pp. 181–190.

Tyrer, P., Owen, R.T. and Cicchetti, D.V. (1984) 'The brief scale for anxiety: a subdivision of the comprehensive psychopathological rating scale', *Journal of Neurology Neurosurgery and Psychiatry*, 47: 970–975.

Tyrer, P., Morgan, J., Van Horn, E. *et al.* (1995) 'A randomized controlled study of close monitoring of vulnerable psychiatric patients', *Lancet*, 345: 756–759.

Uchtenhagen, A., Gutzwiller, F. and Dobler-Mikola, A. (1998) *Medical Prescription of Narcotics Research Programme: Final Report of the Principal Investigators*, Zurich: Institution fur Sozial-und praventivmedizin der Universitat Zurich.

UKATT Research Team (2005) 'Effectiveness of treatment for alcohol problems: findings of the randomized UK alcohol treatment trial (UKATT)', *British Medical Journal*, 331: 541–544.

UKCBTMM Project Group (2005) 'The effectiveness and cost-effectiveness of cognitive behavioural therapy for opiate misusers in methadone maintenance treatment: a multi-centre, randomized, controlled trial', *Drugs: Education, Prevention and Policy*, 12(S1): 69–76.

UKDPC (United Kingdom Drug Policy Commission) (2008) *Reducing Drug Use, Reducing Offending: Are Programmes for Problem Drug-using Offenders in the UK Supported by the Evidence?* London: UKDPC.

van den Brink, W., Hendricks, V.M., Blanken, P., Koeter, M.W.J., van Zwieten, B.J. and van Ree, J.M. (2003) 'Medical prescription of heroin to treatment resistant heroin addicts: two randomized controlled trials', *British Medical Journal*, 327: 310–316.

van der Waals, F.W., Mohrs, J. and Foets, M. (1993) 'Sex differences among recipients of benzodiazepines in Dutch general practice', *British Medical Journal*, 307: 363–366.

van Os, J., Bak, M., Hanssen, M., Bijl, R.V., de Graaf, R. and Verdoux, H. (2002) 'Cannabis use and psychosis: a longitudinal population-based study', *American Journal of Epidemiology*, 156: 319–327.

Verthein, U., Bonoorden-Kleij, K., Degkwitz, P., Dilg, C., Kohler, W.K., Passie, T., Soyka, M., Tanger, S., Vogel, M. and Haasen, C. (2008) 'Long-term effects of heroin assisted treatment in Germany', *Addiction*, 103(6): 960–966.

Wanigaratne, S., Dar, K., Abdulrahim, D. and Strang, J. (2003) 'Ethnicity and drug use: exploring the nature of particular relationships among diverse populations in the United Kingdom', *Drugs: Education, Prevention and Policy*, 10: 39–55.

Weaver, T., Renton, A., Stimson, G. and Tyrer, P. (1999) 'Severe mental illness and substance misuse co-morbidity', *British Medical Journal*, 318: 137–138.

Weaver, T., Madden, P., Charles, V., Stimson, G., Renton, A., Tyrer, P., Barnes, T., Bench, C., Middleton, H., Wright, N., Paterson, S., Shanahan, W., Seivewright, N. and Ford, C. (2003) 'Comorbidity of substance misuse and mental illness in community mental health and substance misuse services', *British Journal of Psychiatry*, 183: 304–313.

Webster, C. (2007) 'Drug treatment', in M. Simpson, T. Shildrick and R. MacDonald (eds), *Drugs in Britain: Supply, Consumption and Control*, London: Palgrave Macmillan.

Weir, A. and Douglas, A. (eds) (1999) *Child Protection and Adult Mental Health: Conflict of Interests?* Oxford: Butterworth Heinemann.

Weiser, C. (1995) 'Championing the customer', *Harvard Business Review*, November/December 113–117.

Weiss, S.H., Betts Weston, C. and Quirinale, J. (1993) 'Safe sex? Misconceptions, gender differences and barriers among injection drug users: a focus group approach', *AIDS Education and Prevention*, 5: 279–293.

Wild, T., Roberts, A. and Cooper, E. (2002) 'Compulsory substance abuse treatment: an overview of recent findings and issues', *European Addiction Research*, 8(2): 84–93.

Wiles, N.J., Zammit, S., Bebbington, P., Singleton, N., Meltzer, H. and Lewis, G. (2006) 'Self-reported psychotic symptoms in the general population: results from the longitudinal study of the British National Psychiatric Morbidity Survey', *British Journal of Psychiatry*, 188: 519–526.

Williamson, E., Smith, M., Orford, J., Copello, A. and Day, E. (2007) 'Social behaviour and network therapy for drug problems: evidence of benefits and challenges', *Addictive Disorders and Their Treatment*, 6: 167–179.

Wilson, A. (1992) *Evaluation of North Manchester Community Drugs Team: Service Accessibility and the Place of Outreach*, North Manchester District Health Authority.

Wodak, A., Reinerman, C., Cohen, P.D.A. and Drummond, C. (2002) 'Cannabis control: costs outweigh the benefits. For and against', *British Medical Journal*, 324: 105–108.

Wolff, K., Farrell, M., Marsden, J., Monteiro, M.G., Ali, R., Welch, S. and Strang, J. (1999) 'A review of biological indicators of illicit drug use, practical considerations and clinical usefulness', *Addiction*, 94: 1279–1298.

Wood, E., Tyndall, M.W., Spittal, P.M., Li, K., Hogg, R.S., O'Shaughnessy, M.V. and Schechter, M.T. (2002) 'Needle exchange and difficulty with needle access during an ongoing HIV epidemic', *International Journal of Drug Policy*, 13: 95–102.

Wood, E., Li, K., Palepu, A., Marsh, D., Schechter, M., Hogg, R., Montaner, J. and Kerr, T. (2005) 'Sociodemographic disparities in access to addiction treatment among a cohort of Vancouver injection drug users', *Substance Use and Misuse*, 40: 1153–1167.

Woody, G.E., Luborsky, L., McLellan, A., O'Brien, C.P., Beck, A.T., Blaine, J., Herman, I. and Hole, A. (1983) 'Psychotherapy for opiate addicts: does it help?' *Archives of General Psychiatry*, 40: 639–645.

Woody, G.E., McLellan, A.T., Luborsky, L. and O'Brien, C.P. (1995) 'Psychotherapy in community methadone programs: a validation study', *American Journal of Psychiatry*, 152: 1302–1308.

Wright, S., Gournay, K., Glorney, E. and Thornicroft, G. (2000) 'Dual diagnosis in the suburbs: prevalence, need and in-patient service use', *Social Psychiatry and Psychiatric Epidemiology*, 35: 297–304.

Young, J. and Beck, A.T. (1980) *The Cognitive Therapy Checklist*, Philadelphia, PA: Center for Cognitive Therapy.

Zammit, S., Allebeck, P., Andreasson, S., Lundberg, I. and Lewis, G. (2002) 'Self reported cannabis use as a risk factor for schizophrenia in Swedish conscripts of 1969: historical cohort study', *British Medical Journal*, 325: 1199–1201.

Ziedonis, D.M., Smelson, D., Rosenthal, R.N. *et al.* (2005) 'Improving the care of individuals with schizophrenia and substance use disorders: consensus recommendations', *Journal of Psychiatric Practice*, 11: 315–406.

Index